Special Issues from the *Teachers College Record*
JONAS F. SOLTIS, Series Editor

SCHOOL DROPOUTS
Patterns and Policies

GARY NATRIELLO, Editor
Teachers College, Columbia University

Teachers College, Columbia University
New York and London

Published by Teachers College Press, 1234 Amsterdam Avenue,
New York, NY 10027

Library of Congress Cataloging-in-Publication Data

School dropouts.

   Reprint of an issue of Teachers College record, with
new and revised articles.
   Includes index.
   1. High school dropouts — United States. 2. Personnel
service in secondary education — United States.
I. Natriello, Gary.
LC143.S26 1987   373.12'913'0973   86-22978
ISBN 0-8077-2835-7

Manufactured in the United States of America

92 91 90 89 88 87   1 2 3 4 5 6

Contents

Introduction

GARY NATRIELLO
Teachers College, Columbia University

This volume brings together a set of articles that call attention to a continuing problem in American education, the significant numbers of students who fail to graduate from high school. Amid the chorus of reports calling for excellence in education, the authors included here join their voices with only a few others who have urged researchers, policymakers, and educators not to lose sight of the very real problems of those students for whom continued attendance at school is doubtful. The articles cover two general aspects of the dropout phenomenon: the patterns of dropping out evident among American youth and the policies developed and implemented to reduce the incidence of dropping out.

In the first article, Dale Mann alerts us to the multiple problems involved in dropping out and sensitizes us to the need for a multitude of policies to attack these problems. He makes clear the urgency of the problem and the need for action. Valid and reliable measurement of dropping out among American students, however, is a prerequisite to understanding the problem. The next two articles pay special attention to the processes by which data on the patterns of dropping out are collected and the implications of the data-collection process for the quality of data available. As part of a larger study of the incidence of dropping out among students in New York City high schools, Floyd Hammack examines the dropout reports produced by school districts in large U.S. cities. His analysis reveals great diversity in data-collection procedures and more than a few practices used in individual districts that might be applied profitably in all districts. In a second article on the development of school district data on dropouts, George Morrow presents the results of simulations of divergent methods of calculating dropout statistics based on data from operating school districts. These simulations demonstrate the implications of different methods of calculating such statistics. He goes on to propose a set of standard procedures for districts to use in collecting and tabulating data on dropouts.

The next pair of articles present analyses of what is arguably the best national sample of data on high school dropouts, the High School and Beyond study conducted by the National Center for Education Statistics. High School and Beyond followed students who were sophomores in 1980 and surveyed them again in 1982 when some had remained in school and others had dropped out. Thus, the study contains data on the background

1

and school experiences of a sizable sample of dropouts. In a wide-ranging analysis of the High School and Beyond data, Ruth Ekstrom, Margaret Goertz, Judith Pollack, and Donald Rock provide some basic insights into the characteristics of the dropout population followed in that study. Gary Wehlage and Robert Rutter, using the same data set, engage in a more directed analysis designed to assess the potential contribution of schools to the dropout problem. Both articles demonstrate the usefulness of the High School and Beyond data for a range of inquiries into the dropout problem.

In the next article, Michelle Fine takes us into and out of a New York City high school by means of a careful ethnographic study of its students and its dropouts. Fine provides a close look at the process by which students are allowed or forced to leave the school. Her interviews with students provide a vibrant image of the plight of these youngsters both in and out of school.

Two articles pay particular attention to the likely impact of recent efforts to reform schools on those students least likely to graduate from high school. Edward McDill, Aaron Pallas, and I consider the likely positive and negative effects of the types of higher standards proposed in recent school reform efforts in light of what is known about the characteristics of students most likely to leave school early. We then identify school characteristics that might be altered to minimize the adverse effects of higher standards on potential dropouts and propose recommendations to raise standards and mitigate the dropout problem simultaneously. In a similar vein, Stephen Hamilton concludes that simply raising standards without making other organizational and instructional changes would lead to an increase in the numbers of students dropping out. Hamilton examines dropout-prevention programs to ascertain the characteristics of educational programs that might retain students in school in the wake of higher standards. Moving beyond particular programs, he examines secondary education in West Germany in a search for another alternative to keep students in school.

In the final article, Aaron Pallas, Edward McDill, and I consider the implications of the themes in this volume for the development of an agenda for further research on the dropout phenomenon. We spell out the key components of a comprehensive research program.

Together the articles in this volume present a panorama of the current thinking of researchers and policymakers concerned with the dropout problem in our schools. They remind us that steps must be taken to see to it that large numbers of students are not left behind in the pursuit of excellence.

Can We Help Dropouts? Thinking about the Undoable

DALE MANN

Teachers College, Columbia University

Recognizing that we live in a complex world, Dale Mann reminds us that there are few simple answers to persistent educational problems. He argues that the dropout problem calls for imaginative and multiple approaches to what is really a diverse set of problems preventing students from completing high school. His overview sets the stage for the articles that follow.

Dropping out of high school is again nearing the much-to-be-desired status of a scandal in education. The competition is tough — teacher inadequacy, too little character development, too much values clarification, a tide of mediocrity, bureaucratic rigidity, and so forth — but most of those things can be related to dropping out. A local headline, "26 Percent Never Graduate," will trigger the demand that "something" be done about "the problem." This article suggests that "the problem" is not singular and that the solution must be complex. But the nearly intractable problem of early school leaving requires more resources than it has ever attracted. We may have to think about dropouts the way John Lindsay thought about his responsibilities as mayor of New York City: "Insoluble problems masquerading as wonderful opportunities." The accuracy of that bleak diagnosis depends on our skills as educators and as politicians.

THE NESTED PROBLEMS OF DROPPING OUT

A national estimate suggests that 25 percent of fifth graders will not make it through high school graduation.[1] Local estimates vary depending on purpose. A district that wants more money to start a program can derive a high figure; a similar district pressed to defend itself will use different procedures and produce a low rate. The most common defense is to count the number of students who dropped out in a given year as a percent of the total high school

This article was prepared in connection with a grant to the Center for Education and the American Economy at Teachers College, Columbia University, by the American Can Company Foundation. The analysis and conclusions are the author's responsibility.

Table 1. Reasons for Leaving High School
without a Degree: Percents Responding by
Gender

	Male	Female
A. School-related	51	33
B. Work-related	21	9
C. Family-related	5	37
D. Other	23	21
Totals	100	100

Source: William R. Morgan, "The High School
Dropout in an Overeducated Society," Table 5.8,
"Reason Given for Leaving High School Without
a Degree, for All Youth Who Ever Dropped Out,
in Year First-Reported Having Dropped Out, by
Sex" (Center for Human Resource Research,
Ohio State University, February 1984, Mimeo-
graphed). Data are from National Longitudinal
Survey of Labor Market Experience, The Youth
Cohort, Ohio State University.

enrollment. In any case, the size of the number is less important than how
policymakers feel about it.

One of the best sources of information about dropouts is the National
Longitudinal Survey of Labor Market Experience (NLS) Youth Cohort.
During its first four years (1979–1982), 5,880,000 youth dropped out. But
the nearly million and a half who left school each year without a degree did so
for various reasons (see Table 1). William R. Morgan estimates that, for boys
(who constitute 54 percent of the dropout population although they loom
larger in the public eye), 51 percent disappear because of things about the
school: 21 percent for economic reasons; 5 percent for family reasons; and 23
percent for other reasons. Youth older than the compulsory attendance age
who have been retained in grade and then simply walk away are the largest
component of the "other" group.[2] But what are the practical implications of
the big, school-centered set of reasons? Vocational programs have a higher
dropout rate than academic programs,[3] which might support the Committee
on Economic Development's (CED) recent attack on vocational education.[4]
But the difference is probably due to prior preparation of young people in the
two tracks: Forcing everyone into academic programs might accelerate the
dropout rate. In pursuit of reform, schools have raised standards and will
hold more children back. Being retained one grade increases the risk of
dropping out later by 40–50 percent, two grades by 90 percent.[5] Fifty-one

percent of the males but only 33 percent of the females who drop out do so because they "dislike school." Can we, should we change the gender-related experiences of schooling? Black youth who are poor stay in school more than do white youth who are poor, but is that because of perseverance in school or discrimination in the labor market?

Everyone agrees that the way young people experience school is the most frequently cited reason for quitting early. But what does that mean? Children who failed to learn? Or schools that failed to teach? The first are called "dropouts," the second are called "pushouts." Interestingly, youngsters blame the school less for their failures than might be expected. When asked why they dropped out, more than a third of all the boys say, "Because I had bad grades," "Because I did not like school." Only one in five drop out because they could not get along with the teacher and only 13 percent are expelled. The figures underestimate the institution's willful decision not to teach all children. Referrals to special education have become a common way to solve class control problems by pushing some youth out of the mainstream. One district suspended additional referrals because at then current rates, the entire pupil population would have been placed in special education within three years.[6]

Saying that schools push out some young people is a harsh statement of a painful responsibility. When schools give everyone a diploma (one consequence of social promotion), employers are inconvenienced and will force schools to discriminate among, for example, young people who do and do not have basic academic skills. In the search to make high school diplomas "meaningful," thirty-five states have raised graduation standards and twenty-nine have required passage of statewide minimum-competency tests, often as a condition of graduation.[7] But as Robert Crain discovered, business is more interested in the attitudes and habits of potential employees than in their academic skills.[8] Thus, schools are increasingly expected to teach children not only how to think but how to act. The Committee for Economic Development has said,

> If schools tolerate excessive absenteeism, truancy, tardiness, or misbehavior, we cannot expect students to meet standards of minimum performance or behavior either in school or as adults. It is not surprising that a student who is allowed to graduate with numerous unexcused absences, regular patterns of tardiness, and a history of uncompleted assignments will make a poor employee.[9]

Eighty percent of teacher criticism is now directed at 20 percent of the students. Blacks are already suspended from high school three times as often as whites.[10] Nonetheless, CED's message is clear: Schools should get tougher and kids should work harder. A recent study looked at the "time budgets" of young people, especially at how many from which groups were going to school full-time and simultaneously trying to make some money with outside jobs. The analysis indicated clearly that young people from minority backgrounds are fully engaged not just in school but also in paid employment. At least these young people are "Chasing the American Dream" (the report's title) with the same kind of overtime investment that previous upwardly mobile groups have done. There remains a real question of whether, given the quality of their school experience and the nature of labor markets, they will catch it.[11]

Work-related reasons for leaving school are cited by 21 percent of the boys and 9 percent of the girls.[12] This is a push-pull situation: Some are pushed by family necessity (about 14 percent of the boys in the High School and Beyond data set gave this explanation). Some are pulled by the lure of cash now (27 percent of the boys in High School and Beyond data). [13] Either way, being in paid employment poses a cruel choice for young people already at risk. Given limited time and energy, schoolwork suffers. Barro says, "Both males and females are more likely to drop out if they work longer hours."[14] Up to fourteen hours of paid employment a week, there is little effect. Fifteen to twenty-one hours a week increases the dropout rate by 50 percent; twenty-two hours or more increases the risk by 100 percent. Then there is the question of the quality of the jobs. Some may be full-time but dead end. These often temporary or seasonal jobs contrast with others that are threshold or entry-level jobs leading to a career. The jobs most likely to be held by the youth most at risk have been "dumbed down" and thus, again, hard work leads nowhere.[15] On the other hand, "High school completion . . . substantially boost[s] the earnings of youth." Morgan estimates that in 1981 high school graduates earned $60 a week more than those who quit.[16]

Looking at data about dropouts ought to teach us some things about the fragility of school completion, the competing forces that press young people away from that, and the very different impact of those forces on different kinds of youth. If only nine percent of girls leave school for economic reasons, only five percent of boys leave school for family reasons. But while boys drop out to support their families and girls to take care of them, both are helping. Between 1979 and 1982, 2.7 million young women left American high schools without graduating. One million of that group did so for family reasons: 45 percent left because they were pregnant, 37 percent because they got married, 18 percent because of home care responsibilities, especially for siblings.[17]

The closer one looks at the data, the less adequate are simple (if popular) explanations — "They're lazy," "Kids drop out because they don't fit in," "They're all on drugs," ". . . having babies," ". . . hanging out," and so forth. Variations in the experience ought to invalidate simple explanations. Why do southern high schools have half the holding power of northern schools? Why are black rates 40 percent greater than white rates while Hispanic rates are 250 percent higher than white rates?[18]

The singular outcome — not finishing high school — is in fact a nest of problems. A migrant child jerked from one curriculum to another suggests a pedagogical problem. A black girl, angry at real or imagined slights, would benefit from counseling for herself and her teachers. The son of a single mother who works because his family needs the income is caught in an economic vise, and so is the daughter who is chronically truant in order to help with younger siblings. Across all dropouts, the range of circumstances is impressive, even daunting. Equipping any system (from a junior high school through a state) to cope with them means accepting the multiplicity of causes. But they are nested in another way.

Most students quit because of the compounded impact of, for example, being poor, growing up in a broken home, having been held back in the fourth grade, and finally having slugged "Mr. Fairlee," the school's legendary vice-principal for enforcement. These young people need a range of things, just as any system's at-risk population will need services that fit their hurts. If the problem is complex, so will be the solutions.

MULTIPLE PALLIATIVES, MULTIPLE PLAYERS

Peng reports that the high school dropout rate for pupils entering the fifth grade has been 25 percent since 1958.[19] When an indicator is that sticky — 25 percent for twenty-five years — it says something about the power of the interventions being applied. Despite the amazing array of things that have been and are being tried, no one should talk about solutions.

In the list below, check the programs that are for dropouts.

( ) Enhancing the self-image of elementary school children
( ) An alternative high school
( ) A "Big Brother" program run by the Chamber of Commerce for low-achieving high school students
( ) Minicomputers for math instruction
( ) A storefront street academy with an experience-based career education component
( ) A school-improvement project to upgrade basic skills acquisition in a middle school
( ) Drug abuse counseling
( ) A foundation-supported study of occupational education
( ) Smaller class sizes
( ) T-shirts, notebooks, pencils (with corporate logos), and dictionaries given at a ceremony where three hundred ninth graders take a public oath to graduate
( ) An ombudsman

( ) A computerized index of commercially available curricula organized
by objectives for academic skills, attitudes, and job-performance skills

If you doubt that the list can be extended endlessly and that everything can
be related to dropouts, ask any schooling agency staff to report what they are
doing about the area. (An obvious way to make sense out of any list is to ask
that only programs "that work" be reported, about which more later.) The
up-side of the astonishing array is a measure of the sincerity and creativity of
the system. The down-side is chaos.

Asking "what works" is good for students who will continue to be at risk
until we have better answers, and for a public that would like to maximize
outcomes from tax dollars. But knowing what works requires knowing what
was done (the interventions applied) to whom (recall the variations in etiol-
ogy) and with what effect. Education agencies — not just schools — are trying
a galaxy of things that deserve serious inquiry. Even sorting the preventive
from the remedial interventions (i.e., before and after dropping out) would
help, but this is seldom done. A second step is to apply a framework that
captures differences among programs that may be related to differences in
outcomes. For example, does a program work directly with at-risk youth or is
it staff-focused, family focused, or organizationally focused in order then to
get at the at-risk youth? Such a taxonomy was used recently to analyze dropout-related activities reported by a dozen U.S. public school districts. The
categories most often used for the analysis of curriculum require data about
objectives, learner diagnosis, program content, program delivery, resources,
and pupil progress evaluation. Those six major headings were further divided into seventy-one subcategories. For example, was the program's content "academic" (enrichment, remedial, interdisciplinary), "vocational"
(work-study, career education, career exploration, job-specific vocational
training), or "guidance" (family counseling, life skills, social skills)? The construction of such taxonomies is the first step in finding out what works best:
academic, vocational, or guidance approaches. But a content analysis of programs submitted by just a dozen districts resulted in 360-plus entries scattered almost randomly over the major and minor headings.[20] Without even
addressing the outcomes question, the only thing that is clear is that most
districts are doing lots of things. From the program-improvement perspective, that is a very weak finding. Said another way, considering just in-school
programs, a dozen school districts were using sixty-three of the seventy-one
logically possible approaches to dropout prevention and/or remediation. If
those activities constituted a "naturally occurring experiment," that is, a
chance to use the results of current practice to refine future practice, then the
activities would be a resource.

But they are not. On the one hand, virtually anything can be "related" to
the dropout problem and on the other, we cannot even agree on what consti-

tutes a dropout. Phi Delta Kappa's Center for Evaluation, Development, and Research tried to derive a consensus definition of dropping out by looking at district reporting practices and concluded,

> We simply cannot agree what a dropout is. In some districts death, marriage, taking a job, entering the armed forces, entering college early, being expelled or jailed, going to a deaf school, business school, or vocational school causes one to be considered a dropout. In another district, none of these acts would be considered. . . .
>
> There are at least as many different definitions of a dropout as there are school districts recording dropouts. Some districts solved their problem of who to count as a dropout by not using any definition at all, whereas other districts had three or four definitions, and neither we nor they seemed to know which one was used.[21]

What have we learned? First, people feel that too many students leave school without graduating. Second, students are impelled to do that by a wide range of circumstances. Third, practical improvements depend on knowing what was done to whom, but (a) virtually everything is being done and (b) at the delivery level we cannot yet tell to whom or with what effect.[22] Thus, we are doing a lot and learning a little about the multiple palliatives.

Some will dissent from this interpretation. Professionals often form strong attachments and strong beliefs about their programs, and well they should. But conclusive evidence documenting significant program effects is even more rare than careful evaluation in this field. The point here is not that nothing works — some things probably do, and some approaches are preferable to others. We ought to maintain some version of the array of things now being tried but we ought also to learn from them, including what Hodgkinson calls "negative knowledge," that is, the candid admission that R, S, and T simply did not work and ought not to be tried again.[23] Given the protean shape of the dropout problem(s), there are no magic wands that, when waved, will turn chronic truants into college scholarship winners. People who believe in simple solutions here also believe that break dancing cures arthritis. Obviously, it is easier to be candid about program noneffects from the outside than the inside. Managers need success to increase budgets, leaders need hope to motivate staffs, and concerned professionals need positive outcomes to justify continuing and expanding their work.

And dropouts are a growth industry. In 1900, the U.S. high school dropout rate was 90 percent and no one cared. In 1940, it was 76 percent, but so what.[24] Now our national rate seems stuck at 25 percent — objectively better than ever and subjectively worse than ever. Schools are not the only interested agencies. For example, community colleges have begun to tell state legislatures that there is a message about the high school when young people vote with their feet. Instead of more money to that repudiated institution, states are being told to fund "Middle College Schools" that pull adolescents out of the tenth grade and bring them to the college campus for grades ten through fourteen. Such schemes try to combine the holding power of the high school with the pulling power of the college. They also move social missions, staffs, and budgets from secondary to postsecondary institutions.

For a time, school people did not mind. Awash in the baby boom, confident in the illusion that schools were society's primary educators, and discouraged by critics of their efficacy (both things were happening), it seemed just as well that the most difficult of the high school's clientele would serendipitously "solve" the institution's problem by disappearing. And if they went to a manpower training experience, a community-based agency, an alternative setting, or a private training vendor, so much the better. With too few resources for too much work, let the difficult cases tarnish someone else's reputation. In most places there are a lot of agencies that work with youth at risk. One result of this otherwise wholesome social invention has been a diminution in the responsibility for these youth felt by the core secondary school and with that diminution an insensitivity to signals of needed improvement that have been ignored until recently.

If school districts can produce long catalogs of dropout-related projects, so can other municipal agencies. In New York City, less than half of every youth-serving dollar is spent by the board of education. Taking just the employment-related piece of the dropout puzzle, the board of education spends more than $200 million on work experience and occupational training (the figure does not include activities in the city's ninety-plus academic secondary schools) but the department of employment spends another $80 million to work with in-school and out-of-school youth toward the same goals.[25] Trainers blame teachers for having failed to make young people job-ready. Teachers respond that if they had the luxury of a single mission (vocational preparation) and the resources of the training community, youth would be better served. Everyone suspects labor unions of sabotaging training efforts if a successful program would increase competition, decrease the value of union members' labor, or displace members' relatives who might otherwise have the inside track on new hires.

Coordinating policies to improve the programs available to young people is surreal in its complexity. Public sector agencies are the federal and state departments of labor and of education, the municipal department of employment, the multiple programs within the board of education, and public postsecondary institutions. The private sector has nonaffiliated independent and parochial schools; private, for-profit vocational schools; colleges and universities; and community-based organizations. Obviously both unions and employers should be represented and at one seat each, that is thirteen chairs around a conference table. The employment/economic facet of dropping out is just one dimension.[26]

Doing better than current practice is going to rest on convincing politicians that it is important and school people that it is doable. The next sections take up those topics.

BARRIERS TO BETTER PRACTICE

The fact that the dropout rate has not changed in such a long time suggests that not everyone regards this as a crisis. Teenage unemployment in central cities may be twice the unemployment rate of the Great Depression, but when an administration representative describes out-of-work youth as the "industrial reserve of America," it does not take too much imagination to understand that cheap labor, available to practically any enterprise, has its uses and so by extension does a system that emits undertrained youth. A child at risk is not likely to be the captain of the cheerleading squad, a Westinghouse semi-finalist, or the nephew of the school board president. Beneath the flurry of reform and the easy rhetoric about having excellence and equity (more of both for everyone!), there is real competition. "Twenty-nine states have established new *academic enrichment programs* . . . for gifted students."[27] But "as of 1984, virtually no state passed 'reform' legislation that contained specific plans to provide remediation to those who did not meet the higher standards on the first try."[28] Most young people at risk will be what some describe as the undeserving poor.

Consider that 10 percent of those who quit also drop back in ("stopouts") and that of those returnees, 90 percent go on to postsecondary education.[29] Some do not rejoin high school but try another sort of postsecondary institution. One might imagine that such diligence would be worth supporting. But rather than reinforce these young people in their investment, the U.S. Department of Education wants to deny the 119,000 young people in this category eligibility for Pell Grants (which grantees later repay). And not only does the administration want to cut them out; Secretary Bennett has stated that "I don't know what the Department can do about [the causes]."[30]

Most policy analysts subscribe to the notion that self-interest is the only reliable motivation. The task of policymakers is to get people to see how government action helps them. At the individual level, one might point out that when my grandfather retired in 1950, his Social Security Trust Fund income was guaranteed by seventeen currently employed workers who were paying into the fund. If I could retire in 1992, my Social Security checks would be supported by only three workers and one of those would be minority.[31] With most of some youth groups both out of school and unemployed, how much wasted human capital can I afford? How much can governments afford? The Appalachian Regional Commission estimates that dropouts will earn $237 billion less over their lifetimes than will high school graduates. Thus, state and local governments will collect $71 billion less in taxes.[32] (Said another way, we could spend $71 billion on dropout programs and still break even.) The majority of inmates in any jail are functionally illiterate yet a year in jail costs three times as much ($25,000) as a year in college.

Not all dropouts are a net drag on society but it is hard to argue that they are the most productive workers either. The U.S. economy is in the shape it is in partly because of the nature of the American labor force. Each day, we lose 3,500 jobs to foreign competition. Lester C. Thurow has noted that "every country in Northern Europe with the exception of Great Britain and Ireland, now has an average level of productivity, an average level of technology which is above the American average." In 1983, Japan made 15 million video recorders and sold them for $13 billion. The United States made none.[33]

The U.S. gross national product is approaching the $4 trillion mark but we have lost the old U.S.-dominated production process markets like basic steel, textiles, clothing, and footwear. In 1950, we made 80 percent of the world's cars; in 1980, 30 percent.[34] The Japanese, who originally moved into those areas, are now shifting out of them, so that simple electronic assembly has gone to Malaysia, Thailand, and the Philippines while complex production processes (color television sets, tape recorders, ship building) are increasingly dominated by Korea, Hong Kong, and Mexico. Every year from now to the year 2000, 36 million new workers will enter the world labor force and 85 percent will be from less-developed countries. Robert Reich, in "The Next American Frontier," suggests that the only way forward for the U.S. economy is in precision manufacturing — technology driven, flexibly produced, custom engineered processes. But what kinds of workers, what skills from young people are necessary for precision manufacturing, custom engineering, and flexible production? One measure of how badly we need reform lies in our current high school curriculum. We may congratulate ourselves that 15 percent of all high school students now take at least a year of French or German, but "the United States now does more trade with the Pacific Rim countries than with all of Europe combined. By 1995, American trade with the Pacific Rim will be double the size of our European trade." How many years of Cantonese instruction does the average high school offer?[35] Overcoming the political barriers to more resources will require that we convince ourselves that the United States cannot waste such a large portion of its youth. It is too expensive in lost taxes, misspent revenues, lost productivity, and lost profits.

Documenting the magnitude of a problem helps in assembling resources for amelioration.[36] In that regard, the notoriously wobbly nature of dropout data is troublesome. Until we can agree on what a dropout is and how to measure that, no one can make a compelling case for more attention to the plight, for example, of out-of-school youth from Central America. If the data are unreliable, misunderstood, and a basis for finger-pointing, it is easy to see why leaders are nervous about this area. Even worse, it is likely that they will be unfairly criticized for something that is beyond their control. Only a fool would accept public accountability for making subway trains run at super-sonic speed. Smart people resist being held responsible for things they cannot deliver. Thus, until answers come along, most districts will concentrate on what they do best, they will fret quietly about dropouts, and they will main-tain a string of activities (often developed for other purposes) that can be trotted out in response to criticism. That may distress some advocates, but it is prudent in that it minimizes criticism and protects the main event, the core part of the institution. Still, most professionals came into public schooling for reasons that connect with the democratic premise that all children can learn and should be taught. Local dissent from a national policy of "teach the best and to hell with the rest" is widespread and encouraging.

You cannot beat something with nothing. Documenting the magnitude of the problem(s) is one step; the next is replacing current practice with better practice. Here, the wild variation in the numbers reported makes it impossi-ble even to ask the "what works?" question. There can be no improvement without measures of success. The private sector calls this "the bottom line"; academics, "the dependent variable"; leaders, "results." By whatever name, the public school dropout field has no data linking programs to outcomes. But it does not have to be that way. Two youth-serving areas have made remarkable progress, in part because common definitions of outcomes have illuminated the process of improvement. The addition of "positive termina-tions" in youth employment training programs (e.g., enrollees who graduate and find and keep jobs) and standardized reading and math achievement scores in schooling for basic skills have both helped refine programs by linking inputs to client outcomes. The measures are controversial and have unintended outcomes but the difference that the absence of comparable standards makes is noticeable in the dropout area.

If better data would help, so would better programs.

BETTER PRACTICES, BRAIDED SOLUTIONS

Earlier we asserted that there are no solutions. But professionals must always make rough judgments about what seems to work. Not very many policy decisions are based exclusively on the evidence. While initiatives are fre-quently resisted on the ostensible grounds that they are "unproven," thank-fully, school people never have waited for the analytic community to resolve the last empirical issue before adopting a probably preferable practice. What follows is one person's summary of what works. It is offered in the hope that the reader's judgment, when combined with my own, might yield better practice than is now the case. And, as Alvin Gouldner once said in another context, "I have not felt compelled to inundate [these] pages with a sea of footnotes. If the substance and logic of what I say here does not convince, neither will the conventional rituals of scholarship."[37]

To begin with, there are great gains in removing or ameliorating the things that later cause students to drop out, especially school failure and a lack of mastery of the basic skills. Howe points out that "it costs only $500 to provide a year of compensatory education to a student before he or she gets into academic trouble. It costs over $3,000 when one such student repeats one grade once." [38] Lawrence J. Schweinhart and David P. Weikart have shown that two years of preschool education for one child cost $5,984 and returned $14,819 in savings from a reduced need for later special education ($3,353), increases in projected lifetime earnings ($10,798), and the mother's income from paid employment during the hours the child was in the program ($668). [39] The best way to avoid dropping out in high school is to make the elementary school more successful. (A special case can be made for the junior high school. Large numbers of already fragile adolescents fail to make the transition either into or out of such middle grades). Going upstream to minimize school failure, maximize school success, and provide a foundation of basic skills pays high dividends. The practical and empirical work going forward under the "effective schools" label is a strong resource in that regard. [40] The earlier we start, the less the damage and the greater the dividends.

Programs that seem to help have four Cs — cash, care, computers, and coalitions. For the first, we ought to understand that basic skills teaching and learning, by itself, is not enough. But then neither is it enough simply to put an at-risk young person into a work-experience program or an On-the-Job Training (OJT) situation. There needs to be a link between learning and earning. There needs to be experience with both schooling and paid employment. Some of the success of Joint Training Partnership (JTPA) program (née Youth Employment Demonstration Program Act [YEDPA], née Comprehensive Employment and Training Act [CETA]) springs from that connection.

The second C is care, or perhaps concern. Asking teachers to care about these children is asking a lot, since teaching them is seldom the system's most sought after assignment and especially since the group at risk is likely to have clarified everyone's incompetence and frustration for years previous. But there is no substitute for adults (probably all adults) knowing young people by name, asking about their lives, assigning homework, grading homework, and returning homework. One consequence is that the institution cannot be very large and the pupil-teacher ratio has to be lower than typically found. One example of what the care/concern precept can do is Atlanta's "Community of Believers," where — unique among U.S. urban public school systems — the lowest achieving youngsters are systematically identified and then paired with someone who has volunteered from the business community. Those adults are trained, tracked, and supported in their work with individual, at-risk youngsters and the early results are encouraging. [41]

Gary Wehlage's analysis of programs that work for marginal high school students supports the care/concern thesis. Wehlage found that successful programs were small with lots of personal contact; teachers had high expectations, used a wide range of instructional techniques, and cared about student progress; and the students were challenged to succeed at feasible tasks and had opportunities to take initiative and to show responsibility.[42]

The property of care or concern is what the futures literature calls "high touch" and that must be coupled with "high tech." The third *C* is computers. The use of computers here is twofold — instructional management and student management. Berlin and Duhl talk about the "second-chance" school system that has grown up around programs of adult basic education, the Job Corps, and the youth employment training area.[43] Many of the youth in such programs have dropped out; most share the sociodemographic characteristics of at-risk youth. Yet the second-chance system has made remarkable progress in recent years in working simultaneously on basic skills, attitudes, and job performance skills. One effort is a computerized index of the competencies necessary to each of these three domains, cross-referenced to the major commercially available curricula. Thus, a district can start at either end — "We'd like to teach these behaviors, how can that be done?" or, "We have these materials, how can they be used?" and use the system to support both teaching and learning. When fully operational, this "Comprehensive Competencies Program" (CCP) uses computer-assisted-instruction techniques to guide both teachers and students.[44] "Some students enrolled in CCP learning centers attain impressive grade gains. At a CCP center run by the Milwaukee Opportunities Industrialization Center, average reading gains of three grades and mathematics gains of 3.9 grades were recorded for the first group of seventy-seven who completed *100 hours* of instruction."[45]

The second use of computers is in identifying young people as they become increasingly at risk and then getting them help. Many students drop out because they cannot bear the cumulative weight of what is happening to them. Most districts have a sense of what those reasons are, and different parts of most systems even collect data about them. Computers can keep track of those multiple impacts and alert a professional before they reach a danger point. Poor grades in Rodney Zagorip's student file are one flag, a second is truancy, a third is retained in grade/older than classmates, a fourth is discipline problems, a fifth is paid employment, a sixth is family problems, and so on. The computer asks (generally based on district-specific profiles), "How many hits can a 14-year old boy stand?" When that point is reached, the file goes to a dropout prevention team whose job it is to find Rodney and see that he gets what he needs.

But recall the nested problems of the dropout. Personally, what Rodney needs may well lie beyond the public school. Organizationally, there are nonschool agencies whose budgets depend on helping Rodney. If complex problems require ambitious solutions, the problem of early school leaving ought to implicate everyone — schools, youth employment programs, civic agencies, parents, community-based organizations, business and industry.

Orchestrating different municipal agencies can be like steering the Crab Nebula. Turfs, unions, constituencies, missions, standard operating procedures — everything varies, but despite that, the national "Cities-in-Schools" program seems to be making a difference in Texas, Atlanta, and New York as it puts the schools together with parks and recreation, juvenile justice, family courts, social work, and youth employment.

In the context of coalition-building, the fourth *C*, it is worth repeating how much can be gained for at-risk youth by increasing the interaction between schools and employment-training organizations. The two agencies have much to offer each other. With refreshing candor, federal planners admitted in the 1970s that they did not know how to solve the problem of teen-age unemployment and thus, while they would continue to press for billion-dollar operating appropriations, they recommended that Congress reserve a fixed proportion for evaluating what was done. That simple expedient (plus an enormous amount of program evaluation design and implementation) turned federally supported youth-employment programs into a long-term, multi-site, mega-buck naturally occurring experiment aimed at deriving better practice from current efforts. We need to do the same in the dropout area. We also need to learn from each other. The interpenetration is apparent in the comments of two manpower economists, Berlin and Duhl, writing about summer learning programs:

> Research on the effects of summer learning suggests that schools play a significant role in the education of rich and poor alike, significantly reducing, if not entirely overcoming, differential achievement rates related to socioeconomic status. Viewed in an employment and training context, school effectiveness research may have significant implications for in-school, school-to-work and summer youth employment and training programs.[46]

The final resource in coalition-building can be the business/school partnerships that have been formed in this decade. The Boston Compact is deservedly famous in that the participating businesses were challenged to reserve a specific number of new-hire vacancies to be filled with high school graduates if, in fact, the Boston schools could increase the achievement and preparation of such youth. A related approach with considerable success in finding and deploying new resources for the public schools is the creation of local education foundations, largely assisted by the Pittsburgh-based Public Education Fund.[47]

Classroom teaching is an isolated and lonely business but so is working in a dropout program. Districts maintain them but without much hope for success, and they are seldom promoted. Categorical programs do not target these youth while they are in school, there are no fiscal rewards to organizations that succeed, and there is no network bonding similarly inclined professionals. From the standpoint of career advancement, the area is so risky as to be a disincentive. Where neighboring professionals do try to communicate, the chaos of definitions, the blizzard of approaches, and the lack of agreed-upon outcome measures produce cacophony. The result is not only isolation; it is also good practices that literally cannot be shared. Here again, doing better rests on a coalition. If the lesson of the 1960s was that the system cannot be driven from the top, the lesson of the 1970s should be that it cannot be led from the bottom. No one is going to impose answers on this field but neither are answers going to bubble up unaided. We need a consortium of major players, dedicated to the thoughtful scrutiny of their own practices, convened over time, and with a way to test and share their results. That too suggests a coalition.

The policy area of the dropout is emphatically one in which action creates understanding. The clock that measures our efforts is calibrated with young people. Fifteen percent is a conservative estimate of the dropout rate for a city school system. In middle-sized cities — Boston, St. Louis, San Francisco — that means about twenty students drop out each week. If you are charged to "do something" about that you might begin with a survey of existing practices, which could take a month (and 80 students); a needs assessment will take two more months to circulate and analyze (160 more students); writing a program and getting board approval could be three months (and 240 more young people gone). That is 480 dropouts before anything different and maybe better is even tried. Our efforts here are measured by time and money *and* by what happens and does not happen to children and youth.

Notes

1 Samuel S. Peng, "High School Dropouts: A National Concern" (Washington, D.C.: National Center for Education Statistics, U.S. Department of Education, n.d., Mimeographed), p. 14.

2 William R. Morgan, "The High School Dropout in an Overeducated Society" (Center for Human Resource Research, Ohio State University, February 1984, Mimeographed).

3 Stephen M. Barro, "The Incidence of Dropping Out: A Descriptive Analysis" (Washington, D.C.: SMB Economic Research Inc., October 1984, Mimeographed).

4 Committee for Economic Development, *Investing in Our Children: Business and the Public School* (New York: CED, 1985), pp. 30–35.

5 Jerold G. Bachman et al., *Youth in Transition, Volume III: Dropping Out — Problem or Symptom?* (Ann Arbor, Mich.: Institute for Social Research, 1971). Cited in Gordon Berlin and Joanne Duhl, "Education, Equity and Economic Excellence: The Critical Role of Second Chance Basic Skills and Job Training Programs" (New York: The Ford Foundation, August 30, 1984, Mimeographed).

6 Cf. Gary G. Wehlage and Robert A. Rutter, "Dropping Out: How Much Do Schools Contribute to the Problem?" in this issue.

7 Harold Howe, II, and Marian Wright Edelman, *Barriers to Excellence: Our Children at Risk* (Boston: National Coalition of Advocates for Students, 1985), p. 51.

8   R. L. Crain, "The Quality of American High School Graduates: What Personnel Officers Say and Do about It," Report No. 354 (Baltimore: Center for the Social Organization of Schools, The Johns Hopkins University, 1984).

9   Committee for Economic Development, *Investing in Our Children*, p. 20.

10   Howe and Edelman, *Barriers to Excellence*, p. 10.

11   Dale Mann, "Chasing the American Dream: Jobs, Schools, and Employment Training Programs in New York State," *Teachers College Record* 83, no. 3 (Spring 1982): 341 – 76.

12   Morgan, "The High School Dropout," Table 5.8, p. 14.

13   Peng, "High School Dropouts," Table 8, "Reasons 1980 sophomore dropouts reported for leaving high school before graduation, by sex: February 1982."

14   Barro, "The Incidence of Dropping Out," p. 62.

15   See Mann, "Chasing the American Dream," pp. 24 – 25.

16   Morgan, "The High School Dropout," p. 24.

17   Ibid., Table 5.8

18   Howe and Edelman, *Barriers to Excellence*, pp. 16 – 18.

19   Peng, "High School Dropouts," Table 2, "Estimated dropout rates based on pupils who entered 5th grade," p. 14 (source: *Digest of Education Statistics 1982*).

20   Cf. George Paul Morrow, "Standardizing Practice in the Analysis of School Dropouts" (Ed.D. diss., Teachers College, Columbia University, 1985).

21   Larry Barber, "Dropouts, Transfers, Withdrawn and Removed Students" (Blooming-ton, Ind.: Center for Evaluation, Development, and Research, Phi Delta Kappa, Inc., n.d., Mimeographed), pp. 7, 8.

22   Clinical data developed and used by workers and aggregate, generally national data are very different. The national data sets are fairly good and certainly better developed than the more important clinical data that might inform the improvement of practice. The current state of the art in dropout program management is akin to obstetricians trying to improve their forceps delivery techniques by peering at the "Current Population Survey" from the Bureau of the Census.

23   Harold Hodgkinson points out, "Negative knowledge is very important in making a profession out of a field" (Harold Hodgkinson, *All One System* [Washington, D.C.: Institute for Educational Leadership, 1985], p. 12).

24   Ibid., p. 11.

25   Cf. Dale Mann, "Education," in *Setting Municipal Priorities*, ed. Charles Brecher and Raymond D. Horton (New York: Russell Sage, 1981), pp. 367 – 69.

26   Cf. Jeannette S. Hargroves, "The Youth Training and Employment 'Mess': Boston's Interactive Planning Approach" (Boston: Federal Reserve Bank, n.d., Mimeographed).

27   Howe and Edelman, *Barriers to Excellence*, p. 52. Emphasis in original.

28   Hodgkinson, *All One System*, pp. 11 – 12.

29   Morgan, "The High School Dropout."

30   *Education Week*, May 1, 1985, p. 10.

31   Hodgkinson, *All One System*, p. 3.

32   Research Triangle Institute, "Study of High School Dropouts in Appalachia" (Research Triangle Park, N.C.: Center for Educational Studies, Research Triangle Institute, May 1985).

33   Lester C. Thurow, "A National Industrial Policy" (New York: New York Urban Coali-tion Forums on Political Economics, occasional paper, November 16, 1983).

34   Economic information in this paragraph is based on Robert B. Reich, "The Next Ameri-can Frontier," *The Atlantic Monthly*, March 1983, pp. 43 – 58.

35   Foreign language data are from Valena White Plisko, ed., *The Condition of Education: 1984*, Table 5.6, "Percent of 1982 High School Graduates Who Met Curriculum Recommenda-tions of the National Commission on Excellence in Education by Subject Area and Selected School Characteristics, 1982," (Washington, D.C.: National Center for Education Statistics, NCES 84-401), p. 164; trade data from President's Commission on Industrial Competitiveness,

Global Competition: The New Reality (Washington, D.C.: U.S. Government Printing Office, January 1985), vol. I, p. 10.

36   The distribution of a policy problem is sometimes even more helpful than its magnitude. Nothing guarantees a more favorable reception for a program manager than the fact that the nephew of the chairman of a legislative committee is, for example, enrolled in a drug abuse treatment program.

37   Alvin Gouldner, *The Coming Crisis of Western Sociology* (New York: Basic Books, 1970), p. viii.

38   Howe and Edelman, *Barriers to Excellence*, p. x.

39   Lawrence J. Schweinhart and David P. Weikart, *Young Children Grow Up: The Effects of the Perry Preschool Program on Youth through Age 15* (Ypsilanti, Mich.: Center for the Study of Public Policies for Young Children, High/Scope Educational Research Foundation, 1980). Figures are 1979 dollars.

40   For elementary school applications, see Wilbur Brookover et al., *Creating Effective Schools* (Holmes Beach, Fla.: Learning Publications, Inc., 1982); and Dale Mann, "Excellence? For Whom?" *Equity and Choice* 1, no. 1 (Fall 1984). For secondary schools, see Michael Rutter et al., *Fifteen Thousand Hours: Secondary Schools and Their Effects on Children* (Cambridge: Harvard University Press, 1979).

41   Cf. Boyd Odum, "A Community of Believers," Fourth Anniversary Report of the Atlanta Partnership of Business and Education, Inc., Atlanta, 1985.

42   Gary G. Wehlage, *Effective Programs for the Marginal High School Student* (Bloomington, Ind.: Phi Delta Kappa Educational Foundation, 1983).

43   Berlin and Duhl, "Education, Equity and Economic Excellence."

44   Cf. Robert Taggart, "The Comprehensive Competencies Program: An Overview" (Alexandria, Va.: Remediation and Training Institute, August 1984, Mimeographed).

45   R. C. Smith, "Special Report: Mastery Learning: Catch-up for Students Who Fail," *Ford Foundation Letter* 15, no. 6 (December 1, 1984): 3. Emphasis added.

46   Berlin and Duhl, "Education, Equity and Economic Excellence," p. 50.

47   Cf. *The First Two Years: The Public Education Fund, 1983–1985* (Pittsburgh: Public Education Fund, n.d.).

Large School Systems' Dropout Reports: An Analysis of Definitions, Procedures, and Findings

FLOYD MORGAN HAMMACK
New York University

One basic problem for both researchers and policymakers is obtaining accurate information about dropouts. In this article, Floyd Hammack examines school district reports on the dropout problem in Boston, Los Angeles, Miami, New York City, San Diego, and Chicago. Citing the great diversity in the processes for the classification of students as dropouts, he raises important concerns about the comparability of dropout rates between districts.

Although there is considerable concern about the proportion of young adults who have not completed high school, there have been few efforts to explore in detail how school systems define dropouts and how they arrive at rates of completion. Much of our data regarding rates of completion come from national data-gathering efforts such as the Census Bureau and the Department of Labor, which provide information on the proportion of those at specific years of age who have attained a high school diploma or higher education. Other sources of data include information school systems provide to the National Center for Education Statistics (NCES). The NCES data on dropouts are based on the yearly number of high school graduates compared with the number of freshmen enrolled four years earlier for each state, in addition to data it uses that are provided by other government agencies. This former figure does not, of course, take into consideration in- and out-migration or the number of students held back or advanced a grade during the period. These data, moreover, may not be comparable if districts do not use similar methods of defining dropouts or similar methods for calculating rates of completion. Cooke, Ginsberg, and Smith report on these and similar problems with national educational data.[1] Thus, while we have information,

This article is part of a larger project on New York City dropouts sponsored by the New York City Alliance for the Public Schools. I would like to thank Gary Natriello, Lloyd Bishop, and Deborah Inman for their helpful comments. However, the views presented here are mine, and do not necessarily reflect those of my colleagues or the alliance.

for example, about the proportion of twenty-two-year-olds who have not received a high school diploma, we certainly cannot rely on national data for those who are sixteen.

As we begin to think seriously about ways to hold school systems accountable for their educational efforts, however, we need to pay strict attention to how they measure such important indicators as school completion rates. Relatively small differences in such calculations can produce large differences in rates. Are special education students, however they are identified, included in the rates? Are students attending night school treated as dropouts? These are just two examples of the differences in definition that can lead to rather large differences across systems and consequently different assessments of the degree to which systems are providing effective education for their students.

It is worth noting that research on dropping out seems, like most educational issues, to follow a cyclical pattern. Even a cursory search of the literature reveals considerable activity during the late fifties and early sixties, and a rather sharp decline since then. The problems of specific demographic groups have received attention, especially legislatively, but problems that cut across these and other groups have not been as assiduously attended to in the last fifteen years. In the context of this article, the National Education Association's (NEA) publication *Dropout Studies: Design and Conduct* is illustrative of the noncumulative nature of educational knowledge.[2] Many of the problems of consistency and comparability of reporting found in the current report are also identified in this twenty-year-old NEA publication. Moreover, the 1965 document provides ample examples of how to overcome the limitations of existing (both then and now) data sources.

In an effort to begin the investigation of these differences, and the degree to which they exist, the following report presents information on how several large urban school systems define dropping out (or "early school leaving," as some systems describe it), and on how they process the information and arrive at rates of school completion. A summary of the major findings reported in the documents collected is also provided.

METHOD

School systems were contacted in order to obtain information regarding the nature of their definition of dropouts, the procedures for collecting the necessary information to determine dropout statistics, and the method used in determining the dropout rate. Appropriate school officials were contacted in the following cities to obtain the information reported here: Boston, Los Angeles, Miami, New York City, San Diego, and Chicago.

These cities were chosen because they are large, contain heterogeneous student populations, and have high proportions of students who were recent migrants or whose parents had recently immigrated. These criteria were chosen for several reasons. First, the dropout problem, although important in all districts, is especially acute in large, urban centers with heterogeneous populations. While national estimates of rates of leaving school before a diploma range from 18 to 25% of eighteen-year-olds,[3] estimates from large cities are often double these rates, and, for some subgroups of urban students, rates have been reported at 60% or higher.[4] Second, recent research emphasizes the importance of limited English proficiency as a factor associated with early school leaving.[5] Thus, districts with substantial numbers of immigrants from non – English speaking areas or large groups of non-native-English speaking students are likely to have greater problems with dropping out. Finally, reports prepared by research and/or evaluation offices of five of these systems were obtained and are discussed below. In the case of Chicago, I was referred by officials in the Department of Research and Evaluation, Chicago Board of Education, to a report prepared by the Chicago Panel on Public School Finances.[6] This report was prepared in cooperation with the Department of Research and Evaluation, and was held by them to be the most accurate information available on Chicago dropouts.[7] Additionally, I will refer to a study prepared by another external advocacy group in Chicago, Designs for Change, reported on in *Education Week*,[8] and found in the document *The Bottom Line: Chicago's Failing Schools and How to Save Them.*[9]

Clearly, not all districts that meet the criteria above are included in this paper. Although others were contacted, recent reports were not available or additional needed information could not be obtained by telephone interview. The districts included in this report, therefore, represent only themselves. Nevertheless, the problems they illustrate and the findings they provide are certainly common among districts across the country and can both illuminate what data districts can provide on the dropout phenomenon and point to directions that need to be pursued in improving the collection and use of dropout statistics.

DIFFERENCES IN THE DEFINITION OF A DROPOUT

The issue of noncompletion of high school courses of study has become one of considerable importance to all the school systems contacted. In some cases, it has become enmeshed in local politics and is currently very controversial. In other cases, where politicization has not gone far, the issue is still considered a high priority due to efforts of state education authorities to enhance the statewide performance of local schools. In any case, all those contacted expressed high levels of concern. At a time of increased public interest and legislative focus on education, the fact that a considerable proportion of enrolled students do not achieve what has become the expected minimum level of educational attainment — represented by the high school diploma — is being more closely scrutinized than before. This is especially the case as national and local evidence clearly demonstrates wide variations in completion rates among demographically identifiable groups. Not only, then, are questions of organizational effectiveness involved, but so too are questions of educational equity.

Under these circumstances, the question of how dropouts are identified and counted is important. Procedurally, all school systems contacted begin the process at the building level, where an attendance secretary, or the equivalent, maintains records of attendance of students enrolled at the school. When students formally leave a school, a notation is made regarding why the student is leaving. These notations are usually in the form of a code, perhaps with additional information. Such codes usually include: transferred to another school; entered a private school; moved out of district; entered the military; entered full-time work; and so on. Such codes are standard throughout each system and, along with other student records, are periodically transferred to the central office where systemwide data are collected and processed. However, the thoroughness of such centralized record keeping, its currency and ability to be used for student tracking and report generating, vary, as does the availability of personnel to utilize such systems.

An important issue arises when students do not formally withdraw from school. This can occur when students simply do not appear at the school to which they have been assigned. For example, a number of students who drop out do so during the summer, between academic years. Others stop attending without formal notification to the school that they have withdrawn. How school officials classify these long-truant students depends on the available codes and on their efforts to follow up on such students. "Not found," or a similar phrase, is frequently used for such students, and is usually one of the codes included in the dropout statistics. How long a student may be truant before being classified as a dropout, however, varies widely among districts.

The complexities do not stop here. As school systems have developed special schools, alternative programs, and the like, the collection of data for central record keeping has become very difficult. Consistency of reporting within districts as well as across them becomes problematic. For example, some districts include special education students in their reports, while others do not; some include all students enrolled in any type of program offered by the district, while others include only those enrolled in regular day high schools. The specific dropout codes that are used vary, so that in some districts, a transfer to a business or trade school is not registered as a dropout, while in others it is, at least if the school does not offer a high school diploma program. Finally, as the structure of educational systems varies both within districts and between them, there is no consistency in the grade levels included. Some districts have regular four-year high schools and junior or intermediate schools that include the ninth grade plus senior high schools, while others have only one or the other. The data reported in dropout reports sometimes includes only tenth through twelfth grades; others report ninth through twelfth grades, but only those from regular four-year high schools, leaving unreported ninth-grade students dropping out from junior high schools. The effects of these different definitions on rates reported for systems are not known but undoubtedly account for at least some of the variability between them.

That variability in dropout rates exists is aptly demonstrated by the information collected by Dale Mann and his colleagues at Teachers College, Columbia University, for the National Invitational Working Conference on Holding Power and Drop-outs, sponsored by the American Can Company Foundation and held during February 1985.[10] Dropout rates for eleven school districts varying widely in size and geographic location were presented in the conference report. As reported, the one-year, cross-sectional rates range from .8% in St. Cloud, Minnesota, to 16% in Fort Worth, Texas. Size of district, however, seems not to be directly related, as Houston (the seventh largest district in the country) is reported to have a 5.4% rate, and Cleveland (the twenty-eighth largest) reports a rate of 4.4%, while St. Louis (forty-second largest) reports a rate of 15%. It should be noted that the veracity of these data were questioned by both those who provided them and other conference participants.

School districts also vary in the formulas used to calculate their dropout rates. The most common procedure is simply to divide the number of dropouts by the total enrollment for the grade levels included during a single year (a cross-sectional rate). Other districts follow cohorts, usually across the secondary school years. Still others provide projections from cross-sectional data to four-year rates.

It is useful to note here that the context in which the data gathering and reporting processes just described take place has important implications for the quality of data collected. For example, I was told by a school official in one city that considerable pressure had been exerted on principals in the district to keep the dropout rate low. Performance evaluation systems for school managers used in this system were suggested as providing part of this pressure. One of the ways this was accomplished was for building-level personnel to intentionally mis-code students who were "not found," that is, who were most likely true dropouts. A proportion of such students were coded as "transferred to private schools." Because there was no mechanism to share data between public and private schools, such codes effectively meant that the school's codes could not be checked (had there been an effort to do so), and its dropout rate was recorded as lower than it actually was. Other students who had in fact dropped out were thought to have been coded as having moved out of the district. These suspicions led the district's central research office to be skeptical of the data being forwarded by the individual schools. The magnitude of distortion involved here may be sizable: One school in this system reported an "official dropout rate" of 1.9%, but its actual rate was calculated by the central office as 58.3%.[11]

The quality-of-data question is critical because, although a central office may utilize a definition of dropout, that definition must be adhered to at the point of generation, that is, at the school-building level. The degree of adherence is affected by intentional mis-codes as well as by errors of recording.

To the degree that state legislatures, their departments of education, local boards, and superintendents attempt to increase accountability and focus on attendance and retention, accuracy of data becomes even more problematic. While previously, the lack of data, of whatever quality, had been cited as a problem, educational leaders may now be creating the circumstances that produce plenty of data, but of questionable quality. Because dropouts come predominantly, though by no means entirely, from disadvantaged segments of the population, issues of equity are involved, and these, along with other issues, can lead to politicization. Such politicization can lead to action on this neglected problem, but it can also lead to subversion in data reporting. Designers of school record keeping systems need to be alert to problems of data integrity.

CITY-BY-CITY FINDINGS

BOSTON

Boston public schools, comprising the thirty-seventh largest district in the country, enrolled 62,989 students in the fall of 1981. Of this number, 30,733 were secondary school students.[12] During the 1978–1979 school year (the most recent for which data are available), the racial and ethnic composition of the student body was: 3% Asian, 12% Hispanic, 44% black, and 40% white. A total of 11.5% of all students were identified as having limited English proficiency.[13]

In Boston, any student who leaves school before graduating for one of the following reasons is considered a dropout: work, military service, marriage, over age sixteen, did not report, and other. Special education students as well as those enrolled in alternative schools are included. The rate reported in the Office of Counseling and Pupil Services' "Drop-Out Information Paper"[14] is calculated by dividing the total number of high school (grades nine to twelve) dropouts for a school year by the total enrollment for that year. This cross-sectional rate for 1983–1984 was 14.2%. The rates for individual high schools vary from 0% at Boston Latin Academy (a selective public school) to 24.5% at Dorchester High School (a comprehensive high school). By far the largest number of dropouts were found in the "over age sixteen" category.

Considering only male dropouts, the rates by race were: white: 15.6%; black: 14.7%; Hispanic: 19.9%; Asian: 11.4%. The corresponding rates for females were 12.8%, 13.7%, 14.7%, and 7.6%.

LOS ANGELES

The Los Angeles Unified School District enrolled 540,903 students in the fall of 1981, 161,907 of whom were secondary school students. It is the second largest district, behind New York City, in the country.[15] The U.S. Department of Education reports that for the 1978–1979 school year, Asians comprised 6% of the student body; Hispanics, 38%; blacks, 25%; and whites, 30%. Those students with limited English proficiency comprised 16.5% of all students.[16]

The most recent data available from Los Angeles are for the academic year 1981–1982, and are reported in the document "Early School Leavers: High School Students Who Left before Graduating, 1981–1982."[17] Only senior high school students (grades ten to twelve) are included in the report. The term "dropout" is not employed by this school system; rather, they refer to "early school leavers." Those early school leavers who are included in the data are those whose codes were: overage, whereabouts unknown, full-time employment, institutionalized, medical exclusion, enlisted military, marriage, and other. The "other" category included such reasons as nonattendance or excessive absence, in custody of parent at home, or "dropped to parent, deceased, expelled, child care, and miscellaneous." Miscellaneous included undercover agents, no statement, emancipated minor, and runaway. The most frequent code was overage, with whereabouts unknown a very close second and all others far behind.

Overall, the proportion of early school leavers was 7% of the total school enrollment for the year. Included in these numbers are students attending all types of secondary school programs. Males comprised 55% of dropouts. Hispanic students constituted 43% of the early leavers, and their cross-sectional rate was 8.6%; white students constituted 26% of the early leavers and had a cross-sectional rate of 6.0%; black students also comprised 26% of those identified as early leavers and had a rate of 7.6%; Asian students were 4% of the leavers and had a rate of 7.4%.[18]

MIAMI

The Dade County school district enrolled 224,580 students in the fall of 1981, of whom 105,137 were enrolled in secondary schools. It is the fourth largest system in the country.[19] According to the U.S. Department of Education, the district's student body in 1978–1979 was comprised of 1% Asian students; 32% Hispanic students; 29% black students; and 38% white students. Students with limited English proficiency comprised 5.3% of the total enrollment.[20]

The Miami report was unique (except for the report prepared by a Chicago advocacy group, discussed below) among those examined in that it reported on a longitudinal study of the June 1980 eighth-grade cohort followed through February 1985.[21] All students who were in the eighth grade in June 1980 in the school system are included. The definition of dropout was any student who left the ninth-to-twelfth-grade program before completing a program of studies and receiving either a certificate of completion or a diploma. Exceptional students, retained students, "no shows" from one school year to another, and those whose parents are not citizens were included. Excluded from the data were those who graduated, are still enrolled, transferred to another school, died, were transferred to the court or a private agency for purposes of custody, or were expelled. Of the students followed, 29.5% had dropped out by the end of the follow-up period. The rate for whites was 26.4%, for blacks 33.9%, for Hispanics 29.3%, and for Asians 19.0%. For males, the rate was 32.1%; for females, 26.8%.[22]

There are several other findings from this study that are worth noting. For example, the researchers found that the largest proportion of dropouts left during the freshman and sophomore years;[23] that being overage in the eighth grade (a result, for example, of being held back in earlier grades) was *very* strongly associated with eventual dropping out;[24] and that of those students who do drop out, a large number do so between academic years, during the summer.[25] This report, however, does not provide information of school leaving codes used by schools to report data. Thus, there are no data from which to assess reasons for dropping out or what the young person did after leaving school.

NEW YORK CITY

The New York City school system, the largest by far in the country, enrolled 924,123 students in the fall of 1981, of whom 469,263 were at the secondary school level.[26] Data from the U.S. Department of Education for 1978–1979 reveal that 3% of New York's total enrollment was comprised of Asians, 30% Hispanics, 39% blacks, and 29% whites. Almost 10% of the total enrollment was classified as having limited English proficiency.[27]

The report prepared by the Educational Management Information Unit of the New York City Public Schools, "Dropouts from New York City Public Schools, 1982–1983," is the most thorough of those reviewed in providing details about how the data were collected and the procedures used for arriving at the statistics reported.[28] Where prior reports had included only students discharged as dropouts from day high schools, this report embraces as well all ninth- through twelfth-grade students who dropped out of intermediate and junior high schools, who left special education programs without a diploma, and who dropped out of retrieval settings such as pre-General Equivalency Diploma (GED) and GED programs, Schools for Pregnant Teens, Substance Abuse Programs, and Literacy Programs.

The term "dropout" is defined as any student who left the school system in the 1982–1983 school year prior to graduation, and who did not enter other educational settings leading to a high school diploma within the same year. Students who re-enrolled were not counted as dropouts, but those who, for example, entered a business school program that did not lead to a diploma were included. The discharge codes identifying dropouts are: age seventeen or over with parental consent (the New York City schools are mandated to provide up to high school diploma education for all residents up to the age of twenty-two, although the minimum age of voluntary withdrawal is seventeen with parental consent); employment (requires a certificate and parental consent and can be obtained after age sixteen); not found; transferred to business or trade school. Not included in the dropout category are students who graduated, transferred, were institutionalized, entered college early, entered high school equivalency programs, or attended other (auxiliary) board-sponsored programs. For students from schools below the high school level, the primary code was "not found"; a few left for work or were over seventeen.

The rates calculated in the report are "survival rates." For example, there were 39,040 dropouts during the 1982–1983 school year and a ninth- to twelfth-grade enrollment in the intermediate and high schools of 309,784. Thus, 12.6% dropped out, and 87.4% remained in school. Multiplying the survivor proportion by 4 yields a value of 58.4%, the survivor rate, and 41.6% as the projected four-year dropout rate. When only high school students are included, the rate drops somewhat, to 11.4% dropouts, and a four-year projected rate of 38.4%.[29]

By dropout code, the report finds that among the day high school dropouts, 9.4% entered employment, business or trade schools, or the military; 8.9% were reported to have transferred to auxiliary or outreach centers but did not enroll in them; 74.2% left at age seventeen or over; and 7.5% were not found, after a search by the attendance bureau.[30]

By grade level, the largest group left in the tenth grade, 31.4%; 25.2% left in the ninth grade; 20.8% left in the eleventh grade, and 14.6% were seniors when they dropped out. Of the remainder, 6.1% were special education students not categorized by grade level, and 1.9% did not have their grade level recorded.[31]

Males comprised 55.8% of these dropouts, and females accounted for 44.1%.[32] It is interesting to note that almost 20% of the dropouts were born in 1963 or before, which would have made them almost nineteen years old in September of 1983. Seventeen was the most common age of dropping out

(38.4%), but 17.6% were sixteen (born in 1966), and 23.8% were eighteen (born in 1964).[33]

The report includes no other personal information on students, so racial or ethnic differences are not available from this document. Although a racial and ethnic census is taken by the system, individual student records do not include such information. However, school-by-school dropout data are reported and range from a low of .5% at two selective high schools, Stuyvesant High School and Bronx High School of Science, to 24.9% at a comprehensive high school, Roosevelt.

SAN DIEGO

San Diego City Unified schools, the fourteenth largest system in the country, enrolled 110,904 students in the fall of 1981, of whom 33,465 were in secondary schools.[34] The U.S. Department of Education reported that, for 1978–1979, Asians comprised 7% of the total enrollment; Hispanics, 16%; blacks, 15%; and whites, 62%. A total of 4.5% of enrollees was classified as having limited English proficiency.[35]

The San Diego report was the only one to include student performance data and information about the special advantages and/or disadvantages that characterized its school leavers.[36] The report itself is based on data from 1982–1983, is cross-sectional in nature, reports a "school leaver" rate of 4.5%, and projects a cumulative attrition over four years of 16.5%.[37] The definition of "school leaver" employed includes any student who participated in any grade, nine to twelve, during the school year, had the ability to meet graduation requirements or pass the California High School Proficiency Examination, did not transfer to another school or certified program, and did not reenter the system by October 1983. Males comprised 54% of all school leavers. The rates for specific ethnic groups are as follows: Hispanics, 7.4%; whites, 3.8%; blacks, 5.1%; Asian/Pacific Islanders, 6.8%.[38]

School leavers were classified according to reason for leaving in the following categories: whereabouts unknown, 41.6% of all leavers; married, 3.6%; withdrew, under eighteen, 10.5%; withdrew, over eighteen, 13.4%; full-time employment, 17.0%; mental condition, 10.2%; hardship, 0.5%; pregnant, 3.1%.[39]

By age, of those leaving, 3.2% were thirteen to fourteen years old; 13.1% were fifteen; 23.7% were sixteen; 30.5% were seventeen; 26.0% were eighteen; and 3.4% were nineteen or twenty. By grade level, 3.8% of freshmen left school, 4.6% of sophomores, 6.6% of juniors, and 2.6% of seniors.[40]

Regarding student-performance data, the findings are consistent with previous research. Early leaving is far more characteristic of students who are not doing well in meeting academic expectations than those who are doing average or better. Seventy percent of those who left early had scholastic averages of 2.0 (on a four-point scale) or below; over one-half were below 1.5 and over one-fourth were below 1.0. On the other hand, 7% of leavers had averages over 3.0.[41]

Students with limited English proficiency had higher dropout rates than those who were fluent in English; their rate of leaving was 7.5%. Hispanic students comprised 15.5% of the students enrolled and had a leaving rate of 7.4%. Hispanic limited-English-proficiency students were .9% of the system's students, but left at a rate of 12.5%. The differences are also striking for Indochinese students. They comprised 6.3% of the system's students, and the Indochinese limited-English-proficiency students were 4.1% of the system's students. These limited-English-proficiency students left at a rate of 5.2%, while those fluent in English had a rate of 1.3%, the lowest for any group studied.[42]

Additional data are provided for students enrolled in special programs that were seen as advantageous (gifted, etc.) and for those who had disadvantages not elsewhere included in the report (handicapped, a record of suspension, bottom half of reading scores, etc.). The data for these groups are consistent with the labels associated with the variables: students in gifted, magnet, and other programs associated with success in the schools or those who had high grade-point averages (a sign of success in school) had low leaving rates. On the other hand, students who had been unsuccessful in meeting school expectations or had other disadvantages were far more prone to leave school before obtaining a diploma.

CHICAGO

The City of Chicago school system enrolled 442,889 students in the fall of 1981, of whom 125,255 were at the secondary level. It is the third largest school district in the country.[43] The U.S. Department of Education reported that for the 1978–1979 school year the student body of Chicago's public schools was 2% Asian, 16% Hispanic, 61% black, and 22% white.[44] Those students identified as having limited English proficiency were not reported.

As noted earlier, the dropout report for Chicago was prepared by the Chicago Panel on Public School Finances in cooperation with the Department of Research and Evaluation of the Chicago Board of Education.[45] It differs from the other reports discussed here in that it was prepared by an outside advocacy group. However, the report was cooperatively prepared and was recommended by personnel in the Board of Education who had aided in the data analysis for the report.[46]

Dropouts from Chicago Public Schools provides a longitudinal analysis of the high school classes of 1982, 1983, and 1984. The class of 1982 (which entered the high schools as freshmen in 1978) received the most attention, but comparisons are made between their rates and those of the later years. The 1982 class is studied most intensively because the researchers found that at the end of four years, 10% of this class was still active in the public schools. Thus, a complete analysis of the careers of this class required the inclusion of data from later years. The report follows the 1982 students until September of 1984, or over two years beyond the normal four years.

Because there has been controversy in Chicago about the dropout rate and the methods used to calculate it, this report is very explicit about which categories of students are counted as dropouts. Only those students who transferred to legitimate secondary schools outside of the public system are eliminated from the analysis. Even this exclusion, however, raises questions. The researchers report that the system's follow-up efforts to assure that such transfers actually took place are not vigorous, and thus this modification of the base may act to decrease the actual dropout rate (only slightly, however).[47] Nevertheless, 85% of all members of the class of 1982 attended only one school and remained in the public school system. The 1982 class was comprised of 33,142 students, of whom 140 were still enrolled in the system as of September 1984; 3,060 had transferred out of the system. Of the remaining 29,942, 12,804 were classified as dropouts, for a longitudinal rate of 42.8%, and 17,138 graduated, for a graduation rate of 57.2%.[48]

The report also provides data on dropouts by characteristics: age, race and ethnicity, reading score, and gender. It provides some rates calculated from combinations of these variables, but does not provide extensive multivariate analyses.

Age was found to be an important variable. Fourteen years of age is typical for high school freshmen, and those who entered high school at this age dropped out at a rate of 37%; for those thirteen years of age, the rate was 26%. These two age groups comprised 74.4% of the entering freshman class. However, for those fifteen years of age or older in 1978 (25.6% of the class), the eventual dropout rate was 59.9%, and for those sixteen or older, the rate was 68.8%. The proportion of the class who entered at these two age levels was 23% and 3%, respectively.[49]

By reading level, the rate of dropouts is linear. For those students at or above "normal" reading level (47% of the class) when they entered high school, 23% had dropped out (i.e., not graduated or transferred) by September 1984.[50] For those students whose eighth-grade reading scores were at the 4.7 to 6.7 grade level, the dropout rate was 49.9%, and for those whose scores were lower than that level, the rate was 67.8%. These two groups comprised, respectively, 33.6% and 13.1% of the entering freshman class in 1978.[51]

Considering gender, the differences were consistent with national and other cities' data. Males dropped out more frequently than did females (49.2% against 36.2%).

By race or ethnicity, while black students comprised 63% of the class, their dropout rate was 45.1%; whites were 22% of the class and had a rate of 34.5%; Hispanic students were 14% of the class and dropped out at a rate of 46.9%; Asian students were 2% of the class and dropped out at a rate of 19.4%.[52]

The report finds that entering high school overage, that is, at fifteen or older, is especially potent as a predictor of dropping out, and that this condition is more common for males than females. Holding students back a year or more in elementary school increases the probability of dropping out. The effect of being overage is increased if the student reads below grade level and/or is black. The rates of dropping out for black males who enter at age sixteen or over is 77%; for black males who enter at age fifteen, 63%. These two groups comprised 16.8% of the class of 1982, and provided 25% of the dropouts.[53]

Interestingly, the effects of entering high school at an older than normal age were not present for Hispanics, nor as dramatic for whites or Asians. The authors speculate that language difficulties for Hispanics might account for part of their being held back and that this reason did not carry the stigma or represent the degree of failure that being held back for non-language-related reasons did for black students.[54]

By schools, the dropout rates varied from 62.6% at a 100% black school where 37.6% entered overage, and only 40.3% entered with normal reading scores, to 10.8% at a school with 95.7% white students, 82.7% of whom were reading at or above grade level. As one might expect, the latter school had few students from poverty families (9.0%) while the former school had many (73.2%). Systematic analyses of student body characteristics and performance and dropout rates were not provided for the schools, but much individual school information is presented. From an inspection of these data, however, while the ranking of schools by dropout rates compares closely with the proportion of at-risk students they serve, there are schools that do better and worse than would be expected on the basis of student body characteristics alone. Clearly, these data, although underanalyzed, provide room for optimism about the possibilities of interventions at the school level that may lower the dropout rates.

A report prepared by Designs for Change, a nonprofit advocacy group in Chicago, reports that for "the system as overall, the High School Completion rate is 47%." [55] The rates for predominately black and Hispanic high schools were 65% and 64%.[56] Precise information about which school-leaving codes are included in dropout statistics is not available, nor is information about whether all groups of students and schools (e.g., alternative or special education schools) are included. These data, while lacking the precision of those provided by the Chicago Panel on Public School Finances reviewed here, are generally comparable with them.

CONCLUSIONS

The most important conclusion of this paper is that there is no single or standard definition utilized by the school systems contacted. Moreover, rates are calculated differently and include different data. Under these circumstances, comparisons across school districts must be made very carefully, and only when there is some assurance that data or rates have been adjusted to account for the differences noted here. Such adjustments are often impossible to make.

However, as this review shows, there is much to be learned from the reports of school districts — both about how they gather and process information and from the specifics of their reports. In this regard, special note can be made of the Miami and Chicago reports, which provide information not available elsewhere and may therefore be useful in stimulating thinking about ways to analyze data that inform policy and programs. Furthermore, the San Diego report, although cross-sectional, contains a variety of information not found in the other reports and provides an illustration of the analytical benefits to be derived from a full data base on students and an analysis informed by policy-relevant and explanatory hypotheses. Specifically, the availability of student background, achievement, and discipline data allows for more detailed analyses than were reported by other cities. It may well be that such data were available in at least some of the other systems, but not utilized in the reports. The Miami and Chicago reports illustrate the value of using such annual or periodic reports for more than accountability or evaluation purposes; they can also offer districts information that can be useful for program design and implementation as well as for generating basic research.

One substantive finding that has not received the attention it deserves needs to be highlighted: Students who are overage when they enter high school are far more likely to drop out than are their classmates of normal entering age. School policies of promotion and retention must be carefully examined for their negative effect on dropout propensity, with their positive educational effects better established and balanced against the negative effects shown in these reports. It is clear that being overage is associated with other indicators of problems with school and thus is not, by itself, a variable whose policy manipulation will result in large effects. Nevertheless, the evidence presented here casts doubt on the positive effects on holding students back. Moreover, except for those students who enter a system overage, students who are held back in elementary or junior high schools are known to school officials as already having difficulty in school. They can easily be identified as at risk and targeted for special attention.

Although, as noted, the reports summarized here are very difficult to compare, it is useful to keep in mind information on dropouts provided by national surveys. The November 1983 National Center for Educational Statistics' (NCES) *Bulletin,* entitled "High School Dropouts: Descriptive Information from High School and Beyond," reports data from a longitudinal study begun in 1980. It finds that about 14% of 1980 high school sophomores left school during or after their sophomore year before completing requirements for graduation. Of these, 24% left in their sophomore year, 47% left in their junior year, and 29% left in their senior year. Males had a 15% rate, while females left at a rate of 13%. American Indians and Alaskan natives had the highest rate, at over 29%; Hispanics, 18%; blacks, 17%; whites, 12%; and Asians left school early at a rate of 3.0%. Students whose self-reported grades were "mostly D's or below" had a 42.5% rate, "mostly C's," 18.5%, "mostly B's," 8.1% and "mostly A's," 2.9%.[57]

The survey also asked students for the reasons (post hoc) for dropping out. Of the male students, 36% reported, "I had poor grades; I was not doing well in school." The next largest response was "School was not for me; I did not like school," cited by 35% of the respondents. "I was offered a job and chose to work" was cited by 27%; "I couldn't get along with teachers" was the reason given by 21% of the dropouts; and "I was expelled or suspended" was cited by 13%. For females, the four most frequently cited reasons were "I got married or planned to marry" (31%); "school was not for me" (31%); "had poor grades" (30%); and "pregnancy" (23%).

It is clear that these data are generally comparable with the city school system reports summarized here. These national-sample survey data are useful for providing a measure against which to examine the city data, but explicit comparisons, again, must be made very carefully, especially when comparing the overall rate, as the student composition of the city systems examined here varies widely from that of the nation as a whole. Moreover, freshman students are not included in the NCES report. That exclusion may account for the difference between the figures cited above for the sophomores of 1980 and the percentage of eighteen to nineteen year olds who had dropped out of high school as of October 1981, as reported by the Bureau of the Census (from Current Population Reports). This latter figure was 16.0% for all, 17.9% for white males, 13.2% for white females, 18.9% for black males, and 19.7% for black females. For those twenty and twenty-one years old, the rates were: white males, 16.5%; white females, 12.8%; black males, 24.1%; black females, 22.6%.[58]

Given what we know from previous research about the characteristics of students at greatest risk of dropping out,[59] it is clear that the interpretation of dropout rates for school districts or, for that matter, individual schools must take into account the student body served. Reports of single variable analyses, for example, must be viewed with skepticism.[60]

Finally, the current emphasis on accountability of school managers and teachers and performance-based contracts must be seen as a double-edged sword. While it clearly directs attention to specific aspects of school operations and productivity, it also creates the incentive to misreport relevant data.

This article provides evidence of the problems and also the prospects of district-generated dropout research. We certainly need greater consistency in definitions, and specifically the operational definitions of discharge codes and the grades and categories of students included in the enrollment base used to calculate rates. California, among other states, is moving in this direction, requiring all districts to report data in a consistent fashion. While districts may prefer a particular method, the use of cohorts or at least projected four- or six-year longitudinal rates as provided in the Miami and Chicago reports or the New York City report should also be considered so as to provide both additional information and consistency across districts. The benefits of including demographic and performance data in such reports is clearly demonstrated by the San Diego and Chicago reports. Researchers should be cautious in interpreting data across districts and states, and should begin to build student composition variables into their models. Finally, administrators must be alert to intentional misreporting in the design of student information systems and in the use of accountability data.

Notes

1   C. Cooke, A. Ginsberg, and M. Smith, "Researchers Find That Educational Statistics Are in a Sorry State," *Basic Education* 29 (January 1985): 3–8.

2   National Education Association, *Dropout Studies: Design and Conduct* (Washington, D.C.: National Education Association, 1965).

3   R. W. Rumberger, "Dropping Out of High School: The Influence of Race, Sex, and Family Background," *American Educational Research Journal* 20 (Summer 1983): 199–220; and N. B. Dearman and V. W. Plisko, *The Condition of Education, 1979 Edition* (Washington, D.C.: Government Printing Office, 1979). See Gary G. Wehlage and Robert A. Rutter, "Dropping Out: How Much Do Schools Contribute to the Problem?" in this issue.

4   R. Calitri, *Minority Secondary Education in New York* (New York: Aspiria of New York, Inc., 1983).

5   L. Steinberg, P. L. Blinde, and K. S. Chan, "Dropping Out among Language Minority Youth," *Review of Educational Research* 54 (Spring 1984): 113–32.

6   Chicago Panel on Public School Finances, *Dropouts from the Chicago Public Schools* (Chicago: Chicago Panel on Public School Finances, 1985).

7   William Rice, personal communication, July 23, 1985.

8   Alina Tugent, "Half of Chicago Students Drop Out, Study Finds," *Education Week*, March 6, 1985, p. 10.

9   Designs for Change, *The Bottom Line: Chicago's Failing Schools and How to Save Them* (Chicago: Designs for Change, 1985).

10   Dale Mann, "Report of the National Invitational Working Conference on Holding Power and Drop-outs" (New York: Department of Educational Administration, Teachers College, Columbia University, Mimeographed, 1985).

11   Chicago Panel on Public School Finances, *Dropouts*, p. 6.

12   W. V. Grant and T. D. Snyder, *Digest of Educational Statistics* (Washington, D.C.: National Center for Education Statistics, 1984).

13   U.S. Department of Education, Office of Civil Rights, *Directory of Elementary and Secondary School Districts, and Schools in Selected School Districts, School Year 1978–1979* (Washington, D.C.: U.S. Department of Education, n.d., p. 614).

14   Boston Public Schools, Office of Counseling and Pupil Services, "Drop-out Information Paper" (Boston: Boston Public Schools, n.d.).

15   Grant and Snyder, *Digest,* p. 58.

16   U.S. Department of Education, *Directory,* p. 155.

17   Los Angeles Unified School District, Research and Evaluation Branch, "Early School Leavers: High School Students Who Left Before Graduating, 1981–1982" (Los Angeles: Los Angeles Unified School District, 1983).

18   Ibid., p. 5.

19   Grant and Snyder, *Digest,* p. 58.

20   U.S. Department of Education, *Directory,* p. 258.

21   Dade County Public Schools, Office of Educational Accountability, "A Study of the Longitudinal Dropout Rate: 1980 Eighth-Grade Cohort Followed from June, 1980 through February, 1985" (Miami: Dade County Public Schools, 1985).

22   Ibid., p. 3.

23   Ibid., p. 4.

24   Ibid., p. 11.

25   Ibid., pp. 4, 5.

26   Grant and Snyder, *Digest,* p. 58.

27   U.S. Department of Education, *Directory,* p. 955.

28   New York City Public Schools, Educational Management Information Unit, "Dropouts from New York Public Schools, 1982–1983" (New York: New York City Public Schools, 1984).

29   Ibid., pp. 10, 11.

30   Ibid., p. 20.

31   Ibid., p. 21.

32   Ibid.

33   Ibid., p. 22.

34   Grant and Snyder, *Digest,* p. 58.

35   U.S. Department of Education, *Directory,* p. 186.

36   San Diego City Schools, Planning, Research and Evaluation Division, "The 1982–83 School Leaver Study of the San Diego Unified School District" (San Diego: San Diego City Schools, 1985).

37   Ibid., p. 4.

38   Ibid., p. 13.

39   Ibid., p. 15.

40   Ibid., p. 20.

41   Ibid., p. 23.

42   Ibid., p. 28.

43   Grant and Snyder, *Digest,* p. 58.

44   U.S. Department of Education, *Directory,* p. 366.

45   Chicago Panel on Public School Finance, *Dropouts.*

46   William Rice, personal communication, July 23, 1985.

47   Chicago Panel on Public School Finances, *Dropouts,* pp. 114–15.

48   Ibid., p. 21.

49   Ibid., p. 22.

50   Ibid.

51   Ibid., pp. 22, 23.

52   Ibid., p. 25.

53   Ibid., p. 28.

54   Ibid.

55   Designs for Change, *The Bottom Line*, p. 7.

56   Ibid., p. 8.

57   *National Center for Educational Statistics Bulletin*, "High School Dropouts: Descriptive Information from High School and Beyond" (Washington, D.C.: National Center for Education Statistics, November, 1983), pp. 1–9.

58   Grant and Snyder, *Digest*, p. 71.

59   Rumberger, "Dropping Out of High School"; R. D. Mare, "Social Background and School Continuation Decisions," *Journal of the American Statistical Association* 75 (June 1980): 295–305; A. L. Stroup and L. N. Robbins, "Elementary School Predictors of High School Dropout among Black Males," *Sociology of Education* 45 (Spring 1972): 212–22; Steinberg, Blinde, and Chan, "Dropping Out among Language Minority Youth"; T. S. Sewell, A. J. Palmo, and J. L. Manni, "High School Dropout: Psychological, Academic and Vocational Factors," *Urban Education* 16 (1981): 65–76; W. R. Morgan, "The High School Dropout in an Overeducated Society," in *Pathways to the Future, Volume IV: A Report on the National Longitudinal Surveys of Youth Labor Market Experience in 1982,* ed. P. Baker et al. (Columbus, Ohio: Center for Human Resources Research, Ohio State University, 1984).

60   R. Merritt, "The Effect of Enrollment and School Organization on the Dropout Rate," *Phi Delta Kappan* 65 (November 1983): 224.

Standardizing Practice in the Analysis of School Dropouts

GEORGE MORROW

Columbia High School, Maplewood, New Jersey

After demonstrating the types of problems that arise from using different methods to calculate school dropout rates, Morrow suggests a set of procedures to standardize the process and improve the validity and reliability of data on dropouts.

School dropouts have been a concern among educators for over one hundred years. W. T. Harris initiated the public discussion of why students left school prematurely in an 1872 address to the National Education Association.[1] Since then, hundreds if not thousands of studies have focused on the dropout issue. Thirty years ago Blough reviewed over eight hundred studies on dropouts.[2] The U.S. Bureau of the Census and the National Center for Education Statistics have collected data on dropouts for decades. Wehlage and Rutter reviewed four major longitudinal studies conducted in the past twenty years on U.S. dropouts.[3] Today most of the fifteen thousand school districts in the United States monitor the enrollment and graduation or dropping out of their students. Yet for all this effort there is little agreement on the direction for school dropout programming efforts.

A knowledge base regarding school dropouts, from which programming activities can grow, has not yet been firmly established. The multitude of sources for data and analysis regarding dropouts creates problems of consistency. Reasons for analyzing dropout statistics range from generating ammunition for a change in school policy to school-district comparisons. Differences in defining the target population (dropouts), computing a summary statistic (dropout rate), and collecting and coding primary data create research results and school reports that are incompatible if not misleading. The Illinois State Task Force on Hispanic Student Dropouts recently stated that "the lack of . . . uniformity in a definition has kept policy and lawmakers from understanding the nature, scope, and dimension of the dropout problem."[4]

Two competing approaches to the study and reporting of dropout data have complicated the building of a knowledge base. The approach chosen shapes the collection and manipulation of data and the reporting of results.

38

Schools maintain a dynamic data set. Students enroll, transfer, graduate, drop out, and are readmitted on a daily basis. Accountability is to a public school board and state offices, and is often viewed in an evaluative manner. Several states publish, for comparison purposes, the dropout rates of their school districts and high schools. Special-interest/research groups use static data tapes and consider factors beyond the school walls. Their goal is to obtain results useful to their sponsor. Accountability is to scientific credibility and/or a specific audience.

This article discusses the variety of practices used by researchers and practitioners in two areas that impede the development of a common knowledge base on dropouts: the definition of a school dropout, and the computation of a dropout rate. Placing the possible practices together may help delineate the parameters of a common data set for the study of school dropouts. Solving the "problem" of school dropouts may not be in the immediate future, but achieving a better understanding of the phenomenon of dropping out of school is possible.

DEFINITION OF A DROPOUT

The term "dropout" has been used to designate a variety of early school leavers: (1) pushouts — undesirable students; (2) disaffiliated — students no longer wishing to be associated with the schools; (3) educational mortalities — students failing to complete a program; (4) capable dropouts — family socialization did not agree with school demands;[5] and (5) stopouts — dropouts who return to school, usually within the same academic year. Barber attempted to establish, by majority vote, a common definition of a dropout.[6] His attempt failed, however, because competing concerns overruled the desire for consistency.

Current definitions of dropout can be used to establish the critical elements of a common definition. Good states that dropout

> most often designates an elementary or secondary school pupil who has been in membership during the regular school term and who withdraws or is dropped from membership for any reason except death or transfer to another school before graduating from secondary school (grade 12) or before completing an equivalent program of studies; such an individual is considered a dropout whether his dropping out occurs before or between regular school terms, whether it occurs before or after he has passed the compulsory school attendance age, and where applicable, whether or not he has completed a minimum required amount of school work.[7]

This definition is a refinement of the definition used in the manual by Project: School Dropouts and the National Education Association.[8] Page and

Thomas briefly define dropout as a "person who leaves school/college before completing his/her studies."[9] Many definitions of dropouts are written by state agencies and school districts. These definitions commonly list reasons why students withdraw from school; selected reasons constitute "dropout," others "nondropout." A review of "reasons for dropping out" used by school districts as their working definition of a dropout, and the more formal textbook definitions listed above, suggest three criteria for a definition: (1) Is the student actively enrolled? (2) If not, has the enrollment been formally transferred to another legitimate institution? (3) Has the student earned a high school diploma or its equivalent? A school's dropouts are those students, at one time formally enrolled, for whom all three questions are answered in the negative. These three questions will serve as the framework for discussing variations in defining a school dropout.

NOT CURRENTLY ENROLLED

Both decisions about the enrollment status of individual students and the method of district enrollment record keeping affect a school's total enrollment. Decisions about the enrollment of individual students are influenced by several factors.

States distribute funds based on the number of students a school claims to serve. It is to the financial benefit of a district to have as many students on their enrollment list as possible. State auditors may be used to monitor the actual presence of students reported on school enrollment lists. Problems arise regarding students enrolled at one time who later become less active: truant students, students who may have moved to another district, and deceased students. In each of these cases, classification of the questionable student as a dropout diminishes the district's state funds and may also require the district to add the student to its dropout count. Both are negative sanctions.

Students are absent for various reasons that schools often label as excused or unexcused. Truancy is a student's unexcused absence without a parent's permission.[10] If dropping out is the intentional premature departure from school, then an approved absence (trip, illness), where the intention of the student is clearly to return, should not remove the student from the enrollment list. However, extended truant behavior or continued unexcused absence presents doubts of the student's intention to return. Establishing a specific number of days of continuous unexcused absences would set a clear criterion for determining if a student should be designated a dropout.

Dropout statistics are also affected by the method of enrollment record keeping. Continuous enrollment permits the tracking of students who drop out during the summer break. Barber cites noncontinuous enrollment, where districts close their enrollment books in the spring and start fresh in the fall, as a major problem.[11] In such cases only students dropping out during the school year can be counted as dropouts. A final count of dropouts takes place in the spring; a student who finishes tenth grade and does not enroll in the eleventh grade is never included in the district's dropout count: "School membership should be on-going or continuous. A pupil is a member of a class or school from the date he enters until he withdraws by completing his school work, transferring, dropping out, or dying."[12] Noncontinuous enrollment permits a large gap in accounting for students.

TRANSFER OF ENROLLMENT

A student may attend many schools but the classification of a student as a dropout is associated with the school last attended. Two problems exist in transferring possession of a student's enrollment. First, what proof is needed that a student has enrolled in another school, permitting subsequent dropping out to be associated with the latter school? Second, to what kind of institution is it acceptable to pass on the responsibility for educating a child? Is the school at the state correctional facility for minors an appropriate academic institution, or the Deluxe Travelling Barber College?

It is common practice that new students enrolling in a school district are asked the name of the school and district they previously attended. The receiving school then sends a letter to the administration of the previous school asking for a record of the student's schoolwork. This record (the student's transcript) is mailed to the new district and the initiating letter is stored in the school's files as proof of the student's transfer. Without this certifying letter the student *may* be considered a dropout. This practice places responsibility for a district's dropout count on receiving school districts. Cooperation among districts is crucial.

The definitions noted earlier indicate that a dropout is someone not "graduating from a secondary school (grade 12) or [leaving] before completing an equivalent program of studies,"[13] or "completing high school."[14] All states provide public education and establish standards for high school completion.[15] Educational institutions are licensed by state agencies to provide high school programs and degrees. However, the receiving school's legal status is not always considered when transferring student enrollment. In order for all students to be accounted for (graduated, dropout, or death), it is imperative that any organization being formally approved as offering a public school education or its equivalent be held accountable for reporting the status of all students who enroll.

Some organizations, such as the armed services or the Job Corps, offer and/or encourage formal secondary instruction. Dropouts who join these organizations may be encouraged to finish a high school equivalency program. However, neither of these institutions is held accountable for the formal secondary education of its recruits.

HIGH SCHOOL GRADUATION

The actual criteria used to qualify for high school graduation have become a volatile issue in the past three years.[16] Education is a state function, and as such each state has established its own set of graduation standards.[17] Hence there are a great variety of possible routes to a high school diploma. The names assigned to the award given on completing these standards vary as well. It seems inappropriate if not impossible to demand uniformity across states and districts. Since we use the state educational agencies to approve institutions providing formal education, it seems appropriate to consider their judgment in establishing graduation requirements as well.

Special education students are sometimes permitted variances in their graduation requirements. These students have been recognized, usually by a panel of education professionals, as being hindered in the average attainment of educational skills and abilities. In some cases the state or district may choose to credential students who complete twelve or more years of school without completing the suggested minimum requirements. Such students meet the intention of completing a high school program, and as such ought to be considered valid high school graduates. Other awards include vocational certificates, certificates of attendance, and the Graduate Educational Development (GED) award. As useful as these credentials are to the individuals, they do not signify the sanctioned approval of the state for graduation.

The GED is growing in stature within the educational community and needs to be discussed by the states as a possible equivalent to the high school diploma.[18] Qualifications, however, may be necessary (eighteen years or older) to weaken the perceived competition of the GED with the local public school program.

COMPUTATION OF A DROPOUT RATE

A rate is expressed as a fraction (or ratio) of the incidence of something happening, over the pool of times it could have happened. This ratio is often written as n/d = rate. The numerator (n) is the count of special cases from the total of possible cases (d), the denominator. In computing a dropout rate, the numerator (n) is the number of students fitting the district's definition of a dropout, the denominator (d) is the pool of students from which the dropout originated.

Two mathematical principles are important when dealing with the dropout rate. As a ratio of one number against another, the dropout rate will increase or decrease with a change in the numbers. A change in the numerator (number of dropouts) will create a change in the same direction as the dropout rate, that is, an increase in the number of dropouts also increases the dropout rate. A change in the denominator (pool of students) creates the opposite change in the dropout rate, that is, an increase in the pool of possible dropouts will decrease the dropout rate. The power of this elementary math is significant to a district's reported dropout rate.

Three factors influence the mathematical computation of a dropout rate. First is the *time frame* during which the number of students who drop out is counted. Traditionally the time frame has been one calendar year or an annual dropout rate; districts using noncontinuous enrollment use a nine- or ten-month time frame. An alternative to the annual dropout rate is called the cohort dropout rate, used to monitor a group of students for several years. A second factor is the *range of grade levels* (K – 12, 7 – 12, or 9 – 12) selected by a district to represent its pool of possible dropouts. Third is the *student accounting procedure* used by the district, commonly referred to as either Average Daily Attendance (ADA) or Average Daily Membership (ADM).

In computing a dropout rate, our previous discussion of the definition of a dropout is influential in determining the size of the numerator — the number of students labeled dropouts. A liberal inclusion of students increases the dropout rate, a conservative inclusion decreases the dropout rate.

The denominator of the dropout fraction represents the student population pool from which dropping out is said to occur. The denominator is commonly referred to as the *baseline population,* and is as open to variation in size as the definition of a dropout.

To standardize a dropout rate three practices need to be consistent: (1) a definition of a dropout, (2) a time frame, and (3) a baseline population. The definition of a dropout is used to establish the numerator. Consideration of the denominator, time frame, and baseline population follows.

TIME FRAME

Two time frames are used to compute dropout rates. The most common is the annual dropout rate. This procedure uses a single school year as its time frame. The number of dropouts (n), usually the sum of a district's dropouts across all grade levels, is divided by the baseline population (d) representing a single year for a single grade level or multiple grade levels (see Figure 1a).

The cohort dropout rate has a time frame of several years and is a more statistically involved method that monitors only a segment of the school population. This method is used to follow the dropping out among students who are expected to graduate together. Figure 1b shows how the 1980 freshman may be isolated from other high school students and monitored through their sophomore, junior, and senior years. The cohort dropout rate presents a more accurate picture of the success and failure rate of the dis-

School District X 1983–1984

n = 50 dropouts
d = 1000 students

$$\frac{50}{1000} = 5\% \text{ dropout rate}$$

Figure 1a. Computation of an Annual Dropout Rate

trict's school program. Figure 1b summarizes the likelihood of a freshman's dropping out before graduation at 20 percent. The Project: School Dropouts study offers numerous computational methods for determining both a dropout rate and a district's holding power (ability to hold students in school until graduation).[19] Their manual prefers the term "cumulative rate" to "cohort rate."

BASELINE POPULATION

The powerful effect of controlling the membership in the baseline population was recently shown in the comparison of Scholastic Aptitude Test (SAT) scores state by state.[20] SAT scores may be reported as the mean score of *test takers* within a state. If a state routinely encourages all students to take the SAT, the pool of students begins to represent a cross section of students within the state. If, on the other hand, a state encourages only those students with college potential, it restricts SAT test takers to those most likely to do well. The selective states have SAT score means above their expected norm because of the restricted pool of test takers. Reports using only the states' mean SAT scores cannot be used to rank the scholastic aptitude of a state's youth, or to compare the quality of various state education programs.

The baseline population for dropout computations has two components:

High School Y Class of 84 (1980–1984)

n =   8 (freshman dropouts, 1980–1981)
     29 (sophomore dropouts, 1981–1982)
     46 (junior dropouts, 1982–1983)
     <u>17</u> (senior dropouts, 1983–1984)
    100 total dropouts (1980–1984)

d = 500

$$\frac{d}{n} = \frac{100}{500} = 20\% \text{ dropout rate for the Class of 1984}$$

Figure 1b. Computation of a Cohort Dropout Rate

District XYZ
(1983–1984)

Annual dropout rate $= \dfrac{n}{d}$

n = 3308 dropouts   d = 65272 (K – 12)
                                    = 27317 (7 – 12)
                                    = 22119 (8 – 12)
                                    = 16922 (9 – 12)

K – 12 $\dfrac{3308}{65272} = 5.1\%$

7 – 12 $\dfrac{3308}{27317} = 12.1\%$

8 – 12 $\dfrac{3308}{22119} = 15.0\%$

9 – 12 $\dfrac{3308}{16922} = 19.5\%$

Figure 2a. Annual Dropout Rate Computed Using Different Grade Levels in the Baseline Population

the grade level distribution and the student accounting process. *Grade level* refers to the range of grades most likely to generate dropouts. In fact, students of any grade can drop out, legally or illegally. Our earlier definition of a dropout did not separate elementary students from secondary or high school students, nor will our example school XYZ (Figures 2a through 2e).

Student accounting refers to the approach used to tally the number of students a school district serves. This is traditionally done by Average Daily Attendance or Average Daily Membership. The two methods are related, but reports generated by each are different.

Limiting the range of grade levels represented in the denominator dramatically increases a district's reported dropout rate. The four-year profile of an actual school district (XYZ) is used to show the effect of different baseline options. Figure 2a shows the possible annual dropout rates of District XYZ using different baseline populations. The number of dropouts is kept constant at 3,308 since many districts include dropouts at all levels (K – 12) in computing the dropout rate.

District XYZ's dropout rate varies from 5.1 to 19.5 percent, a jump of 380 percent depending on the grade levels included in the baseline population. Each of the computed dropout rates is an "average" for the entire baseline population. This suggests that in the K – 12 grade example in Figure 2a, 5.1

District XYZ's Dropouts

Elementary*		Secondary	
PreK —	1	7 —	46
K —	10	8 —	89
1 —	26	9 —	286
2 —	11	10 —	1501
3 —	9	11 —	815
4 —	5	12 —	493
5 —	4		3230
6 —	12		
	78		

District Total: 3230 + 78 = 3308

* 66 of the elementary school "dropouts" were "Lost to the System," suggesting procedural error.

Figure 2b. Frequency of Dropouts by Grade Level, in a Sample District

percent of the third graders dropped out as well as 5.1 percent of the tenth graders. This can be misleading if the incidence of dropping out is limited to a portion of the pool. District XYZ's distribution of dropouts looks very different (Figure 2b).

Dropping out appears to be a tenth- and eleventh-grade phenomenon. Spreading the dropout rate over thirteen years of school suggests that all ages have the same potential for dropping out. However, constraining the baseline population to the high school (9 – 12) fails to consider the 421 students who dropped out of junior high. Attention to dropouts has generally been focused on the high school, yet some consider the junior high/middle school years as important, formative years, relevant to future success in school.[21] Many school systems have changes in building, curriculum, and student assignment to courses between the sixth and seventh grades — professionally this is the demarcation between elementary and secondary education. Including the seventh, eighth, and ninth graders in the denominator increases the size of the baseline population, thus lowering the annual dropout rate, but it also focuses attention on these grades as relevant in dropout discussions.

Average Daily Attendance and Average Daily Membership are two common methods to report the number of students a district serves.[22] Membership (ADM) includes all students who are assigned to a school; attendance (ADA) is the average number of students who enter the school building on a daily basis. A school's ADA number is a percent of the ADM number. This percentage is called the attendance rate (see Figure 2c). As in dropout rates, a districtwide attendance rate hides variations in grade-level attendance patterns. Nationwide the school attendance rate in 1981 – 1982 was about 92

1983–1984 District XYZ

ADM = 34035

Attendance Rate = 80.3%

ADA = ADM × Attendance Rate

ADA = 34035 × .803 = 27317

ADA = 27317

Figure 2c. Relationship of Average Daily Attendance to Average Daily Membership

percent.[23] Since attendance is seldom perfect, a district using attendance for its baseline has a smaller denominator than one using membership. A district using school membership, ADM (a larger number in the denominator), would report a lower dropout rate than the same district using ADA (Figure 2d). The lower the attendance rate the greater the difference in a district's reported ADA versus ADM dropout rate; ADA always produces a larger dropout rate. In district XYZ the high schools have a lower percentage of students attending than the elementary schools. A districtwide attendance rate would be between these two levels.

The earlier example of the effect of grade-level groupings in the baseline population on the dropout rate (Figure 2a) used ADA as the baseline population; a comparison using ADM is shown in Figure 2e. District XYZ's annual dropout rate is shown to vary from 4.4 to 19.5 percent depending on how the baseline population is determined. Such a range gives a great deal of flexibility to those wishing the numbers to say what they want them to say. The increase in the annual dropout rate calculated in ADA over the ADM dropout rate rises from 16 percent higher in K–12 (4.4 vs. 5.1 percent) to 26 percent higher in 9–12 (15.5 vs. 19.5 percent). This rise is a function of the different attendance rates for each group.

One additional factor to consider in comparing ADA and ADM is the

District Y

n = 50 (dropouts)

d = 1000 (ADM)

Attendance Rate = 92%

Dropout Rate (ADM) $\dfrac{50}{1000}$ = 5.0%

Dropout Rate (ADA) $\dfrac{50}{1000 \times .92} = \dfrac{50}{920}$ = 5.4%

Figure 2d. Example of Difference in Annual Dropout Rate Using Both ADA and ADM

District XYZ
(1983 – 1984)

d = 3308 (dropouts)

	ADM	ADA	Attendance Rate
K–12	n = 75427	n = 65272	86.5
7–12	= 34035	= 27317	80.2
8–12	= 27690	= 22119	79.8
9–12	= 21344	= 16922	79.2

K–12 $\dfrac{3308}{75427} = 4.4$ $\dfrac{3308}{65272} = 5.1\%$

7–12 $\dfrac{3308}{34035} = 9.8$ $\dfrac{3308}{27317} = 12.1\%$

8–12 $\dfrac{3308}{27690} = 11.9$ $\dfrac{3308}{22119} = 15.0\%$

9–12 $\dfrac{3308}{21344} = 15.5$ $\dfrac{3308}{16922} = 19.5\%$

Figure 2e. Comparison of District Annual Dropout Rates Using Different Grade Levels and Student Accounting Procedures

maximum number of days used to define an unexcused student as a dropout. A district using ADM and permitting a student truant for sixty days to remain on the rolls maintains an inflated baseline population. A truant student in an ADA district is not in attendance and as such is not added to the district's baseline population. Thus, by using ADA, a district's handling of unexcused absences does not skew the baseline population (reduce the dropout rate). A district using ADM is rewarded with a low dropout rate because long-term truants are included in the student count (denominator).

In summary, both time frames — annual dropout rate and cohort dropout rate — seem to serve a function. The annual dropout rate is more reflective of current district efforts to reduce dropping out, and it is the method with which most people are familiar. The cohort dropout rate needs to be used to display accurately the chances of dropping out for a secondary school student. Both rates should use grade levels seven through twelve; the annual dropout rate should use ADA; the cohort dropout rate needs to be restricted to those entering the seventh grade together.

RECOMMENDATIONS

Schools, consciously used as centers of inquiry,[24] can produce data, programs, and human energy directed toward a greater understanding of school dropouts. To this end I propose the following points of departure for discussions leading to a uniform definition and dropout computation procedure.

1. *Definition of a dropout.* A dropout is any student, previously enrolled in a school, who is no longer actively enrolled as indicated by fifteen days of consecutive unexcused absence, who has not satisfied local standards for graduation, and for whom no formal request has been received signifying enrollment in another state-licensed educational institution. A student death is not tallied as a dropout. The designation of dropout can be removed by proof of enrollment in a state-licensed educational institution or by presentation of an approved high school graduation certificate.

2. *Computation of dropout rates.* Two dropout rates should be produced each year. The annual dropout rate is the total number of students (grades K – 12) qualifying for the status of dropout within a full calendar year (July 1 to June 30), divided by the average daily attendance (ADA) of all secondary school students (grades 7 – 12).

The cohort dropout rate is the total number of students qualifying for the status of dropout who, at the time of dropping out, were members of a cohort of students (grades 7 through 12), divided by the absolute number of students assigned to the cohort minus those students who died or were formally transferred to another state-licensed educational institution. Students are assigned to a cohort at the beginning of the seventh grade or upon transfer into the district. Cohort members and cohort dropout rates are associated with the year of expected graduation from high school.

3. *District-level data.* Data assembly should be organized around computer storage and retrieval. Two types of data are to be maintained: the personal characteristics the student brings to school, and school performance and attitude data. The personal data can be collected at the time of initial enrollment and updated as needed. Minimum personal data to be maintained include: birth date, sex, ethnicity, family status, number of brothers and sisters, language spoken at home, acceptance in free/reduced lunch program, and education obtained by each parent. School data are to be collected and stored on an annual basis creating a longitudinal record of the student's activities. Minimum school data to be maintained each year include: days present and absent, aggregate national test scores, courses taken and grades received, assignment to special programs, behavioral history, and basic health data. If a student drops out, the date and reason for dropping out are recorded as well as a forwarding address. A student transfer should have the name and address of the new school placed in the computer file.

4. *State-level tracking systems and incentives for accurate reporting.* State-level student tracking systems are needed to monitor the enrollment and transfer of students. Individual districts would benefit from efforts by the state's education bureaucracy to establish a statewide student tracking system. An existing program, the Migrant Student Record Transfer System (MSRTS), may serve as a useful model.[25] Moreover, state funding for school districts

should encourage the accurate collection and reporting of data regarding dropouts, possibly by funding recruitment and alternative education programs on a per-dropout basis.

The creative educational programming needed for improved education of today's youth cannot thrive until common, meaningful measures of success are accepted and input variables are controlled. A standardized definition and computation procedure provides the measure of success; the collection of additional data provides the means for monitoring variations in program input.

Many districts have been legitimately leery of announcing the truth of their dropout problem. School dropouts are a recurring dilemma that has not gone away. Without admitting the problem and making it a priority, efforts to improve it are not considered. "We learn to measure those things which are important to us: calories, GNP, RBI's. . . ."[26] The use of a standardized definition of a dropout and procedures for computing a dropout rate provide the hope for progress and may encourage districts to confront the problem.

Notes

1   W. T. Harris, "The Early Withdrawal of Pupils from School: Its Causes and Its Remedies," *Addresses and Journal of Proceedings* 12 (1872): 260–73.

2   T. B. Blough, "A Critical Analysis of Selected Research Literature on the Problem of School Dropouts" (Ph.D. diss., University of Pittsburgh, 1956).

3   See Gary G. Wehlage and Robert A. Rutter, "Dropping Out: How Much Do Schools Contribute to the Problem?" in this issue.

4   "Hispanic Dropouts 'Critical' Problem, Task Force Finds," *Education Week,* April 10, 1985, p. 3.

5   D. S. Elliott, H. L. Voss, and A. Wendling, "Capable Dropouts and the Social Milieu of the High School," *The Journal of Educational Research* 4, no. 60 (1966): 180–86.

6   L. Barber, "Dropouts, Transfers, Withdrawn and Removed Students" (manuscript, Phi Delta Kappa, Center on Evaluation, Development, and Research, 1984).

7   C. V. Good, ed., *Dictionary of Education,* 3rd ed. (New York: McGraw-Hill, 1973), p. 198.

8   Project: School Dropouts and National Educational Association, *Dropout Studies: Design and Conduct* (Washington, D.C.: National Educational Association, 1965), pp. 71–72.

9   G. T. Page and J. B. Thomas, *International Dictionary of Education* (New York: Kogan Page/Nicholas Publishing Company, 1977).

10   Good, *Dictionary of Education,* p. 625.

11   Barber, "Dropouts, Transfers, Withdrawn and Removed Students."

12   *Dropout Studies: Design and Conduct,* p. 25.

13   Good, *Dictionary of Education,* p. 198.

14   Page, *International Dictionary of Education,* p. 109.

15   C. Pipho and P. Flakus-Mosqueda, *Minimum High School Graduation Requirements in the States, Clearinghouse Notes* (Denver: Education Commission of the States, 1984).

16   M. J. Adler, *The Paideia Proposal: An Educational Manifesto* (New York: Macmillan, 1982); E. L. Boyer, *High School: A Report on Secondary Education in America* (New York: Harper & Row, 1983); and National Commission on Excellence in Education, *A Nation at Risk: The Imperative for Educational Reform* (Washington, D.C.: Government Printing Office, 1983).

17   Pipho and Flakus-Mosqueda, *Minimum High School Graduation Requirements in the States.*

18   A. Tugend. "Half of Chicago Students Drop Out, Study Finds," *Education Week,* March 6, 1985, p. 10.

19   *Dropout Studies: Design and Conduct.*

20   B. Powell and L. C. Steelman. "Variations in State SAT Performance: Meaningful or Misleading?" *Harvard Educational Review* 54 (1984): 389–412.

21   J. Lipsitz, "Early Adolescence — Social/Psychological Issues" (talk presented at the Association for Supervision and Curriculum Development, St. Louis, 1981 Annual Conference).

22   W. I. Garms, J. W. Guthrie, and L. C. Pierce, *School Finance: The Economics and Politics of Public Education* (Englewood Cliffs, N.J.: Prentice-Hall, 1978), pp. 233–34.

23   *Digest of Educational Statistics: 1983–84* (Washington, D.C.: Government Printing Office, 1984), p.45.

24   R. J. Schaefer, *The School as a Center of Inquiry* (New York: Harper & Row, 1967).

25   M. Webb, *Technology Programs That Work* (New York: Teachers College, Columbia University, Institute of Urban and Minority Education, 1984), p. 40.

26   D. Mann "Opening Remarks," National Invitational Working Conference on Holding Power and Drop-Outs (New York: Teachers College, Columbia University, February 13, 1985).

Who Drops Out of High School and Why? Findings from a National Study

RUTH B. EKSTROM, MARGARET E. GOERTZ,
JUDITH M. POLLACK, DONALD A. ROCK
Educational Testing Service

Using the most comprehensive data set on school dropouts that we have to date, the High School and Beyond study, Ruth Ekstrom, Margaret Goertz, Judith Pollack, and Donald Rock provide an analysis of the salient characteristics of the dropout population.

In 1983, the National Center for Education Statistics (NCES) contracted with Educational Testing Service (ETS) to conduct a study using NCES's High School and Beyond (HS&B) data base. This study, which was part of NCES's Study of Excellence in High School Education, included a longitudinal analysis relating growth and development of 1980 high school sophomores to their school experience over the period 1980–1982. Since these data provide information on administrative practices and school policy, on curriculum and requirements, and on student outcomes, a thorough investigation of models of the process of schooling and of casual relationships among school and student characteristics was possible.

One of the issues examined in the longitudinal study was: How did the cognitive achievement and attitudes of high school dropouts differ from those of teenagers who chose to stay in high school? The research focused on four questions:

Who drops out?
Why does one student and not another drop out?
What happens to dropouts during the time that their peers remain in school?
What is the impact of dropping out on gains in tested achievement?

The research on which this paper is based was supported under Contract No. 300-83-0247 for the U.S. Department of Education, National Center for Education Statistics (NCES). The opinions and findings expressed here do not necessarily reflect the position or policy of NCES and no official endorsement should be inferred. The authors contributed jointly and equally to this paper: the order of listing is alphabetical.

This article summarizes the answers to these questions.[1]

Previous research has indicated that high school attrition is related to background, achievement and attitudes, and individual behaviors.

The two background characteristics that are most strongly related to dropping out are socioeconomic status (SES) and race/ethnicity. Students of lower socioeconomic status have been consistently shown to have higher dropout rates than high socioeconomic status students.[2] Dropout occurs more often among Hispanics than among blacks, and more often among blacks than whites.[3] Other background factors associated with dropout include coming from a single-parent family,[4] coming from a large family,[5] and living in the South or in a large city.[6]

Low academic achievement, as indicated by low test scores and low grades, has also been consistently associated with high school attrition. Low scores on standardized tests have been found to be good predictors of dropout.[7] Academic failure, as indicated by low grades, is also consistently related to dropout.[8] Students who become dropouts have been shown to be dissatisfied with school and to have lower self-esteem.[9] Students with no plans for postsecondary education have also been shown more likely to become dropouts.[10]

Student behaviors that have been found to be associated with dropout include enrollment in a nonacademic (vocational or general) curriculum[11] and problem behaviors such as delinquency and truancy.[12] Other researchers have pointed out the role that employment during high school[13] and pregnancy[14] play in dropout.

METHODOLOGY

The analyses were conducted using data from High School and Beyond, a national longitudinal study of American high school students sponsored by NCES. The data in HS&B are drawn from a highly stratified national probability sample of about thirty thousand high school sophomores who attended about one thousand public and private high schools in 1980. Students were administered base-year survey and achievement tests in vocabulary, reading, mathematics, science, writing, and civics. A follow-up survey collected data from and retested over twenty-two thousand of these students who were seniors in 1982 and over two thousand of the individuals who had dropped out of school by 1982.

The findings reported in this article are based on three different kinds of analysis. First, descriptive analysis was used to describe who stayed in school and who dropped out between the sophomore and senior years. Students who stayed in school ("stayers") were compared with those who did not complete school ("dropouts") on a number of dimensions: race/ethnicity, socioeconomic status, family structure, home educational support system, ability and attitudes, and school behaviors. Second, path analysis was used to explain why some students and not others drop out of school. The robustness of some of the estimates in the path-analysis results was further verified by comparing these estimates with those of a propensity analysis.[15] Third, a value-added analysis was conducted to estimate the relative impact of staying in or dropping out of school on gains in tested achievement.

WHO DROPS OUT OF SCHOOL?

Students who later became dropouts differed significantly in their sophomore year from those who chose to remain in school. These differences include background, educational achievement and other school-related behaviors, out-of-school activities, educational aspirations, and attitudes toward self and society. Thirty percent of the dropouts reported leaving school during or before the end of tenth grade, 44 percent during or before the end of eleventh grade, and 26 percent during twelfth grade.

BACKGROUND

As shown in Figure 1, dropouts are disproportionately from low SES families and racial/ethnic minority groups. While 15 percent of students who were sophomores in 1980 did not complete high school two years later, nearly 25 percent of black students dropped out. Dropouts were also more likely to be older, to be males rather than females, and to attend public schools in urban areas in the South or West.

Dropouts tended to come from homes with a weaker educational support system. Compared with stayers, dropouts: (1) had fewer study aids present in their homes, (2) had less opportunity for non-school related learning, (3) were less likely to have both natural parents living at home, (4) had mothers with lower levels of formal education, (5) had mothers with lower educational expectations for their offspring, (6) had mothers who were more likely to be working, and (7) had parents who were less likely to be interested in or to monitor both in-school and out-of-school activities.

EDUCATIONAL ACHIEVEMENT AND OTHER SCHOOL-RELATED BEHAVIORS AND ATTITUDES

Dropouts exhibited different school behaviors. They had lower school grades and lower test scores, did less homework, and reported more disciplinary problems in school.

It appears that the gap between stayers and dropouts is greater in the area of school performance (as measured by reported school grades) than it is in tested achievement. The typical sophomore who remained in school reported a grade average of B, while those who dropped out reported grades of "mostly Cs," a difference of about one standard deviation. The typical drop-

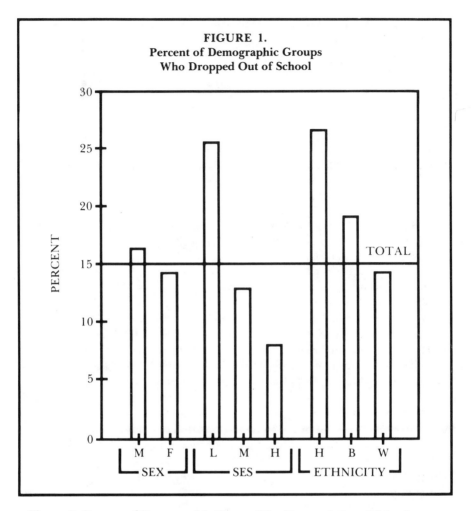

Figure 1. Percent of Demographic Groups Who Dropped Out of School

out's grades were at approximately the sixteenth percentile of the school stayers.

The dropouts had lower sophomore-year scores on all of the HS&B achievement tests than the stayers. The mean score differences were smallest in science and largest in mathematics. The dropouts' science test scores placed them at about the twenty-eighth percentile of school stayers while their mathematics scores placed them at about the twenty-third percentile of the stayers.

Not surprisingly, the dropouts reported doing less homework as sopho-

Table 1. Frequency of Behavior Problems among Dropouts and Stayers
(Percent Yes)

	Sophomores Who Stayed in School	Sophomores Who Dropped Out	Dropouts Minus Stayers
Cut classes	25	54	29[a]
Had disciplinary problems	16	41	25[a]
Suspended or put on probation	10	31	21[a]
Serious trouble with law	4	13	9[a]

[a] Statistically significant difference at .05 level or greater.

mores than did the school stayers (an average of 2.2 hours of homework a week compared with 3.4 hours a week reported by stayers).

The dropouts were also more likely to report having behavior problems while in school. As shown in Table 1, dropouts were more likely than stayers to have cut classes, to have had disciplinary problems, to have been suspended from school, or to have had trouble with the police. The dropouts also reported higher rates of absenteeism and tardiness.

The dropouts appear to feel alienated from school life. They report lower levels of participation in most extracurricular activities, especially in athletics. They are less likely to feel satisfied with the way their education is going, to be interested in school, or to like working hard in school (see Table 2). They are also less likely to feel that they are popular with other students, to feel that other students see them as good students, as athletes, or as important, and more likely to feel that other students see them as troublemakers.

The dropouts appear to have chosen friends who are also more alienated from school than the friends of the stayers (see Table 3). The largest dropout-stayer differences in close friends involve plans to attend college and being interested in school.

Table 2. Attitudes about School among Dropouts and Stayers
(Percent True)

	Sophomores Who Stayed in School	Sophomores Who Dropped Out	Dropouts Minus Stayers
Interested in school	79	60	−19[a]
Satisfied with way education is going	69	45	−24[a]
Like to work hard in school	56	40	−16[a]

[a] Significant difference.

Table 3. Behaviors and Attitudes of Closest Friend
(Percent True)

	Sophomores Who Stayed in School	Sophomores Who Dropped Out	Dropouts Minus Stayers
Attends classes regularly	93	82	−11[a]
Is popular	88	81	− 7[a]
Gets good grades	83	73	−10[a]
Is interested in school	69	51	−18[a]
Plans to go to college	67	44	−23[a]

[a] Significant difference.

OUT-OF-SCHOOL BEHAVIOR

Students who later became dropouts reported spending more time in their sophomore year "riding around" or "going on dates" than students who stayed in school (see Table 4). Dropouts were less likely than stayers to discuss their experiences with their parents and, as indicated earlier, parents of dropouts are reported doing less monitoring of the students' activities both in school and out. Dropouts also reported spending less time reading than did stayers.

Dropouts were slightly more likely to be working for pay during their

Table 4. Relative Amount of Time Spent on Nonschool Activities
(Scale: 0 = rarely to 3 = every day)

	Sophomores Who Stayed in School		Sophomores Who Dropped Out		Dropouts Minus Stayers
	Mean	SD	Mean	SD	
Meeting/talking with friends	2.45	0.8	2.50	0.9	.04
Thinking/daydreaming alone	1.91	1.2	1.76	1.2	−.15[a]
Reading newspaper	1.72	1.2	1.42	1.2	−.31[a]
Talking with mother/ father about personal experiences	1.26	1.2	1.03	1.1	−.23[a]
Driving around	1.25	1.1	1.67	1.1	.43[a]
Reading for pleasure	1.21	1.1	1.01	1.1	−.20[a]
Going on dates	1.01	0.9	1.45	1.0	.44[a]

[a] Significant difference.

sophomore year (47 percent) than were stayers (42 percent). The future dropouts reported working more hours per week than the stayers and receiving a higher hourly wage. The dropouts were more likely to report finding their current or most recent job more enjoyable than school (66 percent) than the stayers (54 percent). The dropouts also reported that their job was more important to them than school more often than did the stayers (23 percent vs. 10 percent).

EDUCATIONAL EXPECTATIONS

As sophomores the future dropouts expected to attain less education than did the stayers. The typical stayer thought he or she would complete between two and four years of college, while the typical dropout thought he or she would finish high school and take some junior college training.

ATTITUDES TOWARD SELF AND SOCIETY

The HS&B questionnaires included scales to measure self-esteem, locus of control, gender role attitudes, and life values. Dropouts differed from stayers on most of these scales.

Self-esteem items that focused on whether the students had a positive attitude toward themselves or felt of equal worth compared with others showed no practical or significant differences between dropouts and stayers. However, when asked if they were satisfied with themselves or if they had much to be proud of, dropouts were significantly more likely than stayers to show lower self-concept.

On most of the locus-of-control items, dropouts responded with a significantly more externalized sense of control, indicating that they are more likely than stayers to feel that their destiny is out of their hands.

The gender-role-attitudes scale showed that the females who became dropouts were significantly more likely to agree with items such as "Most women are happiest when making a home" and "It is usually better if the man is the achiever and the woman takes care of the home" than were female stayers.

The contrast in life values of stayers and dropouts is shown in Table 5. Dropouts are more likely than stayers to give importance to "getting away from this part of the country" and to "having lots of money."

WHY DOES ONE STUDENT AND NOT ANOTHER DROP OUT OF SCHOOL?

The preceding section provides a descriptive summary of how the populations of stayers and dropouts differed in their sophomore year in high school. In this section, the question of why one student rather than another drops out

Table 5. Contrast in Life Values of Stayers and Dropouts
(Scale: 1 = Not Important to 3 = Very Important)

	Sophomores Who Stayed in School	Sophomores Who Dropped Out	Dropouts Minus Stayers
Finding steady work	2.83	2.77	−.06[a]
Having strong friendships	2.81	2.74	−.07[a]
Having lots of money	2.24	2.30	.07[a]
Living close to parents	1.98	1.87	−.11[a]
Being a community leader	1.66	1.59	−.07[a]
Getting away from this area of the country	1.54	1.72	.18[a]

[a] Significant difference.

will be examined by analyzing: (1) their self-reported reasons for dropping out of school and (2) the results of a path analysis.

SELF-REPORT OF REASONS FOR DROPPING OUT OF HIGH SCHOOL

In 1982, students who dropped out of school were asked their reason(s) for leaving. The students could check as many reasons as they felt relevant. The major reasons, chosen by 10 percent or more of the dropouts, are shown in Table 6, both for the group as a whole and separately for males and females. Other minor reasons for dropping out included travel (7 percent), and inability to get into desired program, inability to get along with other students, and illness (all 6 percent).

The most frequently reported reasons for leaving school for the total

Table 6. Major Reasons for Dropping Out of School
(Percent responding "Yes" to each item)

	Total	Males	Females
Did not like school	33%	35%	31%
Poor grades	33%	36%	30%
Offered job and chose to work	19%	27%	11%
Getting married	18%	7%	31%
Could not get along with teachers	15%	21%	9%
Had to help support family	11%	14%	8%
Pregnancy	11%	—	23%
Expelled or suspended	10%	13%	5%

group were poor grades and not liking school. This suggests that about one-third of all dropouts leave high school because they do not achieve in school and/or because they are alienated from school. Males are somewhat more likely to leave school for these reasons than are females.

Males are also more than twice as likely as females to report leaving high school because of behavior problems, including not being able to get along with teachers (21 percent of male dropouts) and being expelled or suspended (13 percent of male dropouts). Males were also more likely than females to leave high school because of economic-related issues. Fourteen percent of the males, as contrasted with 8 percent of the females, said they left school because they had to help support the family; 27 percent of the males and 11 percent of the females said they left school because they were offered a job. Females, in contrast, are more likely than males to leave high school for personal/family formation reasons. Nearly a third (31 percent) of female dropouts reported that they left high school to marry and nearly a quarter (23 percent) stated that they left school because of pregnancy.

The diversity of the reasons given for dropping out of high school, encompassing academic, behavioral, economic, and personal factors, suggested that there is no single, simple cause underlying this problem and led to the development of a complex path-analysis model that was tested in the next phase of this study.

PATH ANALYSIS

Student self-reports provide a list of reasons for leaving school, but they do not yield much insight into the causal factors that led a student to drop out of school. A path model was developed that relates demographics, family educational support, behavior, sophomore-year ability and attitudes, and student school behaviors to the student's decision to stay in or drop out of school. The model, summarized in Figure 2, contrasts whites with blacks, and whites with Mexican-Americans and Puerto Ricans, to identify possible level differences in home educational support systems and student behaviors. In addition, the model was run separately within racial/ethnic groups to determine whether the educational process works the same way for minority as for white students.

The direct effects of the explanatory variables that had the largest standardized path coefficients, for total group or for the racial/ethnic subgroups, are shown in Table 7.

The demographic variables related to the decision to stay in or drop out of high school were, in approximate order of importance:

Intact family: White and Hispanic, but not black, students who came from an intact, two-parent family were less likely to drop out of school.

SES: Students of higher socioeconomic status were less likely to drop out.

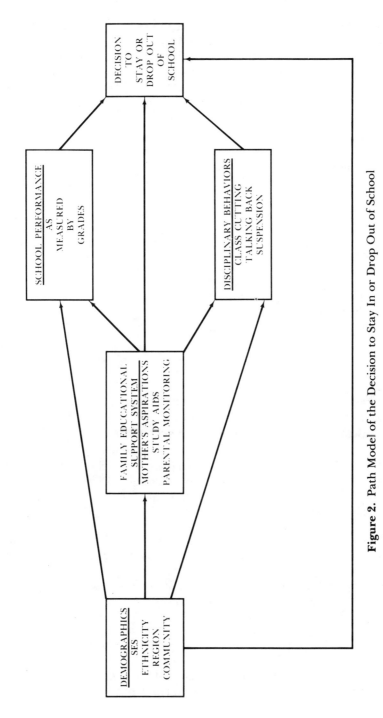

Figure 2. Path Model of the Decision to Stay In or Drop Out of School

Table 7. Direct Effects of Explanatory Variables on Decision to Stay in or Drop
Out of School
(0 = Dropout, 1 = Stay)

	Standardized Regression Weights			
	Total	White	Black	Hispanic
Demographics				
Intact family	.07[a]	.06[a]	.07	.11[a]
SES	.06[a]	.07[a]	.02	.08
Race/ethnicity-white	−.07[a]			
Race/ethnicity-Hispanic	−.04[a]			
Region	.03[a]	.06[a]	−.08[a]	−.03
Sex	.03	.04[a]	−.04	.06
Family educational support				
Study aids	.03	.04[a]	−.01	.01
Sophomore ability & attitudes				
Grades	.17[a]	.18[a]	.07	.19[a]
Math test score	.08[a]	.07[a]	.09	.02
Locus of control	−.03	−.01	−.06	−.10[a]
Student school behavior				
Behavior problems	−.22[a]	−.22[a]	−.21[a]	−.28[a]

[a] Variables whose associated raw weights are at least four times their standard
error.

Race/ethnicity: Other things being equal, whites and Hispanics were more
likely to drop out of school than blacks. The critical control variables
here are sophomore-year grades and achievement test scores.

Region: Whites in the South were more likely to drop out than whites in
other regions, assuming all other variables were held constant. Blacks in
the South were less likely to drop out than blacks in other regions.

Sex: White and Hispanic males were more likely to drop out than females;
black females were more likely to drop out than black males.

The only family-education support variable related to dropping out was
study aids in the home. The more study aids available, the less likely white
students were to drop out.

Three sophomore-year ability and attitude variables were related to staying in or dropping out of school. They were:

Grades: Students with low grades were more likely to drop out. Grades
appear to be more important in the dropping out decision for whites and
Hispanics than for blacks.

Mathematics test score: Poor mathematics skills, as measured by the sophomore-year achievement test, were related to dropout, especially for
whites.

Locus of control: An externalized locus of control, or the feeling that one can do little to control one's destiny, was negatively related to dropout, especially among minority students.

One school behavior variable, having behavioral problems, was also related to dropout. Students who cut classes, had disciplinary problems, had been suspended, and/or had trouble with the police were much more likely to drop out.

It is clear that having behavior problems and having low grades are the major determinants of dropout. What factors affect these behaviors? The same path analysis showed that several demographic and family variables were related to behavioral problems and to grades.

Behavior Problems Students exhibiting problem behaviors, such as cutting classes and having disciplinary problems, during their sophomore year tended to be males with low verbal ability (as measured by the vocabulary test scores) and with a sense that they had little control over their lives (externalized locus of control). They tended to come from homes that failed to provide a supportive educational environment. The mothers had low educational aspirations for these students and the parents were not involved in helping the student select a high school curriculum. The major direct effects of the demographic, family, and ability and attitude variables on sophomore-year problem behavior are shown in Table 8.

Grades Self-reported grades thus far in high school, as of the sophomore year, were highest for students with high verbal ability (as measured by the vocabulary test) who did not engage in problem behavior and who spent more time doing homework. The typical student with high grades was a female whose family provided strong educational support (as indicated by the mother's educational aspirations for the student and by parental involvement in the selection of the student's high school curriculum). These sophomores also tended to be enrolled in the academic curriculum, to do more homework, to have fewer behavior problems, to be involved in extracurricular activities, and to have an internalized locus of control. Other things being equal, grades in the South and in rural schools tended to be higher. The major direct effects of the demographic, family, ability and attitude, and school-behavior variables on grades are shown in Table 9.

WHAT HAPPENED TO DROPOUTS
BETWEEN 1980 AND 1982?

HS&B included a follow-up survey of dropouts that collected information on their activities, attitudes, and behaviors between the time they dropped out of school and 1982.

At the time of the follow-up survey, 47 percent of the dropouts were working full-time or part-time, 10 percent were taking courses or participat-

Table 8. Direct Effects of Explanatory Variables on Behavior Problems,
Sophomore Year
(0 = No, 1 = Yes)

	Standardized Regression Weights			
	Total	White	Black	Hispanic
Demographics				
Sex	.13[a]	.14[a]	.15[a]	.08
SES	.05[a]	.04[a]	.02	.24[a]
Region	.05[a]	.02	.14[a]	.08
Community type	.05[a]	.06[a]	.03	.00
Intact family	−.04[a]	−.04[a]	−.02	−.08
Family educational support				
Mother's aspirations for				
student	−.09[a]	−.08[a]	−.10[a]	−.15[a]
Study aids	−.04[a]	−.04	−.01	−.12
Nonschool learning	.04[a]	.03	.03	.07
Parental role	−.10[a]	−.10[a]	−.13[a]	−.07
Sophomore-year ability & attitudes				
Vocabulary test	−.14[a]	−.13[a]	−.14[a]	−.13[a]
Locus of control	−.08[a]	−.08[a]	−.04[a]	−.19[a]

[a] Variables whose associated raw weights are at least four times their standard
error.

ing in job training programs, 16 percent were homemakers, 3 percent were in
military service, and 29 percent were looking for work. These percentages
varied, however, by gender and by race/ethnicity. For example, more whites
and males reported working for pay than did blacks and females.

Dropouts reduced their educational expectations or plans between 1980
and 1982. As sophomores, 40 percent reported they would be disappointed if
they did not graduate from college. Two years later, this figure was 26
percent. However, 58 percent of the dropouts reported in 1982 that they
planned to complete high school eventually. While dropouts had lowered
their educational aspirations, they had an improved self-concept and, as
indicated by the locus of control scale, more sense of control over life in 1982
than in 1980.

During the 1980 to 1982 period, 21 percent of the dropouts reported that
they had participated in a job training program and/or educational activities
other than formal educational course work. Seventeen percent had enrolled
in an educational institution, and by 1982, 14 percent reported they had
obtained a General Educational Development (GED) high school equivalency
certificate.

Table 9. Direct Effect of Explanatory Variables on Grades in High School as of
Sophomore Year
(1 = Below D; 8 = Mostly A)

	Standardized Regression Weights			
	Total	White	Black	Hispanic
Demographics				
Sex	−.09[a]	−.10[a]	−.08[a]	−.04[a]
Region	−.06[a]	−.05[a]	−.07[a]	−.12[a]
Community type	−.04[a]	−.03[a]	−.07	−.04
Intact family	.03[a]	.03[a]	.02	.04
Family educational support				
Mother's aspiration for student	.08[a]	.09[a]	.04	.07
Study aids	−.03[a]	−.03	−.05	−.01
Parental role	.06[a]	.06[a]	.03	.03
Sophomore-year ability and attitudes				
Vocabulary test	.30[a]	.30[a]	.16[a]	.15
Locus of control	.07[a]	.07[a]	.06[a]	.08
Student school behaviors				
Curriculum	.08[a]	.07[a]	.07	.12[a]
Behavior problems	−.21[a]	−.22[a]	−.20	−.21
Participation in activities	.08[a]	.09[a]	.09[a]	.03
Homework	.14[a]	.13[a]	.18[a]	.21[a]

[a] Variables whose associated raw weights are at least four times their standard error.

THE IMPACT OF DROPPING OUT OF SCHOOL ON GAINS IN TESTED ACHIEVEMENT

A value-added analysis was carried out to estimate the relative impact of early dropout (before the end of the junior year) on achievement gains as contrasted with later dropouts and with stayers in each curriculum. The groups contrasted with the baseline early-dropout group included:

Late dropouts and/or early dropouts who subsequently received additional education or training, such as formal tutoring or GED work
School stayers in the general curriculum
School stayers in the academic curriculum
School stayers in the vocational curriculum

Table 10 presents the standardized adjusted gains averaged across achievement areas by various subgroups and curriculum classifications. The entries in the table indicate the gains in pretest standard deviation units by curriculum type and by racial/ethnic and gender groups.

Table 10. Contrasts of Standardized Achievement Gains for Early Dropouts with Late Dropouts and Stayers by Test for Total Group and Subgroup for Averaged Adjusted Gains across Tests

	By Test					Total
	Vocabulary	Reading	Math	Science	Writing	
Status						
Late Dropouts	.00	.00	.00	−.01	.01	.01
Vocational stayer	.02	.01	.02	.03	.05	.08
General stayer	.05	.03	.05	.05	.08	.12
Academic stayer	.07	.05	.11	.05	.09	.16

	By Subgroup				
	Male	Female	White	Black	Hispanic
Status					
Late Dropouts	.03	−.03	.02	−.01	−.06
Vocational stayer	.04	.12	.07	.10	.11
General stayer	.08	.16	.11	.18	.16
Academic stayer	.13	.21	.16	.25	.16

The results clearly show that staying in school positively impacts one's gains in achievement, and that staying in school in the academic or, to a lesser extent, in the general curriculum leads to larger overall gains than staying in the vocational curriculum.

The results also show that females, and to a lesser extent minorities, are relatively "bigger losers" when they drop out of school. Blacks and females fall the furthest behind in the language development areas of vocabulary, reading, and writing when they leave school early. Because females and minorities tend to take fewer high school courses in science and mathematics than do males and whites, the impact of dropout is less for them in these areas.

SUMMARY

Identifying who drops out of school and why and assessing the impact of this decision on future values, behaviors, and achievement are difficult tasks. Educators and policymakers do not share a common definition of "dropout." Students drop out of school for a variety of personal reasons, and the impact of leaving school is affected by when an individual drops out, what he or she does after dropping out, and the outcome measures employed.

The analyses of the 1980/1982 HS&B data reported in this paper shed some light on the dropout problem. First, the critical variables related to dropping out are school performance, as measured by grades, and extent of problem behavior. These variables are more important in explaining dropout behavior than sophomore ability, as measured by test scores.

Second, problem behavior and grades appear to be determined in part by the home educational support system. The mother's educational aspirations for the student, the number of study aids in the home, parental involvement in curriculum choice, and the provision of opportunities for nonschool learning all affect school academic performance and/or deportment.

Third, regardless of ethnicity, gender, or curriculum choice, staying in school increases achievement gains in all tested areas. Students in the academic curriculum gained most, followed by students in the general and then the vocational curriculum. Females and minorities suffered the greatest with respect to unrealized achievement gains if they dropped out of school. These unrealized achievement gains for women and minorities were largest in the language-development areas of vocabulary, reading, and writing.

These findings have significant implications for the development of policies that deal with the dropout problem. No single program or policy can meet the needs of the diverse dropout population. Three major types of programs are needed: (1) programs to help pregnant teenagers remain in school; (2) programs to help youth with economic needs combine work and education; and (3) programs directed toward students who perform poorly because they are dissatisfied with the school environment.

The study also showed that the students' home environment has a critical, although indirect, impact on the decision to leave school. Policies should be developed to help parents increase their interest in and monitoring of their children's school progress. It is also important to identify potential dropouts prior to the high school years and to begin interventions when the first behavioral signs (e.g., disciplinary problems, poor grades, poor attendance) are noted.

Notes

1   More extensive findings are reported in Donald A. Rock et al., *Determinants of Achievement Gain in High School, 1980–1982* (Washington, D.C.: National Center for Education Statistics, 1985).

2   See K. L. Alexander, B. K. Ackland, and L. J. Griffin, "The Wisconsin Model of Socioeconomic Achievement: A Replication," *American Journal of Sociology* 81 (1976): 324–42; J. G. Bachman, S. Green, and I. D. Wirtanen, *Youth in Transition: Dropping Out — Problem or Symptom?*, Vol. 3 (Ann Arbor: University of Michigan, Institute for Social Research, 1971); J. G. Bachman, P. M. O'Malley, and J. Johnson, *Youth in Transition: Adolescence to Adulthood — Change and Stability in the Lives of Young Men*, Vol. 6 (Ann Arbor: University of Michigan, Institute for Social Research, n.d.); Childrens' Defense Fund, *Children Out of School in America* (Cambridge, Mass.: Children's Defense Fund, 1974); J. Combs and W. W. Cooley, "Dropouts in High School and after School," *American Educational Research Journal* 5 (1986): 343–63; M. A. P. Howard and R. J. Anderson, "Early Identification of Potential Dropouts: A Literature Review," *Childrens Welfare* 57 (1978): 221–31; K. B. Hoyt, "The Counselor and the Dropout," *The Clearinghouse* 36 (1962): 515–22; D. N. Lloyd, "Prediction of School Failure from Third-Grade Data," *Educational and Psychological Measurement* 38 (1978): 1191–200; R. D. Mare, "Social Background and School Continuation Decisions," *Journal of American Statistical Association* 75 (1980): 295–305: A. M. Pallas, "The Determinants of High School Dropout" (Ph.D. diss., Johns

Hopkins University, 1984); R. W. Rumberger, "Dropping Out of High School: The Influence of Race, Sex, and Family Background," *American Educational Research Journal* 20 (1983): 199 – 220; D. Schriber, "The School Dropout — Fugitive from Failure," *The Bulletin of the National Association of Secondary School Principals* 46 (1962): 233 – 41; L. Steinberg, P. L. Blinde, and K. S. Chan, "Dropping Out among Language Minority Youth," *Review of Educational Research* 54 (1984): 113 – 32; G. Stice and R. B. Ekstrom, *High School Attrition*, Research Bulletin No. RB – 64 – 53 (Princeton, N.J.: Educational Testing Service, 1964); and A. L. Stroup and L. N. Robins, "Research Notes: Elementary School Predictors of High School Dropout among Black Males," *Sociology of Education* 45 (1972): 212 – 22.

3   G. H. Brown et al., *The Condition of Education for Hispanic Americans* (Washington, D.C.: Government Printing Office, 1980); Rumberger, "Dropping Out of High School"; and U.S. Bureau of the Census, *Current Population Reports, School Enrollment — Social and Economic Characteristics of Students*, Pp. 20, No. 373 (Washington, D.C.: Government Printing Office, 1982).

4   S. B. Neill, *Keeping Students in School: Problems and Solutions* (Arlington, Va.: American Association of School Administrators, 1979); and Rumberger, "Dropping Out of High School."

5   Rumberger, "Dropping Out of High School."

6   Stice and Ekstrom, *High School Attrition.*

7   Alexander et al., "The Wisconsin Model"; Combs and Cooley, "Dropouts in High School"; E. S. Cook, "An Analysis of Factors Related to Withdrawal from High School Prior to Graduation," *Journal of Educational Research* 50 (1956): 191 – 96; Lloyd, "Prediction of School Failure from Third-Grade Data"; Pallas, "The Determinants of High School Dropout"; R. C. Penty, *Reading Ability and High School Dropouts* (New York: Teachers College, Columbia University, 1956); Stice and Ekstrom, *High School Attrition;* and H. E. Walters and G. D. Kranzler, "Early Identification of School Dropout," *School Counselor* 18 (1970): 97 – 1

8   Bachman, Green, and Wirtanen, *Dropping Out;* L. F. Cervantes, *The Dropouts: Causes and Cures* (Ann Arbor: University of Michigan Press, 1965); Pallas, "The Determinants of High School Dropout"; Steinberg, Blinde, and Chan, "Dropping Out"; and Stice and Ekstrom, *High School Attrition.*

9   Bachman, Green, and Wirtanen, *Dropping Out;* Bachman, O'Malley, and Johnson, *Adolescence to Adulthood;* Cervantes, *The Dropouts;* N. Hunt and J. Woods, *Interrupted Education: Students Who Drop Out* (Brooklyn: New York City Board of Education, September 1979); S. A. Takesian, "A Comparative Study of the Mexican-American Graduate and Dropout" (Ph.D., diss., University of Southern California, Los Angeles, 1967); and L. W. Yudin et al., "School Dropout or College Bound: Study in Contrast," *Journal of Education Research* 67 (1973): 85 – 95.

10   Stice and Ekstrom, *High School Attrition.*

11   Ibid.

12   Bachman, Green, and Wirtanen, *Dropping Out;* Bachman, O'Malley, and Johnson, *Adolescence to Adulthood;* Camp, *School Dropouts;* Carnegie Council on Policy Studies in Higher Education, *Giving Youth a Better Chance: Options for Education, Work and Service* (San Francisco: Jossey-Bass, 1979); D. Elliot and H. Voss, *Delinquency and Dropouts* (Lexington, Mass.: Lexington Books, 1974); Lucas, *Puerto Rican Dropouts;* G. Natriello, *Organizational Evaluation Systems and Student Disengagement in Secondary Schools: A Final Report to the National Institute of Education* (St. Louis, Mo.: Washington University, 1982); idem, "Problems in the Evaluation of Students and Student Disengagement from Secondary Schools," *Journal of Research and Development in Education* 17 (1984): 14 – 24; Neill, *Keeping Students in School;* Pallas, *The Determinants of High School Dropout;* H. C. Quay and L. B. Allen, "Truants and Dropouts," *Encyclopedia of Educational Research*, vol. 5 (New York: John Wiley, 1982); and L. N. Robins and K. S. Ratcliffe, "The Long Term Outcome of Truancy," in *Out of School: Modern Perspectives in Truancy and School Refusal,* ed. L. Hersov and I. Berg (New York: John Wiley, 1980).

13   L. Steinberg et al., "High School Students in the Labor Force: Some Costs and Benefits to Schooling and Learning," *Educational Evaluation and Policy Analysis* 4 (1982): 363 – 72.

14   Camp, *School Dropouts;* Center for Human Resource Research, *The National Longitudinal*

Studies Handbook (Columbus: Ohio State University, Center for Human Resource Research, 1980); Children's Defense Fund, *Children Out of School;* Combs and Cooley, *Dropouts;* Elliot and Voss, *Delinquency and Dropouts;* Lucas, *Puerto Rican Dropouts;* Rumberger, "Dropping Out of High School"; and L. J. Waite and K. A. Moore, "The Impact of an Early First Birth on Young Women's Educational Attainment," *Social Forces* 56 (1978): 845–65.

15 Paul R. Rosenbaum, "Dropping Out of High School in the United States: The Analysis of an Observational Study Embedded in a Complex Sample Survey" (paper delivered at the annual meeting of the American Educational Research Association, Chicago, April 1985).

Dropping Out: How Much Do Schools Contribute to the Problem?

GARY G. WEHLAGE, ROBERT A. RUTTER
University of Wisconsin, Madison

Arguing that educators have little control over a dropout's background characteristics, Gary Wehlage and Robert Rutter probe the High School and Beyond data for insights into the characteristics of students' school experiences that may contribute to dropping out and that might be altered through policy interventions.

Dropout rates of 40 and 50 percent from the nation's central city high schools are now being reported.[1] While most public schools have a much lower dropout rate, the magnitude of the problem nationwide has caused concern among educators and policymakers. In general this concern is based on the prediction that serious economic and social consequences will result for those who fail to obtain a high school diploma. Moreover, it is argued that the civic and economic welfare of the nation is dependent on a universally high level of education attainment. Thus for the benefit of both individuals and society, it is assumed that youth should remain in school until high school graduation.

Although the school dropout rate has been on the rise in recent years, viewed historically it is relatively low even today. In 1900, for example, about 90 percent of the male youth in this country did not receive a high school diploma. By 1920 the noncompletion rate for males was still 80 percent, and it was not until the 1950s that the dropout rate fell below 50 percent. By the mid to late 1960s the dropout rate reached its low point, and since then the rate for early school leaving has risen.

California illustrates the recent trend. In 1967, only 12 percent of the students left school before graduation. By 1970, the rate had risen to 17 percent; by 1972 it had climbed to 20 percent; in 1976 the rate was 22 percent.[2] California seems typical, but a precise figure for the current national dropout rate is difficult to obtain because reporting procedures differ across the country. However, it is reasonable to assume that at least one quarter of our nation's adolescents fail to graduate from high school.[3]

The research reported in this article was funded by the Wisconsin Center for Education Research, which is supported in part by a grant from the National Institute of Education (Grant No. NIE–G084–0008). The opinions expressed here do not necessarily reflect the position, policy, or endorsement of the National Institute of Education.

The problem is not simply to keep educationally at-risk youth from dropping out, but more importantly to provide them with educationally worthwhile experiences. Those who lack basic skills, career skills, and the social presence to be successful in the workplace will encounter unemployment and welfare, with the frustration and indignity this status confers on them. Previously the labor market was able to absorb most of those with a limited education, but increasingly the lack of a high school diploma is tantamount to a denial of employment. In order to be employable in other than the most menial work, those entering the labor market will certainly have to master the core competencies that should be acquired in high school.[4]

WHAT DO WE KNOW ABOUT DROPOUTS?

Most of the research on high school dropouts has been based on the desire to find the causes, correlates, or motives underlying the actions of dropouts. Typically, it begins by looking at the characteristics of those who drop out. The questions guiding the research (as well as the thinking of most educators) are directed at finding those characteristics or qualities of dropouts that make them different from those who complete high school. Social and personal categories are scanned to find those that separate the dropout from the stay-in. Dropping out is construed as a form of social deviance, and an explanation of this deviant action is sought in the characteristics distinctive to the dropout group.

There are several generalizations that describe high school dropouts based on research literature from four national studies utilizing longitudinal data: Project TALENT, Youth in Transition, National Longitudinal Survey of Youth Labor Market Experience, and High School and Beyond.[5] What has been learned about the dropout phenomenon based on these four data sets? All four studies confirm that a family background characterized by low socioeconomic status (SES) is strongly associated with dropping out. However, what it is about this kind of family background that produces youth who are poor risks to finish school is not made clear in the analyses of the data. Another finding is that poor school performance leading to low grades and course failure is associated with dropping out. After controlling for family background, race is not a variable that predicts dropout. Some data indicate that dropouts exhibit social-psychological characteristics that distinguish them from stay-ins. However there are no consistent categories or measures of these variables to sustain any findings. In general, it is not clear if measured characteristics such as low educational/occupational aspiration, weak sociability, negative school attitudes, low self-esteem, and external sense of locus of control are brought to the school or produced by school experiences. There is some evidence in the Youth in Transition study of a relationship between disciplinary problems in school and dropping out, which suggests that the school itself may contribute to negative school experiences leading to dropout.

An important source of information about dropouts is the set of reasons they give for leaving school. Although the major studies sought student views, there is a tendency by researchers to see such information as less important, or at least to treat it as "surface" data as opposed to "underlying" data, which are assumed to be more powerful. Nevertheless, there is a clear trend in what students say. They leave because they do not have much success in school and they do not like it. Many of them choose to accept entry-level work or to care for their children, choices that apparently are seen as more attractive than staying in school.

The problem of females' leaving school because of marriage and/or pregnancy is now a major factor in the dropout rate. The High School and Beyond (HS&B) data indicate that about half of all female dropouts leave for this combined reason. It is an important social phenomenon when children are having children, but it is also a reflection on the holding power of the school for low SES females, since having a child generally means termination of high school. How is it that child care is more attractive than schooling or that schools are unable to entice these young mothers back into the educational stream?

Implicit in much research on school dropouts is the assumption that a better understanding of the characteristics of dropouts will permit educators to develop policies and provide practices that will reduce the number of adolescents who fail to graduate. The intent is noble, but the results have been negligible because the focus on social, family, and personal characteristics does not carry any obvious implications for shaping school policy and practice. Moreover, if the research on dropouts continues to focus on the relatively fixed attributes of students, the effect of such research may well be to give schools an excuse for their lack of success with the dropout. Institutional thinking may go something like this: After all, it is not the school's fault that some of its students are from poor homes and not very talented academically, and since we cannot do anything about these things that interfere with school success, the school is absolved of responsibility for the fact that a sizable portion of its clients find good reasons to leave before graduation.

Since traditional research has tended to identify characteristics least amenable to change, the focus of new research might better be directed toward understanding the institutional character of schools and how this affects the potential dropout. While institutional character has broad meaning, the focus can be narrowed to those policies and practices that have impact on the institution's holding power. This holding power ought to be part of our definition of school excellence in a democratic society, where schools are to serve all of its citizens, not just the academically agile.

A new focus for research can go beyond the findings, now confirmed by a broad base of research, that those youth most likely to drop out come disproportionately from low SES backgrounds. Researchers need now to ask why these youth are educationally at risk and, further, what policies and practices of public schools can be constructive in reducing the chances that these students will drop out. It is important to conceive this new research in a way that looks for the cause of dropping out not only in the characteristics of the dropout, but also in relation to those institutional characteristics that affect the marginal student in a negative manner. Presumably the school is obligated to create an environment in which these youth can experience some kind of success, find institutional participation rewarding, and develop aspirations for additional schooling that can lead to satisfying employment. We will sketch this new focus for research as a way of making problematic the policies and practices of schools affecting the marginal student.

DROPPING OUT AS A PROBLEM OF SCHOOL POLICY AND PRACTICE

While the major longitudinal studies of dropouts have paid little attention to the role played by school factors, there is empirical evidence as well as theoretical support for redefining the problem to take such factors into account. By searching for school factors that contribute to marginal students' decisions to drop out, such research can provide grounds for school-based reform. Although schools can do nothing about students' SES or innate ability, important contributing factors to dropout that are under the control of the school may be modified to change the school conditions of marginal students.

The High School and Beyond study for the sophomore 1980 cohort provides the most recent longitudinal data in which dropouts are systematically sampled before and after their decision to leave school. Data were obtained from approximately 30,000 sophomores attending 1,105 public and private secondary schools nationwide. Although this data set is rich, our analysis is necessarily constrained by the design of the original study, and should be viewed as exploratory and tentative. Should these data indicate the importance of specific school conditions in predicting dropout, more specific studies will have to be conducted to determine the extent to which schools can be said to contribute to the dropout problem.

Data for the HS&B study were first gathered in 1980 when the subjects were sophomores. In 1982, a follow-up questionnaire was given to the same students. Those who dropped out were located and asked to fill out a slightly different questionnaire. To determine the extent to which certain variables available from HS&B differentiate among three groups — dropouts, stay-ins, and college-bound — a multivariate discriminant analysis was run. This procedure analyzes a set of independent variables to determine if differences in student responses provide a basis for discriminating among two or more known groups.

Students were assigned to one of the three groups on the basis of data gathered in 1982. Dropouts were those known to have dropped out of school between 1980 and 1982. Assignment to the stay-in and college-bound categories was based on student self-descriptions of plans for the next year. It was assumed that late in their senior year, having gained acceptance to a college, students' projections for college would closely reflect their actual status after graduation.

Each independent variable is tested to determine whether it makes a statistically significant contribution to identifying group membership. When comparing three groups, the test produces two discriminant functions that have separate weights (coefficients) for each independent variable. The first function accounts for most of the explained variance, and the second accounts for the remaining explained variance.

The independent variables used in the discriminant analysis were carefully selected from the HS&B data set to represent a range of factors likely to influence the decision to drop out. Items identified as important in prior research were included, such as SES, race, academic ability/performance, self-esteem, and locus of control. Variables in the second set were chosen because they reflect a range of school conditions experienced by students that might influence them to drop out. These include peer relationships, sociability, disciplinary problems, and the amount of formal schooling they expect to attain. The selection of these two sets of variables provides a basis for determining the importance of relatively fixed characteristics brought to the school as compared with social conditions encountered by students while in school.

The analysis was carried out on a 40 percent random, weighted[6] sample of HS&B public school students who filled out a questionnaire in both 1980 and 1982. The two functions are found in Table 1 listing the variables and their coefficients. Some conceptual clarifications are in order for several of the variables. *SES* is divided into quartiles based on student reports of five family characteristics including father's occupation, father's and mother's education, family income, and the presence of certain household items. *Test* refers to quartile placement based on a battery of HS&B tests at tenth grade that include mathematics, vocabulary, language and grammar usage, science, and civics. The type of information gained from these tests is a measure both of ability and of achievement that accrues from taking standard school subjects. *Grades* refers to the self-reported letter grades students have achieved in high school. *Self-esteem* is a four-item composite scale based on the extent to which students strongly agree, agree, disagree, or strongly disagree with statements such as "I am able to do things as well as most other people." The *Locus of Control* scale is also a four-item scale based on student agreement or disagreement with such statements as "Good luck is more important than hard work for success." *Hours Worked* is the self-reported number of hours a week the student works at a job. *Truancy* refers to the self-reported number of school days missed when not sick. *Late* is a measure of the number of days a student

Table 1. Discriminant Analysis (Standardized canonical coefficients)

Independent Variables	Function 1 Academic	Function 2 Social Context of School
Sex	.09	−.07
Hispanic	−.08	.03
Black	.02	−.03
White	−.15	.13
SES/Q	.25	−.07
Test/Q	.29	.05
Grades	.22	−.20
S/Esteem	.04	−.20
Loc/Control	−.00	−.00
Hours/Wrkd	−.11	.22
Truancy	−.12	.47
Late	.07	.25
Sub/Feels	.05	.13
Others/C/Me	−.01	.08
Acdm/Instr	.03	−.04
Reput/Com	−.03	.16
Sch/Clim	.01	.07
Schl/Probs	.01	.00
Intr/Schl	.01	−.09
Discipline	−.10	.41
Law/Probs	−.07	.51
Exp/Schl/Atn	.61	.45
Group Centroids		
Group 1 Dropouts	−1.20	.69
Group 2 Stay-ins	−.56	−.26
Group 3 College-bound	1.08	.09

Classification Results (based on above variables)

Actual Group Membership	Predicted Group Membership		
	1	2	3
1 Dropouts (n = 439)	63%[a]	24%	13%
2 Stay-ins (n = 1599)	22%	54%[a]	24%
3 College-bound (n = 1317)	5%	11%	84%[a]

Overall: 67% correct

Note: For the discriminant analysis, 7,539 cases were processed; the above sample sizes reflect cases where complete data were available.

[a] Percent of accurate predictions for each group.

was late to school. *Discipline* is a three-item scale asking the student about discipline problems in the past year, about being suspended or placed on probation, and about cutting classes every once in a while. Students indicate whether statements are true or false for them. Finally, *Expected School Attainment* is a single item asking students how much formal schooling they expect to get in the future. This item provides for nine levels of possible responses from "less than high school graduation" to "Ph.D. or M.D."

Function 1 accounts for 89 percent of the variance between groups. Expected School Attainment is by far the most powerful variable (.61) in discriminating among the three groups. Test (.29), SES (.25), and Grades (.22) are also powerful predictors and are positively correlated with Expected School Attainment. The fact that Expected School Attainment, Tests, SES, and Grades emerge as powerful predictors in Function 1 suggests that it can be interpreted as an academic function.

Group centroids show that Function 1 spreads the three groups along the horizontal axis with the greatest difference between dropouts (group 1) and college-bound (group 3). This finding is consistent with previous literature and offers the following picture of the college-bound student: high expectations, high achievement/ability, high SES, and high grades. Conversely, the dropout is characterized as one who has low expectations, low achievement/ability, low SES, and low grades.

Once the academic function is partialed out, new variables emerge as important predictors: Truancy (.47), Expectations (.45), Discipline Problems (.41), Lateness (.25), and Hours Worked (.22). Function 2 accounts for 11 percent of the pooled variance and seems to discriminate best between dropouts (group 1) and stay-ins (group 2). This function may be regarded as a social context of schooling function. The picture that emerges in Function 2 is of dropouts who differ from their academically similar peers in terms of their high truancy, discipline problems, lateness, and hours worked. Interestingly, students exhibiting these unconventional behaviors have fairly high expectations about future schooling.

The two-function model described above successfully predicted 63 percent of the dropouts, 54 percent of the stay-ins, and 84 percent of the college-bound for the combined sample. We would expect stay-ins to be the most difficult group to predict in that this group includes students with widely varied backgrounds, abilities, and behaviors. We can imagine students at the tails of this group choosing to drop out or go to college for reasons not explained by the model.[7]

IMPLICATIONS OF THE ANALYSIS FOR SCHOOLS

From the standpoint of school policy and practice, it is essential for educators to become knowledgeable about the way school can be perceived differently and can affect different groups of adolescents in different ways. The exploration of cultural, ethnic, and social-class differences regarding school can provide a basis for understanding and acting on the problem of differential school achievement by these groups.

From an institutional perspective, the data from Functions 1 and 2 suggest that there is a serious problem with the holding power of school for some youth. Dropouts do not expect to get as much schooling as their peers and this is quite understandable. They do not perform as well as their peers on school tests, their grades are lower than those of their peers, they are more often truant both in and out of school, and generally they get into more disciplinary trouble than other students. Given this rather negative set of experiences, it should not be surprising that these students leave school for a different environment. For most the intent is to enter the world of work, which must look more rewarding than the situation they find in school.

While the discriminant analysis using the variables available in the HS&B data base does have a margin of error in identifying the three groups of students, it is more powerful than those analyses that rely primarily on family-background and academic-ability variables. This is particularly evident when distinguishing dropouts from non-college-bound graduates. It also suggests that in addition to the characteristics brought to school by the student, there are several institutional characteristics that are problematic if one wishes to affect the number of students leaving school early.

It can be argued, of course, that discipline problems are associated with low SES and other background factors. Even if this is the case, it is crucial to view the dropout problem as growing out of conflict with and estrangement from institutional norms and rules that are represented in various discipline problems. If the intent of social policy is to reduce the number of dropouts, then policies and practices of schools will need to respond to this conflict with and estrangement from the institution arising out of the social and family background of students. Certainly public schooling in a democratic society is obligated to respond constructively to children from all backgrounds and social conditions. It may be that some kinds of children are more difficult to teach than others, but the school has no less of a mandate to do its best to provide all the schooling such children can profitably use. This is precisely the mandate that has been accepted by the schools for educating handicapped children.

Based on HS&B data, many tenth graders indicate their intentions not only to graduate but also to pursue postsecondary schooling. However, their experiences during the junior and senior years do not lead to fulfillment of these expectations. This is unfortunate for both individuals and society since the diversity of postsecondary education available in this country can provide worthwhile alternatives for most youth. It appears that rather than broadly promoting the realization of youthful expectations schools now work to undermine them, except for those students who are most obviously facile with a

Table 2. Marginal Students' Views of School (Percentage responses for each item; sample size for each group is indicated in parentheses)

Item	Response	Hispanics (294,105) N-CB DO[a]		Blacks (245,100) N-CB DO		Whites (1,632,531) N-CB DO	
Rate teacher	Poor	10	17	14	20	12	20
interest in	Fair	39	39	33	30	37	39
students	Good	36	31	38	24	40	30
	Excellent	11	7	8	11	7	7
	Don't know	4	6	7	15	4	4
Rate effec-	Poor	13	21	12	16	11	12
tiveness of	Fair	42	28	40	47	41	38
school dis-	Good	33	34	24	16	35	33
cipline	Excellent	6	14	12	6	8	11
	Don't know	8	6	11	15	5	6
Rate fairness	Poor	19	22	22	28	21	26
of school	Fair	37	27	39	31	38	38
discipline	Good	29	22	25	19	33	25
	Excellent	6	10	6	5	5	5
	Don't know	9	8	7	17	4	6

[a] N-CB = Non-College-Bound Graduates; DO = Dropouts

restricted conception of learning. Again, we argue that it is a responsibility of school to enhance and reinforce the expectations of all youth regarding their attainment of schooling.

MARGINAL STUDENTS' VIEWS: EVIDENCE OF SCHOOL FAILURE

The most difficult task in selecting dropouts from a group of students is distinguishing between the dropout and the terminal graduate. A clearer picture of who drops out can be obtained by inspecting the pattern of responses to specific items for both dropouts and stay-ins. The question being asked is the extent to which dropouts and stay-ins are similar or different, particularly in terms of their experiences and views regarding school.

Three variables can be seen as measures of student alienation and rejection of school – Teacher Interest in Students, Effectiveness of Discipline, and Fairness of Discipline (see Table 2). These items reveal a general student discontent over the relations students have with the institution and its adults. When those who eventually became dropouts were asked to rate Teacher Interest in Students on a four-point scale, marks of fair to poor were given by

56 percent of the Hispanics, 50 percent of the blacks, and 59 percent of the whites. Non-college-bound students are not much more positive, in view of the fair-to-poor ratings given by each racial group (Hispanics 49 percent, blacks 47 percent, and whites 49 percent).

In terms of Effectiveness of Discipline, schools again receive rather negative ratings. Using a four-point scale, about half of both the stay-ins and dropouts among Hispanics gave poor or fair ratings to their schools. Among blacks, 52 percent of the stay-ins and 63 percent of the dropouts rated discipline effectiveness as poor or fair. Among whites, the rating of poor or fair was given by 52 percent of the stay-ins and 50 percent of the dropouts. These data show consistency across all combinations of groups regarding the relative ineffectiveness of school discipline, nor is there any indication of any important differences between stay-ins and dropouts.

On the question of Fairness of Discipline the schools rated even more negative responses from students across the board, regardless of race or status as a student. Hispanics and blacks gave nearly identical responses. The ratings of poor or fair ranged from 56 to 61 percent for both the stay-ins and the dropouts in both groups. Whites were even more critical; 59 percent of the non-college-bound and 64 percent of the dropouts rated the fairness of their school's discipline as poor or fair.

Taken as a whole, the response of a broad range of students on the issues of effectiveness and fairness indicates a consistently negative view. While both minority groups are critical of the discipline in their schools, it is the whites who are most unhappy. Some might conclude that these responses simply reflect the distorted biases of those most often in conflict with the school, but further inspection of the data revealed that 48 percent of the white college-bound students gave poor or fair ratings to their schools on discipline fairness. This suggests that schools have a serious problem with how students perceive the discipline system.

Up to this point most of the categories of student responses have not revealed substantial differences in responses when comparing the non-college-bound stay-in and the dropout. However, when the statement "I am satisfied with the way my education is going" is presented, clearer separation for these two groups appears. Among Hispanic dropouts, 58 percent answered false, while 38 percent of the stay-ins said false. Among whites the response was 52 and 33 percent respectively. These data indicate an unhappiness over the schooling the soon-to-be dropout has experienced.

Another category that reveals marked differences between dropouts and stay-ins is whether they have ever been suspended or on probation. For Hispanics, 31 percent of the dropouts and 17 percent of the stay-ins report such disciplinary actions. Black dropouts gave 44 percent affirmative response while their non-college-bound peers gave a 19 percent response. For whites the differential between dropouts and stay-ins is 26 and 11 percent respectively. This self-report data indicates that dropouts do have greater disciplinary problems than other students, with blacks having the greatest likelihood of serious discipline problems in school. In view of the generally negative responses by all students regarding the effectiveness and fairness of the discipline system, it is not unreasonable to assume that marginal students doing poorly in academics who also experience disciplinary trouble will acquire negative attitudes.

One variable that clearly separates stay-ins from dropouts across all three racial groups, and that is related to disciplinary problems, concerns cutting classes. Almost two-thirds of the Hispanics and more than half of the black and white dropouts admitted to cutting classes now and then, while their stay-in counterparts were substantially lower at 32, 29, and 27 percent respectively. This difference concerning in-school truancy suggests one way in which the dropout becomes embroiled in both academic and disciplinary problems that can lead to discouragement and lessen the probability of graduation.

In the area of expected school attainment, students were asked, "How far in school do you expect to get?" They were given nine levels ranging from less than high school graduation to Ph.D. or M.D. It should be pointed out that among those who actually dropped out very few anticipated doing so. Among eventual dropouts only 8 percent of the Hispanics, 10 percent of the blacks, and 9 percent of the whites projected that they would not complete high school.

Among those who eventually left before graduation, 49 percent of the Hispanics, 31 percent of the blacks, and 45 percent of the whites saw high school graduation as the end of their schooling. It should be noted that these figures are very similar to the responses of those who graduated. It also means that among dropouts about 44 percent of the Hispanics, 60 percent of the blacks, and 45 percent of the whites projected formal education *beyond* high school.

One interpretation of these data is that the norm of pursuing formal education is firmly embedded in our culture. While Hispanics project somewhat less education for themselves and blacks substantially more — even more than whites — both the dropout and the stay-in anticipate graduating from high school at the time of data gathering, that is, the sophomore year in high school. Since few see themselves dropping out and most see themselves continuing education beyond high school, something happens to dissuade these adolescents from attaining their expectations. One plausible explanation is that those who become dropouts see all schooling in relation to their experiences in high school, and in view of their lack of academic success and disciplinary problems, opt to terminate this negative situation and thereby foreclose opportunities to pursue formal schooling.

In summary, the picture of high school that emerges for most students is a place where teachers are not particularly interested in students, and the discipline system is perceived as neither effective nor fair. Dropouts are not satisfied with their schooling. For the dropout, school is a place where one gets into trouble; suspension, probation, and cutting classes are much more frequent for this group. Almost all of the youth who eventually drop out see themselves finishing high school, suggesting that dropping out is not a conscious decision already made that can be identified in the early years of high school. While dropouts do not see themselves attaining as many years of schooling as their stay-in counterparts, it should be noted that among black dropouts more than 50 percent see themselves going beyond high school for additional education.

Taken as a whole these data suggest that school factors related to discipline are significant in developing a tendency to drop out. If one comes from a low SES background, which may signify various forms of family stress or instability, and if one is consistently discouraged by the school because of signals about academic inadequacies and failures, and if one perceives little interest or caring on the part of teachers, and if one sees the institution's discipline system as both ineffective and unfair but one has serious encounters with that discipline system, then it is not unreasonable to expect such individuals to become alienated and lose their commitment to the goals of graduating from high school and pursuing more education.

The process of becoming a dropout is complex because the act of rejecting an institution as fundamental to the society as school must also be accompanied by the belief that the institution has rejected the person. The process is probably cumulative for most youth. It begins with negative messages from the school concerning academic and discipline problems. As these messages accumulate into concrete problems — failing courses and thereby lacking credits required for graduation — the choice is between continuing an extra year or more in a setting that offers increasingly negative experiences and dropping out. Some do elect to stay to graduation, but as many as 50 percent of the youth in some schools elect to escape to the perceived opportunities and experiences outside.

For the adolescent who has dropped out of high school, the psychological effect is to drop out of all formal schooling. Although there are several routes a dropout can use to reenter the system of formal education, these youth generally believe that school is not for them — a decision that precludes many opportunities for personal and economic advancement in the future.

SELF-ESTEEM AND LOCUS OF CONTROL: FURTHER EVIDENCE OF SCHOOL FAILURE

In this study the variables Self-esteem and Locus of Control are conceived as outcomes of formal schooling. This is based, in part, on the explicit goal

Table 3. Sample Means for Self-Esteem Scale by Group and Race
(Sample size for each group is indicated in parentheses)

	Dropouts		Non-college-bound		College-bound	
	1980	1982	1980	1982	1980	1982
	(95)		(257)		(86)	
Hispanic	1.84	1.65[b]	1.91	1.79[b]	1.84	1.69[a]
	(82)		(187)		(154)	
Black	1.76	1.66	1.74	1.65[a]	1.71	1.55[b]
	(476)		(1453)		(1212)	
White	1.90	1.77[b]	1.93	1.83[b]	1.81	1.68[b]
Overall	1.87	1.74	1.91	1.80[b]	1.80	1.67[b]

Note: Lower numerical values indicate more positive self-esteem.

[a] Significant at .05 level.
[b] Significant at .01 level.

statements of public schools that students should acquire positive self-concepts and learn to take responsibility for their actions. These general school goals are also found in more specific form in the rationales of individual courses. If not always stated explicitly, there is implicit in the purpose of public schooling the goals of self-development, self-management, rational decision making, and control of one's circumstances and opportunities through the acquisition of knowledge and skills.

To see these two factors as outcomes of schooling is not to deny that other influences from the home and community have an important effect on them. Parenting, for example, has a great impact on an adolescent's sense of self but sorting out such influences is extremely difficult. We can, however, look at students both before and after they have dropped out of school and compare them with their peers who continue to graduation and beyond, allowing us an indication of the relative contribution school can make in developing self-esteem and establishing locus of control. The HS&B data permit the comparison of racial groups and student status over time (1980–1982) as sophomores become either seniors or dropouts. This provides information on the effects of staying in school or dropping out as measured by Self-esteem and Locus of Control. It is also an indirect measure of the effectiveness of school policies and practices for different groups of students.

Self-esteem is comprised of four items with which students either agree or disagree on a five-point scale — for example, "I am able to do things as well as other people." Locus of Control has four items, and students are also asked to agree or disagree on a five-point scale with such statements as "Good luck is more important than hard work for success."

The data in Table 3 indicate that all three student status groups and all three races increased their sense of self-esteem in a positive direction over the three-year period. For all but black dropouts the change is statistically significant, and in this case the change score is similar and parallel to those changes for the comparison groups. Dropouts begin with slightly higher self-esteem than the non-college-bound and actually increase the differential by 1982 even though they have left school. This is true for each racial group. The overall gain in self-esteem by dropouts is exactly the same as for the group with greatest self-esteem, the college-bound. These data make it difficult to argue that dropping out of school has a negative effect on youth. The largest score gain for any group (.19) is achieved by Hispanic dropouts. For youth who have been receiving negative signals from the school in the form of poor grades and/or unhappy experiences with the discipline system, dropping out to a different environment is a positive experience. Those youth who are similar to the dropouts in some respects, but who stay to graduation, report less growth in self-esteem than either the dropouts or college-bound.

The question of whether each group's locus of control changes between 1980 and 1982 can be answered from the data in Table 4. Generally, there is movement toward a more internal locus of control. The amount of change varies considerably by group. College-bound Hispanics show the largest change toward internal control, and Hispanic dropouts show a similar movement although they remain relatively externally oriented. Overall changes show an increase of .15 for dropouts, .09 for non-college stay-ins, and .11 for the college-bound group. While dropouts make up some of the difference between themselves and stay-ins, they still project a more external locus of control than do their peers. For blacks, the difference between dropouts and stay-ins widens substantially.

Table 4. Sample Means for Locus of Control by Group and Race
(Sample size for each group is indicated in parentheses)

	Dropouts		Non-college-bound		College-bound	
	1980	1982	1980	1982	1980	1982
Hispanic	(90)		(251)		(83)	
	2.48	2.66[b]	2.60	2.66	2.72	2.92[b]
Black	(81)		(177)		(151)	
	2.59	2.59	2.55	2.74[b]	2.88	2.98[b]
White	(478)		(1430)		(1199)	
	2.65	2.82[b]	2.79	2.87[b]	3.03	3.12[b]
Overall	2.61	2.76[b]	2.74	2.83[b]	2.99	3.10[b]

Note: Higher numerical values indicate greater sense of internal control.

[a] Significant at .05 level.
[b] Significant at .01 level.

Despite beginning with the most internal control orientation, the college-bound group shows substantial change. School appears to be good for this group. Those who are academically successful enough to be going to college begin with an enhanced sense of control over conditions in their lives. Staying in school to graduation also results in gains for each racial group, but the stay-ins lag far behind the college-bound. Using the amount of change toward internal control as a standard, these data do not support the argument that dropouts would have benefited by staying in school (except in the case of blacks). The dropouts begin with a significantly different orientation toward control, and it may be that school with its present reward structure cannot be expected to have much impact on this factor. Dropping out may be good in the sense that it gives these youth an opportunity to gain a sense of control through participation in adult activities. Unless one is very good at doing those academic tasks rewarded by schools, one is not likely to gain a greater sense of internal control through schooling. If this is the case, then schools can be seen as reinforcing the existing dispositions of students rather than helping those most in need of an increased sense of control over plans, decisions, and circumstances.

In most respects our findings from the HS&B data parallel or at least do not contradict the findings of previous studies. For example, SES was found to be an important predictor of dropout by Combs and Cooley, Bachman, Rumberger, and Peng.[8] School ability and performance persist as important predictors of student status. Like Bachman, who found "in-school delinquency"[9] a strong predictor of dropping out, we found several more specific variables indicating conflict between students and the institution to be important predictors. Our analysis of the HS&B data depart from earlier findings, however, in that SES and school performance are reduced in relative importance while Expected School Attainment, along with the conflict variables, is more powerful.

Furthermore, our analysis sees student and school interacting to produce dropouts. Unlike many researchers, we see the school as having an opportunity for initiative and a responsibility to respond constructively to those students whose continued education is at risk. In contrast, Bachman concludes that "dropping out is a symptom which signifies a mis-match between certain individuals and the typical high school environment." The mis-match exists because of limited academic ability, school failure, and delinquent behavior. These problems are not likely to be resolved by staying in school longer, according to Bachman, who concludes that the campaign against dropping out seems questionable because research on the longitudinal effects of dropping out indicate "that some young men can manage reasonably well on the basis of ten or eleven years of education. Perhaps others would do so if they were not branded as 'dropouts.' "[10]

We believe this conclusion is irresponsible because it suggests that schools need not attempt to provide effective education for all students. It argues, instead, for legitimizing a "push-out" strategy by schools for those who are least able to benefit from a traditional academic curriculum. This position tends to absolve the school of responsibility for the least advantaged in our society. It suggests that public education is for some youth but not for all.

While most of the literature on dropouts is directed only at the deficiencies found in the marginal student, we see those same characteristics as a reflection on the institution. More precisely, we consider the possibility that certain student characteristics in combination with certain school conditions are responsible for students' decisions to leave school early. We do not want to minimize the fact that students differ markedly on a range of personal and social characteristics; how could it be otherwise? However, schools are obliged to accept these differences as a fact of life and respond in a constructive manner. We believe this stance, along with our findings, provides grounds for recommending general policy and practice reforms that would make school more responsive not only to those who drop out, but also to a large body of students who now stay in school reluctantly.

Our reform recommendations stem from several specific findings. Three of these are the perceived lack of teacher interest in students, the perception that the discipline system is ineffective and unfair, and the presence of widespread truancy. These findings form a pattern that we believe cannot be easily dismissed because they reflect a fundamental problem with the perceived legitimacy of the institution. We see them as the tip of the iceberg, indicating institutional problems that go much deeper than dropouts. The findings have implications for the degree of engagement by even those who stay to graduation.

In addition to revealing problems in the area of discipline, there is also the more general finding regarding expected school attainment for a large number of youth. Some may dismiss this finding as the product of unrealistic expectations by naive students, and there may be an element of truth in this view. On the other hand, it also suggests that schools in performing their sorting function for society may be unnecessarily harsh and discouraging to many adolescents. The sorting and selecting function does not require schools to be negative and alienating. Moreover, after the selection of those who will go to prestigious colleges is completed, there is a range of possibilities for additional education to which many youth could aspire. Selecting the college-bound elite is one task schools should be engaged in; the remaining body of students should receive the kind of attention that will allow them to pursue all the schooling they can profitably use.

Three general reforms of policy and practice are necessary if schools are to respond to these problems and perform the social mandate with which they are entrusted: (1) an enhanced sense of professional accountability among educators toward all students; (2) a renewed effort to establish legitimate authority within the institution; (3) a redefinition of school work for students and teachers that will allow a greater number of students to achieve success and satisfaction and to continue their schooling.

The enhanced sense of professional accountability speaks to the problem of providing equity in public schooling. This does not mean that all students will receive the same curriculum or achieve at the same level, but it does imply that all youth must be given an opportunity to receive some reasonably attractive benefits from a publicly financed school system. Educators must be responsible for those students who are not ideal academic performers as well as for those who are talented. There is evidence now that many students do not believe teachers are very interested in them. To the extent that those who come from disadvantaged backgrounds perceive a less than firm commitment by the institution to educate them, their school effort is not likely to be sincere. Professional accountability to those who are least advantaged is the only responsible stance educators can take. The profession must work to establish a variety of mechanisms to ensure that such students receive all the personal and social benefits possible. Professional accountability must begin with a general belief on the part of educators that such a commitment is important and a social responsibility. In addition, specific institutional mechanisms must be developed to define this accountability and make it a matter of both policy and practice.

One implication of our study is that schools are in serious trouble with respect to the maintenance of authority when many students are skeptical of the discipline system. One can view the problem of legitimate authority as an extension of accountability. It may be that the impersonal bureaucratic structure of large high schools has created a sense of alienation among students, who feel that the adults do not care for them and that they are likely to be treated in an unfair or arbitrary manner. The comprehensive high school of today may create adult/student relationships that result in skepticism and cynicism in both parties. More personal and authentic relationships are probably necessary to reestablish widespread belief in the legitimacy of the institution.

Some reforms in the discipline system are necessary if schools are to avoid creating a sizable group of deviants who can see no alternative to resisting the school's authority if they are to retain their own dignity. At minimum schools must find ways of preventing the widespread truancy that has become a norm in many schools. The very students most at risk must not be allowed to undermine their own chances of success through either misguided permissivism or outright neglect on the part of educators. If the marginal academic student is to benefit from formal schooling, he or she must be in class. Part of the route to professional accountability is through the establishment of legitimate authority in the educational process for those who are to benefit from educators' efforts. The evidence from case studies of effective alternative programs for marginal students indicates that such students respond positively to an environment that combines a caring relationship and personalized teaching with a high degree of program structure characterized by clear, demanding, but attainable expectations.[11]

Finally, a redefinition of school work is needed to be responsible to the broad range of youth the school is mandated to serve. A central problem with schools today is that success is narrowly defined and restricted to the few at the top of their class ranking who are destined for college. Such a restricted notion of competence and success for youth is indefensible in terms of both the individuals involved and society as a whole. While proficiency in traditional academic subjects is important and serves to stimulate some youth, there are many more who should be encouraged to develop proficiency in other domains. Unfortunately, vocational education, the most obvious alternative, is currently in a dismal state in many schools. Moreover, where there are strong vocational programs, they often exclude those students most in need of an alternative that provides success and positive roles.

Schools do have available to them a variety of exemplars using nontraditional conceptions of curriculum and learning. Some of these have been dramatically successful with a range of students. One specific example is *Foxfire* magazine, published by high school students. In addition, we have examples of schools focused on the performing arts, health care and medicine, and human services. There are excellent programs that have youth developing and managing small businesses. There are also exemplary vocational programs that involve youth in the building trades or other skilled fields where the curriculum is based on an "experiential" conception of learning. Such diverse opportunities for success and development can change the view that many youth now have that "school is not for me."

Those who are pessimistic about the willingness and/or ability of schools to respond constructively to the marginal student with both a more caring relationship and a more stimulating curriculum may want to argue that this is an opportunity to try some form of voucher to generate new conceptions of schooling.[12] A voucher plan need not supplant existing public schools. Instead it could be used as a supplemental strategy to create opportunities for students to have planned educational experiences in community-based programs. Some of these could be explicitly vocational while others could provide direct exploration in the arts, science, medicine, and law, as well as performance of public services. The use of the voucher idea may be necessary to attenuate the nearly monopolistic control schools now have over the education of youth.

While none of the recent studies and reports about the conditions of secondary schools have advocated alternatives to public schooling as a reform measure, such an option seems reasonable in light of the severe school problems faced by potential dropouts. In view of the many factors that keep schools from changing quickly and substantially — restricted budgets, state regulations, union contracts, public expectations — it appears that an end-run around these obstacles may be necessary. The use of community-based educational resources may well provide the environment that stimulates those students who now find school an unrewarding place to learn.

Notes

1   *Ford Foundation Letter* 15, no. 3 (1984): 1.

2   C. Camp, *School Dropouts* (Sacramento: California Legislature: Assembly Office of Research, May 1980).

3   The most recent data from the National Center for Education Statistics indicates a 27 percent dropout rate (*Christian Science Monitor*, May 9, 1985).

4   The Committee on Science, Engineering and Public Policy, "Skills for Tomorrow: High School and the Changing Workplace" (draft report, National Academy of Science, Engineering and Institute of Medicine, n.d.); and G. Berlin and J. Duhl, "Education, Equity, and Economic Excellence: The Critical Role of Second Chance Basic Skills and Job Training Programs," (unpublished paper, Ford Foundation, 1984).

5   For Project TALENT, see J. Combs and W. Cooley, "Dropouts: In High School and after High School," *American Educational Research Journal* 5, no. 3 (1968): 343–63; for Youth in Transition, J. G. Bachman, S. Green, and I. D. Wirtanen, *Dropping Out — Problem or Symptom?* Youth in Transition Series, Vol. 3 (Ann Arbor, Mich.: Institute for Social Research, 1971); the National Longitudinal Survey of Youth Labor Market Experience is discussed in R. Rumberger, "Dropping Out of High School: The Influences of Race, Sex, and Family Background," *American Educational Research Journal* 20, no. 2 (1983): 199–220; and High School and Beyond in S. Peng, *High School Dropouts: Descriptive Information from High School and Beyond* (Washington, D.C.: National Center for Education Statistics, 1983).

6   HS&B includes a set of weights that adjust for the over- or under-sampling of certain groups and allows the sample responses to be used to reflect the views of all sophomores nationwide. When a subsample of the original is used (as in this case), a correction factor must be applied to the original weights so that the subsample may again be used to represent the nation.

7   A discriminant analysis was run for each of three racial groups — Hispanics, blacks, whites. Results were similar to those reported above, which are based on a combination of the three groups.

8   Combs and Cooley, "Dropouts"; Bachman, Green, and Wirtanen, *Dropping Out;* Rumberger, "Dropping Out of High School"; and Peng, *High School Dropouts.*

9   Bachman, Green, and Wirtanen, *Dropping Out.*

10   Ibid, pp. 181–82.

11   G. Wehlage, *Effective Programs for the Marginal High School Student* (Bloomington, Ind.: Phi Delta Kappa, 1983).

12   G. Wehlage, "The Marginal High School Student: Defining the Problem and Searching for Policy," *Children and Youth Services Review* 5 (1983): 321–42.

Why Urban Adolescents Drop into and out of Public High School

MICHELLE FINE

University of Pennsylvania

Statistics on school experiences of dropouts provide one sort of picture of the problem. In this article Michelle Fine provides another. Using ethnographic techniques, she describes through the eyes and words of actual dropouts the factors that led them to leave school.

This article contains the words and stories of black and Latin urban adolescents who have dropped out of high school, and of some who stayed in. This ethnography locates the "dropout problem" in the context of a comprehensive high school in New York City, as well as in the homes of these adolescents and on their streets. The analysis tries to unravel the threads of economic and social arrangements, school policies and practices, and individual and collective psychologies of adolescents as they contribute to the extraordinary dropout rate in New York City.[1]

In September 1984 this research, funded by the W. T. Grant Foundation, was driven by the question "Why do urban students drop out of high school?" By December, a parallel but equally compelling question surfaced, "And why do they stay?" One comprehensive zoned high school in upper Manhattan was selected for this study. The student body is predominantly black and Latin, largely lower-income and working-class. The school is, by reputation, "good" according to representatives at the board of education and teachers/administrators throughout the city. To some this means *safe* (the school ranked quite well in the board's analysis of disciplinary incidents in city schools); to others this means *stable* (the principal is one of the senior principals in the city, and has been the prime administrator of this school for twenty-five years); and to many it means the school is basically *pleasant* (the school is situated in a newly gentrified, largely white, upper-middle-class section of the city, although a pocket of lower-income tenements survives in the immediate vicinity).

In the fall, observations were conducted throughout the school, in the deans' offices, the guidance office, the attendance room, the lunchroom, and the library. Some classes, such as English, English as a Second Language,

Sociology, and Hygiene were attended regularly; other classes, including Bookkeeping, Remedial Reading, Typing, History, Chemistry, and Music, sporadically. Autobiographies were written by twenty-two students in their Sociology class, and two students in English class volunteered elaborate fictional accounts of why students drop out of high school.

To determine a dropout and survival rate, a cohort analysis was undertaken in which the 1,221 students who were in the ninth grade in 1978 – 1979 were tracked through their school records, specifying how many of this cohort graduated, dropped out, and transferred; where official transcripts were sent; and which students under what circumstances left this school prior to graduation.

In the spring, 30 adolescents who dropped out in the past four months and another 15 discharged over four years ago were interviewed, primarily in their homes. A survey was mailed to 350 students who were in the ninth grade at this school in 1978 – 1979, some of whom participated in follow-up interviews.

Across the year a number of General Equivalency Diploma (GED) programs were visited, as was one of the city's "pregnancy schools." A young woman was hired to interview at four private business schools — for example, secretarial, cosmetology, and computer schools — to document promises made, kept, and broken. In addition, I attended most of this high school's Parents' Association executive and general meetings and met with representatives of a number of community-based organizations and dropout-prevention programs.

PLACING THE PROBLEM IN CONTEXT

Others have written that public schools both reproduce the gender, class, and race/ethnicity stratifications that organize our society and make possible moments of truly critical thinking, democratic process, and liberatory education.[2] In the school studied here, attended by low-income and working-class black and Latin youths, there are no SAT preparation courses, few honors classes, overcrowded classrooms, old and damaged textbooks that cannot be taken home by students because there aren't enough.[3] The "hidden curriculum" of corporate America is anything but hidden.[4] To illustrate: A mural on one wall lists qualities of a good student, including loyalty, attractive appearance, cheerfulness, poise, attendance. A major banking/finance firm runs an academy of finance within the school. A few years back, students were given a "choice" of a course on black studies or one on Wall Street finance. The latter won and, according to one teacher, the black studies books were thrown out.

It is not only in curriculum that social inequities are reproduced, even as they are masked. The differential outcomes of schooling also reflect the social reproduction wrought by the public education system. Carnoy and Levin describe the contradictions and tensions embodied in contemporary schooling, and remind readers that in our society "schooling tends to be distributed more equally than capital, income or employment status."[5] Yet having a degree is more valuable for those already privileged by class, race/ethnicity, and gender. Women's returns on education have been estimated at 40 percent of men's, and blacks' approximately 63 percent of whites.[6] High school dropouts who live in the highest income areas of New York City have a 42.4 percent employment-to-population ratio compared with a 31 percent ratio for high school graduates in the poorest neighborhoods.[7]

Indeed, schools do little to disrupt and much to reproduce existing social arrangements. Even with the same level of education — the high school diploma — whites, men, and upper-middle-class students reap consistently more per additional year of education than do blacks, women, and working-class/low-income students, respectively. Among white women and men and black women and men age 22 – 34 who have one to three years of high school, 15 percent of the white men, 28 percent of the white women, 37 percent of the black men, and 62 percent of the black women live in poverty.[8]

Low-income groups, particularly blacks and Latins, do not even have equal access to a degree that disproportionately advantages white upper-income groups. For whites living below the poverty line, 45 percent of the females and 46 percent of the males graduated from high school. For blacks living below the poverty line, 36 percent of the females and 31 percent of the males graduated.[9]

It was startling, in this context, to discover that of the 1,221 students in the ninth-grade cohort at this New York City high school, only 20 percent ultimately graduated from this school. A full two-thirds of these ninth graders never graduated from *any* high school. Of the 1,221, 43.8 percent were discharged (that is, dropped out or transferred) and no records were sent to another educational institution. Another 17.7 percent transferred to another educational facility to which records were sent (of these twenty-nine students moved to Puerto Rico, the Dominican Republic, or Nicaragua, and thirty-one students moved out of state within mainland United States). Six percent ended up in GED programs; 7 percent were considered "not found," and the remaining 5.7 percent were discharged with records sent to the military or a private business school. It is interesting to note that in this cohort there were very few "terminal graduates." Students were either discharged or graduated and applied to college.

To determine a dropout rate, the Discharged No Records Sent were combined with the Not Founds, adding a generous estimate of 50 percent of the transfers, military/business schools, and GEDs who might graduate. Using this calculation, a 65.6 percent dropout rate results for this cohort. This figure stands in striking contrast to the principal's claim that "80 percent of our graduates go onto college." But both "facts" are true and coexist as the central contradiction of the school. Public schools not only reproduce but actually exacerbate existing social inequities, while creaming, in this case, a

20 percent elite who truly benefit from their public education. Dropping out of high school can be analyzed as an act that reflects in some cases a student's articulated politic of resistance, in other cases merely the outcome of a student's disappointment with the promise of education. In most cases dropping out results in the worst of social reproduction.

PERSPECTIVES ON DROPPING OUT: VOICES OF URBAN ADOLESCENTS

From information obtained in interviews with many adolescents in and out of school and spending a considerable amount of time in a public high school, it is possible to argue that some adolescents leave high school with an articulated critique of schooling and pedagogy, and/or a negative appraisal of the relation of schooling to labor market success.[10]

Leo, who left high school in his senior year after receiving 1200 on his SATs, reflected on his Social Studies class:

> Everytime she would write something on the board, even if students contradicted it and made a good point, if it was in her notes we had to write it down. Like there was no discussion. Remember she asked who read the *New York Times* magazine article on teenagers in Harlem, by the guy who wrote *Manchild in the Promised Land?* She asked what was the main point and Louis said it was that those boys are trying to survive, and are frustrated in their lives. She said, no that wasn't the main point. The main point was that they were killing people senselessly, without reason. Then why did she ask us our opinions? I couldn't go to that class.

Leo left school with a powerful and quite obvious critique of traditional pedagogy.

Broderick left because he simply saw no relation between schooling and future income. He dropped out at age sixteen to sell drugs at a "spot" in upper Manhattan. "Where else am I gonna make this money even with a diploma? . . . I know it's a risk, I just got off Riker's Island. I worry about how my mother feels 'bout it. . . . Sometimes I feel its immoral, when I sold Angel Dust to a pregnant girl. Won't do that again, but you can't have a heart up there . . . I don't get it to her, somebody will."

Others leave because family, economic, and social obligations call. Going to school conflicts with their commitment to being what is usually a "good daughter." Diana is seventeen, and her family recently arrived from the Dominican Republic: "My mother has lupus. She's dying and those doctors are killing her. Nobody speaks English good in my family and she wants me there. My brothers and sisters, they little and need me." For lower-income and working-class adolescents, the popularized luxury of extended childhood is inaccessible. Ambivalent about leaving school, Diana felt she had no choice.

"For me, later. Now my mother is ill and I must go." No articulated politic, no resistance, and no critique. Only picking up the pieces in a class-, race-, and gender-stratified society.

There is another group that leaves without a critical analysis of schooling or its economic benefits, and with no immediate crisis. These adolescents leave school because they live surrounded by unemployment and poverty, have experienced failure in school and have been held back at least once, feel terrible about themselves, and see little hope. Most of their friends are out of school, also without diplomas. Their words speak mostly of disappointment over the promises of schooling that turned out to be a lie. Monique ended her interview, "It's a shame, ain't it? I'm seventeen and got nothin' to show for it. Too late for me, but I want a better life for my baby. A house in New Jersey and Catholic schools." These adolescents carry none of the pride, power, or possibility embodied by the first critical group; none of the passion of the crisis group.

Finally, there is a group of unspecified size that is literally thrown out of school. The routinization and bureacratization of the "discharge" process obscures the reality that large numbers of students are actively discharged and not informed of their legal right to an education until the age of twenty-two, as specified in New York State's Education Law S3202. Roy found himself "thrown out. Yeah I cut out some but I didn't think they was gonna throw me out in the twelfth grade. He told me I couldn't come back." Many others are passively discharged, that is, allowed to be dropped from the register once they are absent for twenty consecutive days and have been sent the required letters and received some telephone calls. Yancy explained, "I just couldn't go back there. I was held over three times in ninth grade so I stopped goin' after the first time. You feel so 'shamed and stupid. I guess they figured it out. Got a letter sayin' I can't go back no more to that school."

In many ways these four types embody the range of circumstances under which students leave high school prior to graduation. Some leave with a powerful critique of schooling and/or its labor market potential. Some must attend to their families' social and health needs, making schooling irrelevant and/or disruptive. Others have internalized social ideologies about their inabilities, their uselessness, and they "opt" to leave schools. And finally many, perhaps most, are severed in their connection from schools by those schools they have a legal right to attend.

STRUCTURAL CONDITIONS FACING A COMPREHENSIVE URBAN HIGH SCHOOL: THE CONTEXT FOR DROPPING OUT

Whether dropping out is a personal act of rejection, assertion, joining one's peers, or giving up, it presumes a structural context that is being rejected, critiqued, and/or experienced as defeating by the actor. Therefore we must try to understand such structural conditions as the nature of the student body at this school, the level of overcrowding that marks this and other urban schools, fiscal arrangements that encourage the early dismissal and virtual neglect of dropouts, and the level of empowerment or disempowerment experienced by staff.

The mean reading level of entering ninth graders at this school is 7.0, with math at 6.8, lower than any other high school in Manhattan.[11] The recent proliferation of New York City "theme" schools, which dictate their entrance criteria, has skewed the distribution of low-skill students into the comprehensive zoned high schools. This school had, on register 1984, 3,500 students and, according to one estimate, operated at 144 percent of capacity.[12] Overcrowding heightened alienation and anonymity. The overenrollment of low-skill students reduced academic possibilities, as when Advanced Placement Biology had to be canceled for lack of students.

The education allocation formula for New York City schools further creates conditions antithetic to effective education for all students, especially those having some difficulty in school.[13] The Educational Priorities Panel (EPP) calculated that comprehensive zoned high schools have above-average student/teacher ratios and lower-than-average entering skills levels. Schools are allocated monies in part on the basis of the Curriculum Index, the average number of courses taken per student, and not per capita. In a comprehensive high school many students enroll in half-credit remedial courses, or require extra assistance with homework, counseling, or tutoring. Comprehensive high schools, therefore, receive relatively lower fiscal allocations. With no fiscal incentive to reduce class size or bring back long-term absentees, truants, or dropouts, schools with high dropout rates are financially punished rather than assisted in efforts to retain students.

Another condition facing this school, and also not unique to it, is the racial distribution of personnel. The administration is white, the teaching faculty largely white with many Hispanics; 6 or 7 of the more than 120 teachers are black. This fact is striking in comparison with a city like Philadelphia, which mandates that high schools have a minimum of 21.3 percent and a maximum of 35.5 percent black teachers.[14] Paraprofessionals and aides in this school are largely black women, many of whom do extraordinary amounts of emotional work in the school and receive little pay and varied levels of respect for their labor. This racial distribution reproduces social arrangements and models for students the fact that even schools, allegedly designed to transform those arrangements, are controlled by white persons who only minimally invite the input of persons of color.

Being oversized and underfinanced, as well as racially organized in the most stereotypic ways, this school embodies a profound sense of disempowerment reported by teachers, paraprofessionals, school aides, students, and parents. According to a 1985 Teachers College survey of this school, to which forty faculty and staff responded, "Approximately 2 out of 3 teachers felt that there was little interest shown in their classroom work either by staff or administrators."[15]

While the precise impact of teacher disempowerment on education and students remains to be untangled, a 1983 study of 170 teachers and counselors found that such disempowerment correlated highly with disparaging attitudes toward students.[16] Educators who agreed that "no one around here listens to me" and "school policy doesn't reflect what I think about" were also likely to express disparaging and pessimistic views of the students, for example, "These students are bad kids," and "The students can't be helped." The disempowered teacher may help to produce the disempowered student who, more often than not, in city schools, drops out.

DROPPING OUT OF HIGH SCHOOL:
COERCION, "CHOICE," AND CONSEQUENCES

Adolescents leave high school prior to graduation for a variety of reasons. Many leave because they and/or their families need money. According to the National Center for Education Statistics, 26.9 percent of males and 10.7 percent of females dropped out of school to go to work.[17] In 1979, 60 percent of black male and 77 percent of black female students versus 31 percent of white male and 45 percent of white female students with annual family incomes under $10,000 dropped out of high school.[18]

"Ain't No Jobs Waitin' for Me"

Many adolescents in and out of school understand that a high school diploma guarantees neither job security nor income. Chantal remarked: "Ain't no jobs waitin' for me after graduation." At the same time, she fundamentally believes in the importance of a diploma. What may seem a contradictory awareness accurately reflects her reality. Listen to Ronald: "I stay in school cause every morning I get off the subway and I see this man, he's a drunk, sleeping by the side of the station. I think 'not me' and then I think 'I bet he has a high school degree.'" Chantal and Ronald know many high school graduates who do not have jobs, and others who never graduated but nevertheless make a good living.

These adolescents recognize that there are few jobs waiting—diploma or not. But they also realize that without a diploma "it's tough out here. After two weeks of looking for work I started watchin' the stories [soap operas]. They don't want a black girl with no degree for nothin' but Mikkie D's [McDonald's] or maybe some factory work. Not for me."

If this seemingly contradictory consciousness captures accurately the economic realities faced by poor and working-class black and Latin adolescents and young adults in the United States, it is, at the same time, denied vociferously by most of their teachers and counselors. The lack of black teachers means that few students get an opportunity to talk about race and class contradictions in our society. While not all black teachers agree that these conversations belong in the classroom, white teachers appear more reluctant to raise the issues. White teachers explain that they do not want to "demoralize" black and Latin students; black teachers complain about racism in their work relations, in the curriculum, and overheard in lunchroom conversations about *"those* students and their families."

"If my Momma needs me, I go"

In early September Jose entered the attendance office asking for his discharge papers. He was given the papers to sign, just like so many before him. (My field notes read: September 11. Six or seven kids a day come in asking to be discharged. Nobody says "Are you kidding? Where do you think you're going?" There is no hysteria, no upset, just a bureaucratic, even pleasant exchange of papers.) Jose explained, "I live with my grandmother and she just came out of the hospital for triple bypass in her heart. Now she needs a balloon put in. I can't concentrate and got to help her." When asked why no social worker was contacted, his guidance counselor explained, "Jose got overinvolved, and was irresponsible about his own education." Jose left school.

Most of these students and dropouts seek health care in emergency rooms or neighborhood clinics, if at all. A recent study by Simkin of the Welfare Research Institute[19] indicated that of a sample of 1,700 New York City public school students, 4 percent receive health care from private providers, 6 percent from emergency rooms, 12 percent from hospital clinics, 38 percent from neighborhood health clinics; 34 percent did not indicate any provider. When I first arrived at this high school, students in Hygiene class rank-ordered their social values including marriage, sex, education, status, money, health, job security, nice home, fancy car, children, and so forth. Of fourteen students, seven rated health as their first priority. Such is the case when good health conditions cannot be a taken-for-granted aspect of life.

Many adolescents leave high school because their kin need assistance for health or social services. Even those in school will take time off to wait for welfare checks for fear they will be stolen from the mail box; to translate in housing court; to take "el niño" to the clinic; to pick up a sister, brother, niece, or nephew from day care or to sit with grandpa, who may be alone. Good daughters usually contribute in these ways to their working-class and poor families. But I have also witnessed sons or grandsons, as Jose, who are only children and take on this traditionally female level of personal sacrifice.

Today's dismantled social welfare system, along with the dictates of the female sex role, combine to rip adolescent females from the one institution that could make a difference in their economic and social lives. While it is easy to be cynical about the economic advantage of a high school diploma, for women in particular, the relative advantage gained by a high school diploma is substantial: the difference between life as a domestic (59 percent of women working in private households have 1 – 3 years of high school) and as a clerical worker; the difference between a 31 percent chance of living in poverty for the black female high school graduate and a 62 percent chance for the black female high school dropout (11 percent for the white female high school graduate versus 28 percent for the white female high school dropout).[20]

"Let's Compare Hispanics to Americans"

The incidence of parental and sibling death from illness, accident, homicide, or suicide; health problems; residential moves prompted by arson; drug overdoses and drug-related arrests; harassment by welfare agents, landlords, banks, immigration officials, and boyfriends; and domestic and street violence is indeed astonishing to any observer (and participant). However, that these adolescents often suffer overwhelming social and economic pressures is a necessary but not sufficient explanation for why they drop out of high school at such extraordinary rates. We turn now to the structural and pedagogical practices that facilitate the production of the high school dropout.

> *Item from field notes, October 11, Reading Class.* White male teacher to class of black and Latin tenth and eleventh graders: "OK, let's do a cultural comparison. Let's compare Hispanics to Americans." Some eyes roll. Some girls apply mascara and some hands go up enthusiastically.

In the school that served as home for this ethnography, as is true of many New York City public high schools, students are predominantly black and Latin while teachers, also a segregated population, remain predominantly white. Most students take trains from Central and East Harlem. Some walk to school. Most teachers car pool from suburbs or live in largely white, middle-class, gentrified sections of the city. The contrast in life-styles, experiences, histories, and taken-for-granted expectations is extreme.

> *Item from field notes, November 2, English class.* White female teacher in discussion with students about a recent shooting that occurred outside the school.
> TEACHER: If you know who did it, you have a moral obligation to report that.
> EDITH: If I seen it I still wouldn't say nothing.
> TEACHER: That's not right. I can't believe that.
> LOUIS: I'm not getting my mother killed or my sister beat on.
> DARRYL: I'm not sending some black boy to jail, not me. My brother's in jail. It don't help.

ALICIA: I do what I preach. I don't want nobody to mind my business. Why get involved and get someone in trouble? My names Alicia Patterson, not DT [detective].

TEACHER: Can you imagine any circumstances under which killing would be justified?

OPAL: If a guy tries to beat up my mother, I'd kill him.

TEACHER: Well it's not likely that your mother would be walking down the street and out of the blue she would be beat up. She would have to be in a fight with someone she knew.

ALICIA: Shit, Missy, what city you live in?

This scene illustrates the discrepancies in the lives and experiences of students and teachers. Both, for the most part, agree that the curriculum is standard knowledge. This does not mean that students necessarily accept, learn, or respect this knowledge. But the information gained through *their* lives is often split off or subordinated as irrelevant.[21]

Alicia reflects: "I'm not smart, but I'm wise. I understand people and situations. Don't take much for me to know what's going on. I know what people be thinkin'. But I don't know what they be talkin' about in history class."

But schools are by no means monolithic. They are rife with internal contradiction and therefore the possibility of change. With little support and much initiative, despite administrative fallout and scarce resources, some teachers do teach in ways that are demanding, critical, and expansive. Within public schools one finds teacher-created opportunities for critical thinking, social development, and liberatory education. A dynamic discussion of Paul Robeson and the Red Scare in history riveted students. "He's a tough teacher, but excitin'. I never miss." A guest speaker on lesbian and gay rights in Psychology class allowed Cassandra to feel "comfortable, like it's OK for me, to, you know, like girls. I didn't come out in class but I tole them it makes me mad when everybody so worried 'bout touchin' and lookin' to see and callin' out faggots and such."

The sociology teacher asked girls, "Let's say you and your brother were equally smart and your mother could only send one of you to college, who should go?" which stimulated an unusually high level of energy, dissent, and exchange. After much animated conversation, Deidre, always sobering and thought provoking, joined the conversation, "You know, we should both go. But in my community, boys ain't wrapped so tight. They don't go to college, they end up in jail, on drugs or dead. Girls and womens can take care ourselves better. I don't like it but maybe the boy should go." Independent of the teacher, who participated little after her initial question, the class produced the beginnings of a critical analysis of how gender relations are negotiated within their black, working-class community.

For the most part, however, schooling is structured so that student opinions, voices, and critical thoughts remain silenced—by teachers and ultimately by their own inhibitions. This is especially true in classes from which students are most likely to drop out. Classrooms are organized more around control than conversation, more around the authority of teacher than autonomy of students, and more around competition than collaboration.[22] When students talk to each other or cooperate it often provokes accusations of cheating from their teachers.

"I didn't drop out, I was thrown out"

Many adolescents who are no longer in high school were quick to correct the verb in my question "Why did you drop out of high school?" Many students are coerced to leave high school once they reach seventeen, or at least not encouraged to stay if they "choose" to go. Students are discharged for reasons ranging from continually wearing a coat in the hall, "chronic cutting," "mouthin' off," or having been absent for twenty consecutive, unexcused days.

Item from field notes, September, first week in school.
MF to JUANA (school aide/office worker): Are discharges considered dropouts?
JUANA: Yeah but that seems funny. They been put out. They didn't drop out.

The institutionalized discharge process is accomplished by accumulated cut slips, referrals to deans, perhaps going on "contract" (in which one promises not to violate a school rule or suffers the inevitable consequence of discharge). In this high school, the practice of cleansing the school of "bad kids" was quite widely acknowledged and equally appreciated by administrators, teachers, and counselors. Criticisms of the practice were voiced rarely, quietly, and confidentially behind closed doors. To the extent that they were vocalized at all it was by a small group of predominantly black counselors, teachers, paraprofessionals, and aides, but only occasionally by a white or Hispanic counselor or teacher.

One mother reported, "When they discharged my son I thought it was over, until the guidance counselor told me that the dean couldn't do it [i.e., legally keep him out of school]. But she told me not to tell them she told me. I knew it was a cover-up."

There seems to be an organizational commitment to ridding the school of its presumably "difficult students" as soon as they can be released, and to not acknowledging this process. Data provided by the New York City Board of Education confirmed that this school disproportionately discharges students at age seventeen, at which point it is legal to do so.[23] In 1982–1983, 48 percent of the students discharged from this school left at age seventeen, compared with 32 percent city-wide (n=40275). Thirty percent of the females and 34 percent of the males were discharged from this school during their ninth grade as compared with 19 and 18 percent respectively for the city.[24] The same pattern held for 1983–1984. Citywide, 70 percent of the discharges from day high schools were cataloged as "over seventeen" whereas for this school the figure reached 85 percent.

To the question "How can the school routinely discharge such vast numbers of students?" one administrator explained: "It's like I'm a pilot and there is a hijacker on the plane, and it is my job to throw him out of the window. My job is the safety of the rest of the passengers. That's the safety of the school."

Throughout September, students in the "passive discharge" category would enter the attendance office, perhaps six per morning, saying "I'm seventeen and I want to drop out." Appropriate papers were removed from the desk. Usually the student was asked to sign "here" and get her or his mother to sign "there." Given a sheet of paper listing outreach centers and other GED programs, these adolescents were discharged into a world void of the opportunities they anticipated. None was told that New York State has the lowest national GED pass rate, 48.5 percent; none was told that it is difficult to get into military service without a diploma (as many say they plan to do), and that those who are accepted by the military have an extremely high rate of less than honorable discharge,[25] and none was told that the private business schools that many enroll in have extraordinary dropout rates. As one dean explained to me, "In a system like this you need boundaries. I can't worry about kids after they're gone, it's tough enough while they are here."

Most students who are discharged are not explicitly thrown out. They "choose" to leave, rarely encouraged to stay. As Gramsci tells us, one does not require coercion if hegemonic beliefs are sufficiently powerful to convince people that they deserve or have chosen subordinate fates.

Teen pregnancy: "I got to leave cause even if they don't say it, them teachers got hate in their eyes when they look at my belly"

Item from field notes, December 18. White male counselor, speaking to me in attendance office: "This one's dropping out, but it's a good case. She is pregnant and lucky enough to be getting married." This girl is sixteen. Longitudinal studies indicate that married teen mothers often fare worse than those who remain unmarried, educationally and financially. What makes this a "good case"? For whom is it good?

It is no longer legal to expel a pregnant student from public school. The experience of pregnancy and/or the first year of child rearing, however, is usually sufficient to prompt "voluntary exit." While there is controversy over whether pregnancy "causes" dropping out (which it obviously does in some cases) or dropping out precedes pregnancy (which is then the "good" reason to go), the correlation and consequences are staggering. Forty-four percent of female dropouts in the United States indicate pregnancy/marriage as their main reason for dropping out.[26] The negative effects of early pregnancy on babies and mothers are exacerbated in the United States, where inadequate prenatal services, access to contraception and abortion, sex education, child-care facilities, and employment training/opportunities for teen mothers make having a child and the simultaneous pursuit of education/employment nearly impossible. While the "pregnancy school" option, as the adolescents refer to schools for pregnant students and recent mothers, is available to New York City teens, students often find the juggling of school and child rearing nearly impossible, unless another woman—a mother, aunt, sister, or grandmother—helps with child care, which may necessitate her leaving paid employment outside the home.

Over 50 percent of teen mothers do not graduate from high school and teens who identify themselves as fathers are about 40 percent less likely to graduate than their nonparenting peers.[27] One might say to the male counselor in the field note above that a study of high school students and dropouts indicated that 67 percent of teens who got pregnant and *then married* were pregnant again within twenty-six months and fared worse educationally and economically than pregnant teens who did not marry (who had a 39 percent second pregnancy rate).[28]

With a realistic and dismal vision of the future, an uncompelling present, poor educational skills and experiences, and no job training, the drudgery of staying in school seems barely worth the hassle. The range of possibilities for these young women is, in fact, materially and psychologically quite limited. Having a baby at least offers a full-time job and a sense of purpose and competence.

Growing evidence suggests that interventions that combine sex education, contraceptive availability, and life options (e.g., jobs) can stem the dropout and pregnancy rates among teenage girls.[29] Studies indicate that job training and placement can diminish the likelihood of a second pregnancy for teen mothers. The provision of on-site school-based health clinics can reduce pregnancy rates, including first pregnancies, by up to 50 percent.[30]

"You ain't nothin' without that piece of paper"

Through interviews with recent and long-term (four-year) dropouts, it is clear that immediately following separation from high school, by choice or coercion, adolescents scramble around to find something to do with themselves. Of the thirty recently departed, only two "stay home watchin' the stories." Most adolescents just out of school are struggling to get a GED, enrolling in a private business school such as Wilfred Academy of Beauty or Sutton Business School, or trying to get into military service. Boys may be selling drugs, or working as messengers or in supermarkets. A few expect to go to college. Girls, if they are not mothering, are in cosmetology school, applying to computer training programs, working as cashiers, or, in a few cases, too anxious to look for work. To suggest that these adolescents are unmotivated, as many have, is to ignore the energy with which they pursue what they perceive to be their life choices, and to ignore their vulnerability.

At the end of one interview a seventeen-year-old dropout asked me to help her with a letter from the bank about her 8½ percent interest on two student loans for a private computer school: "I got this call saying I was picked, my name was selected from a long list and they want me to come to computer school! All I got to do is get these two student loans and then I can begin in September. Then they'll get me a good job in computers and I can move with my baby to New Jersey." This was the week that the New York State Education Department published an exposé of the unethical practices of private business schools[31]: Over 70 percent of the students never complete their training; 60 percent do not finish one-half of the term; unethical recruitment and retention procedures are standard, and the schools earn more for dropouts from their programs than for those who stay. Another girl the week before told me that a private business school was paying her for neighbors she could recruit for their courses.

The young adults I am now interviewing have been out of school for four years and are in much worse shape than those just recently out. Of the seven interviewed thus far, three of the four females are mothers and unemployed. The fourth was pregnant, was shot, and then had an abortion. Two of the males are legally unemployed. One sells drugs and the other is doing odd jobs and is interested in the Marines: "I don't want to fight, just be one of the Few and the Proud. I've never done anything I was proud of, so I'd try it." One young man is in college. The economic, social, and psychological deficits collected cumulatively after one drops out of high school suggest that even if dropouts have some initial income or psychological advantage over their graduate peers, this advantage is lost by the time they are twenty-five years old.[32]

Many economic and social factors, as well as structural features of schools, contribute to the dropout rates of urban adolescents. It has been argued that even with a high school diploma these very adolescents suffer economically and socially relative to their equally credentialed white middle-class counterparts, and that females fare worse than males. Given these arguments, does it make sense to examine the *causes* of a phenomenon that is a mass experience? That is, many urban adolescents who are black, Latin, and/or working class or low income do not graduate from high school. Looking for individual explanations is clearly inadequate and blames the victim. Looking for structural and social explanations of high dropout rates is obviously more fruitful. But perhaps most compelling is to consider what would happen, in our present-day economy, to these young men and women if they all graduated. Would their employment and/or poverty prospects improve individually as well as collectively? Would the class, race, and gender differentials be eliminated or even reduced? Or does the absence of a high school diploma only obscure what would otherwise be the obvious conditions of structural unemployment, underemployment, and marginal employment disproportionately endured by minorities, women, and low-income individuals?

Historically, policymakers have looked to improving education as the way to solve prevailing social and economic problems.[33] "If only" all students graduated high school, we would have full(er) employment and lower crime rates. "If only" schools were engaging, students would stay through graduation. "If only" sex education were available, we would reduce rates of teen pregnancy.

For each "if only" a number of existing structural conditions would have to be transformed before a dent in the problem would be perceptible, much less enduring. School-based reforms need to be developed in tandem with a package of economic and social reforms, including job programs, provision of child care, funded access to contraception and abortion services, balanced housing development, social and health services, and so forth, and ultimately there needs to be a redistribution of resources and power within society. Targeting schools as the site for social change and the hope for the next generation deflects attention and resources, critique and anger away from insidious economic and social inequities.[34]

National statistics reveal that over 50 percent of inner-city children never graduate from high school.[35] The illusion persists that there is something wrong with these individual young people: a lack of motivation, skills, discipline, "attitude," or intelligence. The institutions they inhabit continue to be unresponsive, at times assaultive and rejecting. The futures they can envision are, at best, constrained.

National reforms allegedly concerned with this generation of youngsters call for recommendations to increase standardized testing, institute promotion policies, lengthen the school day, strengthen requirements and implement the back-to-basics movement, remove sex education from the academic curriculum, and pull back on the progress made by feminist, black, and Latin studies in the curriculum. These "reforms" are precisely the way to divert attention away from unjust social and economic arrangements, to further deform the process of education, and to guarantee a swelling of the ranks of high school dropouts about whom we can then say "If only . . ."

Notes

1   Michelle Fine, "Perspectives on Inequity: Voices from Urban Schools," in *Applied Psychology Annual IV*, ed. L. Bickman (Beverly Hills, Calif.: Sage, 1983).

2   M. Carnoy and H. Levin, *Schooling and Work in the Democratic State* (Stanford: Stanford University Press, 1984); and H. Giroux, *Theory and Resistance: A Pedagogy for the Opposition* (South Hadley, Mass.: Bergin & Garvey, 1983).

3   Ibid.

4.   J. Anyon, "Intersections of Gender and Class: Accommodation and Resistance by Working Class and Affluent Females to Contradictory Sex Role Ideologies," in *Gender, Class and Education*, ed. S. Walker and L. Barton (London: Falmer Press, 1983); and Giroux, *Theory and Resistance.*

5   Carnoy and Levin, *Schooling and Work in the Democratic State*, p. 2.

6   U.S. Commission on Civil Rights, *Unemployment and Underemployment among Blacks, Hispanics and Women* (Washington, D.C.: Government Printing Office, 1982).

7   E. Tobier, *The Changing Face of Poverty: Trends in New York City's Population in Poverty, 1960–1990* (New York: Community Service Society, 1984).

8   U.S. Department of Labor, *Time of Change: 1983 Handbook of Women Workers* (Washington, D.C.: Government Printing Office, 1983).

9   Ibid.

10   Fine, "Perspectives on Inequity."

11   Memo, Office of the Superintendent of Manhattan High Schools, "PSEN Results: Academic Zoned High Schools," June 1985.

12   Personal communication, 1983.

13   Educational Priorities Panel, *Educational Budget Options: Fiscal Year 1985* (New York: Educational Priorities Panel, 1985).

14   School District of Philadelphia, *Faculty Integration Calculations Memo* (Philadelphia: Office of Personnel Operations, May 2, 1985).

15   Pearl R. Kane, Robert Blair, and Terry Eagle, *Results of the Teachers College Survey of the . . . High School* (New York: Teachers College, Columbia University, 1985).

16   Fine, "Perspectives on Inequity."

17   National Center for Education Statistics, *High School and Beyond: The Condition of Education* (Washington, D.C.: National Center for Education Statistics, 1983).

18   J. Weidman and R. Friedman, "The School to Work Transition for High School Dropouts," *The Urban Review* 16 (1984): 25–42.

19   U.S. Department of Labor, *Time of Change.*

20   Linda Simkin, *Evaluation of the New York State School Health Demonstration Project September 1982-June 1983* (Albany, N.Y.: Welfare Research Institute, 1984).

21   Advocates for Children, *Report of the New York Hearings on the Crisis in Public Education* (New York: Advocates for Children, 1985); P. Freire, *Education for Critical Consciousness* (New York: Seabury Press, 1978); and L. McNeil, "Negotiating Classroom Knowledge: Beyond Achievement and Socialization," *Curriculum Studies* 13 (1982): 313–28.

22   See John I. Goodlad, *A Place Called School: Prospects for the Future* (New York: McGraw-Hill, 1984).

23   New York City Board of Education, *Analysis of the Organization of High School: School Year 1983–1984* (New York: New York City Board of Education, 1984); idem, *Dropouts from New York City Public Schools* (New York: Education and Management Information Unit, Board of Education, 1984); and idem, *The 1983–84 Dropout Report* (New York: Board of Education, 1985).

24   New York City Board of Education, *The 1983–84 Dropout Report.*

25   Militarism Resource Project, *High School Military Recruiting: Recent Developments* (Philadelphia: Militarism Resource Project, 1985).

26   See Gary G. Wehlage and Robert A. Rutter, "Dropping Out: How Much Do Schools Contribute to the Problem?" in this issue.

27   Children's Defense Fund, *Preventing Children Having Children* (Washington, D.C.: Children's Defense Fund, 1985).

28   J. Dryfoos, *Prevention Strategies: A Progress Report* (New York: Rockefeller Foundation, 1985).

29   J. Dryfoos, *Review of Interventions in the Field of Prevention of Adolescent Pregnancy*, Rockefeller Foundation Report (New York: Rockefeller Foundation, 1983); and idem, *Prevention Strategies.*

30   See E. Jones et al., "Teenage Pregnancy in Developed Countries: Determinants and Policy Implications," *Family Planning Perspectives* 17 (1985): 53–63.

31   New York State Department of Education, Memo from Dennis Hughes, State Administrator on High School Equivalency Programs (Albany, N.Y.: December 4, 1984).

32   Weidman and Friedman, "The School to Work Transition."

33   Anyon, "Intersections of Gender and Class"; M. Apple, *Power and Ideology* (London: Routledge & Kegan Paul, 1982); Carnoy and Levin, *Schooling and Work in the Democratic State;* Giroux, *Theory and Resistance;* and M. Katz, "The Origins of Public Education: A Reassessment," *History of Education Quarterly,* Winter 1976, pp. 381–407.

34   Aspira, *Racial and Ethnic High School Dropout Rates in New York: A Summary Report* (New York: Aspira, 1983); Full Access and Rights to Education Coalition, *Their "Proper Place": A Report on Sex Discrimination in New York City Vocational High Schools* (New York: Center for Advocacy Research, 1982); and National Coalition of Advocates for Students, *Barriers to Excellence: Our Children at Risk* (Boston, Mass.: National Coalition of Advocates for Students, 1985).

35   Memo from Dennis Hughes.

A Population at Risk: Potential Consequences of Tougher School Standards for Student Dropouts

EDWARD L. McDILL
Johns Hopkins University

GARY NATRIELLO
Teachers College, Columbia University

AARON M. PALLAS
National Center for Education Statistics

This paper considers the potential impact of the recent recommendations for raising standards in American schools on a population at risk, those students likely to leave school prior to high school graduation. The paper proceeds by (1) presenting a systematic review of the empirical evidence on factors that predict dropping out, (2) synthesizing and explicating the recent recommendations for raising standards in American schools, (3) considering the likely positive and negative effects of higher standards on the population at risk in the absence of any other changes in the structure of schools, (4) identifying the school characteristics that can be altered to minimize the adverse effects on potential dropouts of changes in academic standards, and (5) proposing recommendations to raise academic standards and mitigate the dropout problem simultaneously.

In the last three years we have witnessed publication of a spate of reports on the inadequacies of American education from the elementary through the tertiary levels.[1] Each of these documents has proposed major changes in the structure, content, and functioning of schools, that taken together, constitute a sweeping agenda for educational reform. The public debate and discourse generated by these assessments have already led to a substantial number of changes in educational policy at the state and local levels,[2] and the time is rapidly approaching when we must be prepared to take stock of the impact of these reforms.

This article originally appeared in the February 1986 issue of the American Journal of Education. *We contributed jointly and equally to this article; the order of listing is alphabetical.*

In this presentation we join a number of other observers[3] in questioning the results of the new reforms. More specifically, we focus our attention on the consequences for a population "at-risk" — potential dropouts from secondary schools — of implementing the various reforms.

The dropout problem is worthy of careful scrutiny because it is a major educational, social, and economic problem, the dimensions of which are succinctly outlined by Steinberg, Blinde, and Chan: "It is well documented that dropping out of high school is associated with an array of individual and social costs. For the individual, failure to complete high school is associated with limited occupational and economic prospects, disenfranchisement from society and its institutions, and substantial loss of personal income over his or her lifetime. For society, premature school-leaving is associated with increased expenditures for government assistance to individuals and families, higher rates of crime, and maintenance of costly programs for purposes such as employment and training."[4]

In view of the magnitude of the dropout problem and the costs to both the individual school-leaver and society, it is important to examine the likely consequences for potential dropouts of raising academic standards in accordance with the new reforms. Will these new reforms have the unintended consequences of increasing dropout rates and related problems such as school discipline, violence, and vandalism? We address this difficult problem through the following five-step analysis. First, we present a systematic review of the empirical evidence on factors predictive of dropout behavior. Second, we synthesize and explicate the recommendations of the recent reform reports and studies for increasing academic standards. Third, we integrate information from steps one and two to provide an informed perspective on the likely positive and negative effects on the at-risk population in the absence of any other changes in the structure and operation of schools. Fourth, we identify the characteristics of schools that can be altered to minimize the potentially adverse effects of changes in academic standards on potential dropouts. Fifth, and last, we propose specific recommendations to raise academic standards and combat the dropout problem simultaneously.

Before we deal with these tasks, it is important to review briefly some recent currents of social and educational change in American society that help circumscribe the current debate regarding the perceived erosion of academic standards. This controversy directly involves the concepts of equality and quality in education. Are these two ideas incompatible? Can we be equal and excellent too?[5]

THE DUAL QUEST FOR EQUALITY AND QUALITY IN EDUCATION AS A PRECURSOR TO PRESENT CONCERNS

The current debate about excellence[6] is generally viewed as being "more comprehensive and more intense than in the post-Sputnik and post–Great

Society eras, both of which yielded concrete changes in education."[7] In the post-Sputnik period the reform emphasis was on improving the quality of education. The Eisenhower Administration undertook a major effort to strengthen schools through the National Defense Education Act (NDEA) of 1958 and simultaneously increased appropriations appreciably for the educational activities of the National Science Foundation.[8] NDEA upgraded schools' science programs and facilities and improved teaching by providing fellowship funds. Overall, such efforts were viewed as highly instrumental in solving the crisis in science and technology and in allowing the United States to surpass the Soviets in the race to place a man on the moon.[9]

With the advent of President Johnson's Great Society program, the federal government's emphasis on improving the quality of education shifted in the early 1960s to a preoccupation with issues of equality of educational opportunity. Education was a central part of this massive effort. The Civil Rights Act of 1964 focused public attention on school desegregation and on related equity issues such as aid to handicapped children in 1966, which was universally mandated in 1975 with the passage of PL 94-142. This law requires states to provide all handicapped students with a free, appropriate education suited to their individual needs.[10] Furthermore, the Elementary and Secondary Education Act of 1965 and its subsequent amendments provided massive federal aid for compensatory education for economically disadvantaged students.[11]

Legislation such as the above, coupled with a host of federal court decisions and other sources of federal control and the ongoing civil rights revolution, shifted the emphasis in educational policy from quality to equality. In the minds of some this was at least partly responsible for an erosion of academic standards.[12] The "back-to-basics" and minimum competency testing movements have grown in the past decade to counteract a perceived deterioration in academic standards[13] that is believed to be at least partly a consequence of too much emphasis on equity. Furthermore, the reports on the quality of education by the various commissions and study groups of the past three years were motivated to a considerable extent by widespread concerns of the type adumbrated above over the current condition of education.[14]

It is generally acknowledged that much of the attention of the various reform commission reports was different from that of other periods in significant ways. The breadth of commentary is considerable. Topics and issues addressed include the curriculum, pay and salary structure for teachers, school climate (the learning environment), length of school day and year, and classroom activities.[15] Although the reports and studies are diverse in perspective and commentary, there is consensus among them that the quality of our educational system should be improved immediately.[16]

The various reports and volumes produced a set of recommendations for educational excellence designed "to prepare students for a new society — for a future economy based on high-technology, emphasizing information processing and computers. By adopting these recommendations, the commissions believed, the United States could recapture its economic vigor and regain its competitive edge in the world economy."[17]

In general, these reports have been acclaimed by both laypersons and educators. Nevertheless, there is concern from several sources that the reports fail to provide balanced emphasis to the twin goals of excellence and equality in education. This concern, especially as it relates to the reports' recommendations for educational improvement, has led to criticism by a number of respected policy analysts and researchers that the commissions were insensitive to issues of educational equity. For example, Harold Howe, former U.S. Commissioner of Education and former Chairman of the National Council on Educational Research, is pointed in his critique on this topic: "Fairness to both students and taxpayers in the funding of education, along with continued attention to issues of discrimination on the basis of sex, race, and national origin, constitute a continuing equity agenda that is ill attended in the reports and studies or responses to them."[18]

The dropout problem in secondary schools, as both an excellence and equity issue, is prominent in the critiques of several of the reports' critics. Howe, for example, accords neglect of the dropout problem top priority among a list of 10 major criticisms he presents of the recommendations made by the various reform commissions.[19] Similarly, Stedman and Smith[20] point out that the four commission reports that they reviewed either ignored the dropout problem completely or treated it superficially. Moreover, the very recommendations made by the various commissions may exacerbate the unnoted dropout problem. As Edson points out: "As the National Commission today advocates a uniform academic curriculum, longer school years, greater amounts of homework, and more rigorous testing, we should expect greater and greater numbers of drop-outs and grade repeaters."[21] The reports' neglect of the dropout problem together with their recommendations that are likely to aggravate this problem may be a blueprint for failure in the nation's schools.

Clearly, the ideas of excellence and equity have been joined by the critics of the reform reports and studies. Their strong concern with the lack of attention to dropping out in the reports and studies in conjunction with the magnitude of the problem and its consequences emphasize the need for a systematic examination of the phenomenon.

THE DIMENSIONS AND ETIOLOGY
OF THE DROPOUT PROBLEM

The failure of many students to complete high school is seen by both the lay and educational communities as a serious social problem. In a national survey of school administrators, nearly one-third of the respondents cited early dropouts as a problem in their school districts. This problem is even more widespread in larger districts; over one-half of school administrators in districts with more than 25,000 students report that early dropouts are a problem. School administrators indicate the high dropout rates affect not only the individual development of students, but also the school's standards and achievement levels.[22] The dropout problem has even more far-reaching consequences than these, extending to national economic issues. Although the national economic costs of the dropout problem are difficult to estimate, Levin projected the costs for lost tax revenues from high school dropouts ages 25–34 at $71 billion, welfare and unemployment costs at $3 billion, and crime and crime prevention costs at $3 billion.[23]

It is generally recognized that reliable statistics on school attendance are difficult to obtain as different surveys and accounting practices lead to quite different results.[24] Figures from the Census Bureau suggest that graduation rates have been fairly stable since the latter part of the 1960s, although there is considerable year-to-year variability. This stability does mask large racial/ ethnic and sex differences in dropout rates. Hispanics have much higher and blacks somewhat higher dropout rates than whites. The sex differences are less dramatic. White and Hispanic females are substantially less likely to drop out than white or Hispanic males. Black females, however, are slightly more likely to drop out of school than black males.[25] The majority of youngsters who drop out do so after they have entered the ninth grade.[26]

A proper assessment of the potential effects of implementing the reform commissions' recommendations on the dropout problem requires an understanding of the causal factors associated with dropping out. Evidence on these factors derives both from student self-reports and from longitudinal studies of who drops out. The reasons for dropping out of school often are interrelated, and there is considerable overlap. Nevertheless, it is possible to group them into three major categories: school experiences, family circumstances, and economic factors.[27]

School experiences are the major bellwether of the decision to drop out. Poor academic performance,[28] truancy, and in-school delinquency all are strong predictors of early school leaving.[29] It is not surprising that students who are not doing well in school should seek to leave an environment that provides negative feedback. In surveys of students who dropped out of school, poor performance is often accompanied by expressed reasons for leaving such as "I disliked school" or "School was not for me."[30] Expulsion or suspension from school are additional indicators of problems that students experience in school that lead to failure to complete high school.

Although in-school performance and behavior are clearly the most important precursors to dropping out, other factors may come into play as well. Family formation is another factor associated with failure to complete high school. Teenage pregnancy is an important family formation event with well-known negative consequences for schooling.[31] As Neill reports, "About one million adolescent girls—nearly one in 10—conceive each year, and

600,000 young women carry their pregnancies to full term. . . . An estimated 400,000 pregnant teens are under 17 years of age."[32] Eight out of 10
of these mothers under age 17 never finish high school. For these students,
keeping up with school becomes impossible, and many female dropouts report pregnancy as a reason for dropping out.[33]

Many students who drop out also report marriage or marital plans as the
reasons. Many more females than males report marriage or marriage plans as
reasons for dropping out, and the figures vary considerably by race. More
than one-third of white female dropouts indicate that marriage played a role
in their decision to leave school; the figures are somewhat lower for minority
females, and much lower for males of all types.[34] Although many of the
students who marry or bear children do drop out, it is important to re-
member that these events are fairly rare. Only a very small fraction of high-
school-age youth marry.

A third major category of conditions associated with dropping out of
school is economic factors. Many students report leaving high school to go to
work, which could involve supporting the family of origin or the youth's own
family. About one-fifth of minority male dropouts and one-tenth of all other
dropouts reported leaving school because they had to support a family. In
addition to leaving school for work to support a family, many dropouts leave
school because they are offered jobs and choose to work. More than one-
quarter of all male dropouts offer this as one of the reasons that they dropped
out.[35]

Since leaving school to work is so prevalent, we briefly mention the literature on teenage employment. The extent of teenage employment has only
recently been studied carefully. Michael and Tuma[36] use data from the National Longitudinal Survey of Youth (NLS)[37] to document the prevalence of
employment among high-school-age youth. They find that 25 percent of all
14-year-olds in 1979 were employed at least part-time. The rate of employment increases steadily with age, so slightly more than 50 percent of the
17-year-olds in the NLS sample were employed in 1979. Sex differences in
these employment rates are not large, although racial and ethnic disparities
are pronounced, with whites being employed more frequently than blacks or
Hispanics.

The quantity of work involvement also is quite high. D'Amico shows that
working twelfth graders in the NLS sample average 15 – 18 hours of work per
week. His research suggests that working more than half-time while in high
school is associated with higher rates of dropping out for at least some groups
of youth.[38]

Some of the factors implied in the dropout process are more related to
school experiences than others. Our concern is that many of the reform
recommendations may have consequences for factors associated with leaving
school prior to high school graduation. Raising standards for student performance may interact with these factors to both diminish and increase their

impact. Before considering such interactions, we review the specific recommendations of the various reform commissions for raising standards for student performance.

A TYPOLOGY OF THE STANDARDS NOTED IN THE RECENT COMMISSION REPORTS

The recent commission reports on the state of American public schools have called for higher standards for students in three broad areas: the academic content of courses, the use of time for school work, and student achievement.[39] These three quite different types of standards may present different problems for potential dropouts.

Several reports call for higher standards for course content. For example, the National Commission on Excellence advocates five new basics to be taken by all high school students, although Edson points out that these are essentially those recommended by the Committee of Ten in 1893.[40] These basics include four years of English, three years each of mathematics, science, and social studies, and one-half year of computer science. The commission's proposal would represent a more demanding curriculum for the many students who do not currently take such courses. The National Science Board Commission has advocated more courses in science and math, and the Task Force on Education for Economic Growth has called for the elimination of the soft, nonessential courses.[41] Other reports have placed emphasis on other curriculum areas (e.g., Boyer, on writing),[42] but the general message is that students should be pursuing more demanding sequences of basic courses. Of course, there is another side to strengthening requirements in the basics. If these recommendations are implemented—and there is considerable evidence that they are being implemented in a number of states and school districts[43] —students will have fewer choices in selecting courses, and the high school curriculum will have a more restricted range of course offerings.

The use of time for instruction and learning is a second area in which a number of commission reports have advocated higher standards. Longer school days and longer school years are recommended by the National Commission on Excellence in Education and the Task Force on Education for Economic Growth. They are joined in this recommendation by the National Science Board Commission, which, in addition to longer school days and school years, suggests the institution of a longer school week to provide more time for instruction in science and mathematics.[44]

Several reports look beyond in-school time to the prospects for increasing out-of-school learning time. The National Commission on Excellence in Education argues that students should be assigned more homework in high school. The Task Force on Education for Economic Growth recommends firm, explicit, and demanding requirements for homework.[45]

Still another recommendation for increasing the time students spend in school concerns stricter attendance policies. The Task Force on Education for Economic Growth advocates firm and explicit attendance requirements. The National Commission on Excellence in Education recommends attendance policies with clear incentives and sanctions.[46]

Critical of calls for additional time for school, several reports point out that before we add time to the school day, week, or year, in-school time should be used more effectively.[47] Both the National Commission on Excellence in Education and the Task Force on Education for Economic Growth — groups advocating more time in school — argue for better use of time in school. According to the Task Force on Education for Economic Growth, stricter discipline policies would be one way to promote better use of school time.[48]

Higher standards for student achievement is a third area in which recommendations have been made. Several types of new achievement standards have been suggested. One type of recommendation calls for an end to the use of grades as motivational devices reflective of student effort and the use of grades solely as indicators of academic achievement.[49] Rigorous grade promotion policies are a second type of achievement standard under which students would be promoted only when it is academically justified, but not for social reasons.[50] The use of standardized tests at specified intervals is a third type of achievement standard. Boyer, in keeping with his emphasis on the importance of language, argues for the use of a test of language proficiency prior to high school admission, with remediation of any deficiencies during the summer.[51] More generally, the National Commission on Excellence in Education recommends the use of achievement tests at major transition points, particularly in the move from high school to college. Moreover, it urges colleges and universities to participate in the process of raising standards by tying achievement levels for student coursework to college admissions standards.[52] The Task Force on Education for Economic Growth recommends periodic testing to assess student achievement and skills.[53]

Taken as a whole, the call for higher standards in these three areas seems to be based on several assumptions. An initial assumption is that current standards are too low.[54] The first two types of standards, those having to do with content and time, involve a change in the processes experienced by students in school. More demanding content and more student time on school tasks are assumed to require greater student effort, which, in turn, will lead to higher levels of achievement. Thus, a second assumption is that more demanding content and more time allocated to school will lead to greater individual student effort. The higher achievement levels demanded of students are set with the assumption that all or most students will be able to meet them, and thus excellence will be achieved. A third assumption is that greater student effort will lead to improved achievement. Since the commission recommendations are to be applied across the board, a fourth assumption is that the relationships between standards and effort and between effort and achievement will hold for all students. Finally, there is a fifth implicit assumption that no negative consequences will be associated with the more demanding standards. In the next two sections we first assess the likelihood of realizing the intended positive impact of raising standards on students and then the threat of unintended negative consequences that may be associated with more challenging standards.

INTENDED CONSEQUENCES:
THE POTENTIAL BENEFITS OF RAISING STANDARDS

The best evidence for the potential positive impact of the proposed curriculum reforms comes from a series of studies by Alexander and associates.[55] These studies examined the effects of high school curriculum on several important measures, including standardized test performance, goals for the future, and the likelihood of attending college.

Alexander and Pallas[56] take stock of this line of research by pointing out that the early studies in the series[57] seem to show that students who are enrolled in the academic track fare much better than other students on important outcome measures even after controlling for differences in student background. However, more recent work in this area,[58] using a technically more sophisticated method of analysis, finds that high school tracking is "largely a conduit for differences in social background, academic competency, and educational experiences that predate high school."[59]

Alexander and Pallas emphasize that an adequate examination of curriculum effects should involve an evaluation of the coursework of individual students. Using the type of curriculum reforms presented in the report of the National Commission on Excellence in Education,[60] they analyze data from the Educational Testing Service's Study of Academic Prediction and Growth[61] to measure the effects of the "New Basics" recommended by the National Commission regarding student performance on the SAT and English and history achievement tests. Controlling for student background characteristics, student competency prior to high school, and student grades while in high school, they find that students who completed all of the requirements of the New Basics had a 25-point advantage in the verbal section of the SAT over students who did not complete these curricular requirements. Completing the core requirements in math confers a 40-point advantage on the SAT math section, and completing the requirements in science confers a 22-point advantage in the SAT math section. However, their results also reveal that when students have relatively low GPAs, completion of the core requirements seems to have little effect on student test performance. Indeed, they conclude that "the lowest performing youngsters apparently are a little bit better off outside the core."[62] Although these effects for poorly performing students are small, it is disconcerting that completion of a core curriculum similar to that recommended by the National Commission on Excellence in

Education[63] appears not to improve the performance of the very students most likely to be potential dropouts, those with low GPAs.

Research on student time-on-task in elementary classrooms provides evidence in support of the positive effects of more demanding time requirements on student effort and achievement. This work is rooted in the school learning models of Carroll, Bloom, Wiley, and Wiley and Harnischfeger.[64] Studies in this tradition typically have examined the effect of the time that students are engaged in learning on actual achievement. In reviewing these studies, Karweit concludes that "In general, these studies produce a positive association between time and learning. Many of the studies find a statistically significant effect of engaged time on learning. But all the studies have problems with inconsistency and strength."[65]

Although this one measure of student effort, time-on-task, does produce positive effects on learning, Karweit notes four reasons to be cautious in interpreting these results. First, other factors that co-vary with time, such as an orderly student population, may be responsible for the observed effects. Second, although it is possible to manipulate the total time allocated to learning, it is more difficult to manipulate actual time-on-task since such time depends upon individual students and teachers. Thus, it may be difficult to implement policies that will actually increase the time spent on learning. Third, Karweit observes that extrapolating the time-on-task findings to justify longer school days and years may not be appropriate, since longer school days may require additional breaks, and teachers and students may encounter problems with fatigue. Finally, and most important for our purposes, Karweit notes that most of the time-on-task studies have been conducted on elementary students of average ability; the results of greater time-on-task for older students and for students of greater or lesser ability must still be examined.[66] Thus, while the studies of student time-on-task offer some hope that greater student effort will lead to greater achievement, this may not be the case for all students under all circumstances.

At the secondary school level the question of the impact of increased time requirements on student achievement has been examined through a series of studies regarding the relationship between time spent on homework, a readily apprehendible form of student effort, and achievement. Coleman, Hoffer, and Kilgore,[67] using data from the nationally representative sample of students in the High School and Beyond Survey,[68] found that differences in the time spent on homework by high school students accounted for a small but consistent part of the differences in achievement test scores between public and private sector schools. Using this same data set, Keith showed that the amount of time that students spent on homework contributed significantly and positively to their grades.[69] A meta-analysis of 15 empirical studies of the relationship of time spent on homework to learning found a modest, positive effect of homework on learning.[70] Students of all ability levels seem to benefit from effort spent on homework. Using the High School and Beyond data set, Keith found that low ability students who do one to three hours of homework per week achieve grades commensurate with those of students of average ability who do no homework.[71] Natriello and McDill, in an analysis of data from students in 20 high schools nationwide, found that an additional hour of homework each night was associated with a .13 rise in GPA.[72]

Studies at both the elementary and secondary levels provide some sense of the likely impact of higher achievement standards. At the elementary school level the question of the impact of achievement standards on student effort and achievement is addressed, at least indirectly, by research on the impact of teacher expectations on students. Reviewing some of this research, Brophy and Evertson[73] note that the initial work of Rosenthal and Jacobson[74] on the self-fulfilling prophecy in classrooms generated a great deal of interest in the effects of differences in teacher expectations on student behavior and performance in the classroom.[75] Studies that examine actual teacher behavior in classrooms, such as those by Beez, Kester and Letchworth, and Brophy and Good reveal that teachers do display behavior that represents different levels of standards for different students.[76] Teachers differ in terms of the amount of feedback that they give to students, the amount of and the difficulty level of the material that they attempt to teach, and the number of opportunities that students are given to respond to teachers and to ask questions. In general, when teachers have higher expectations for students, and so are more demanding of them, students put forth greater effort and achieve more. Assessing this literature, Brophy and Evertson conclude that "the weight of the evidence from both types of studies [naturalistic and experimental] suggests that teacher expectation effects are real and can occur, although they do not occur necessarily or always and they differ in strength and type of outcome."[77] Although this literature provides support for the proposition that higher standards can lead to somewhat greater student effort and achievement under certain restricted conditions, at present these conditions are not understood in a systematic way.

A series of studies of the evaluation of students at the secondary school level by Natriello and Dornbusch also provides an answer to the question of the impact of achievement standards on student effort.[78] In a survey study of a large sample of students in 12 high schools in San Francisco and nearby suburban areas, they found that in many cases the standards that teachers had for student performance were quite low. Over half of the students reported that they did not usually receive a poor grade for doing inadequate work. In some situations teachers gave students passing grades simply for attending class. Certain groups of students, most notably blacks and Hispanics, were particularly likely to experience low standards for their school performance. These same studies found that students who were not receiving challenging standards often rated themselves as working hard on school tasks even though their own more objective reports revealed them to be exerting minimal effort. Moreover, these students were very likely to have poor grades and low achievement scores. Apparently, because these students had not been presented with challenging standards, they did not fully appreciate the degree of effort required to learn in high school. They devoted relatively little effort to school work despite the fact that they believed that their performance in school was important to their families and friends as well as to their future jobs. Thus low standards for academic performance seem to be a problem in at least some American schools.[79]

But what happens when students are confronted with challenging standards of the type contained in the recent reforms? In this same study of high school students, those who were presented with challenging performance standards did, in general, devote more effort to school tasks. Natriello and Dornbusch report these same relationships in a subsequent observation study in 38 classrooms. Rating these classrooms as high demand, medium demand, and low demand, Natriello and Dornbusch report that the higher the demand level in the classroom, the more likely students were to report paying attention in class and spending time on homework. Particularly interesting for our current analysis, it was in the low-demand classrooms that student cutting was the highest. Natriello and Dornbusch conclude that although the low-demand teacher might think that the lack of academic pressure makes the class more pleasant and reduces cutting, in reality there is little activity going on in the low-demand classroom to merit attendance. Students who feel that they are not missing anything when they cut class are more likely to cut. Thus, standards for student performance that are somewhat higher than the extremely low standards observed in the low-demand classrooms seem both to encourage student effort and to discourage absenteeism, a precursor to dropping out.[80]

Students in general may profit from higher standards, but how will low-achieving students respond to more challenging demands? Natriello and Dornbusch find that a higher demand level in the classroom is associated with greater effort by students, even when the ability level of the students is controlled. Moreover, it is in the low-demand classrooms that the highest proportion of students report feeling that the teacher should make them work harder. However, high-demand classrooms can often lose low-ability students. In response to an overly fast pace, low-ability students report that they try less hard in high-demand classrooms than in medium-demand classrooms. As Natriello and Dornbusch conclude, "Although low-ability students are assisted by increasing the demands upon them, teachers in high-demand classrooms must learn to help these students keep up with the work by encouraging their questions and coming to their aid. Difficult though the task is, teachers in high-demand classrooms must challenge low-ability students without overwhelming them."[81] Although the impact of higher standards on student effort is generally positive, we should not expect dramatic increases in student effort among low-ability students, particularly if higher standards are not accompanied by provisions for additional help for these students.[82]

Overall, results in several different lines of research provide hope that raising standards will lead students to work somewhat harder, at least when standards are originally quite low, and that greater student effort will lead to somewhat higher student achievement. The assumed relationships between standards and effort and between effort and achievement implicit in the commission reports receive some support. However, it is by no means clear that these assumed relationships will hold for all students under all conditions. Certainly, the provision of additional assistance for students experiencing learning difficulties appears to be a key factor in the success of any attempt to raise standards. A variety of characteristics associated with potential dropouts may complicate the picture and may lead to unintended negative consequences. We next consider these potential negative effects of demanding higher standards.

UNINTENDED CONSEQUENCES: THE POTENTIAL COSTS OF RAISING STANDARDS

Our review of the recommendations of the various commissions reveals three categories of standards that have to do with more rigorous content, greater learning time, and higher levels of achievement. Here we consider the potential negative effects associated with each of these types of standards. More specifically, we consider the possibilities that (1) a restricted core of curriculum requirements may lead to greater academic stratification and less student choice in schools, (2) more demanding time requirements in schools may lead to more conflicts between the demands of schools and other demands placed on students, and (3) required higher levels of achievement may lead to more student experience with failure without apparent remedies.

The recommended curriculum reform entails a uniform set of core courses to be taken by all students. Alexander and Pallas[83] fail to find a positive effect of such a curricular pattern on students with low GPAs — those most likely to be potential dropouts. Although their finding has to do with the substance of the "New Basics," our assessment of potential negative effects should also consider the suggested form of the curriculum, a single pattern of courses to be taken by all students. Studies in elementary school classrooms suggest some negative consequences of this particular reform for our population at risk.

The narrowing of curricular offerings that accompanies the emphasis on the basics may present special problems. Studies of the perception or social construction of ability in classrooms suggest that a narrow range of course offerings may carry particularly negative consequences for potential dropouts.[84] These studies in elementary classrooms find that when instruction is organized so that academic task structures are undifferentiated, that is, when all students work on similar tasks and where students have little autonomy to choose among alternative tasks, students are more likely to develop a stable consensus as to the distribution of ability in the group and these ability conceptions are more likely to be general. In contrast, in classrooms in which there is greater task differentiation, students are less likely to conceive of ability as a single dimension, with some students having generally high ability and others having generally low ability. The consequences of the unidimensional classroom structures for potential dropouts are summarized by Rosenholtz and Rosenholtz: "Unidimensional classroom instruction appears to have more negative consequences for the lower-achieving student. Lower teacher and peer evaluations may lead to lower future performance of the student. The integrally related evaluation of self may also contribute to lower performance. To the degree that teacher, peer and self-perceptions influence future performance, ability stratification as affected by classroom organization could have profound consequences for the individual's life chances. Instructional organization, then, may not only provide a framework by which classroom actors define ability, it may also enhance or limit capability."[85]

Although it is not clear whether the findings regarding ability conceptions in elementary classrooms will operate in the wider context of the secondary school, these studies alert us to some potential negative effects of the form of the proposed core curriculum. The courses proposed for inclusion in the core curriculum are academic courses that tap ability along a narrow range. Thus, implementation of the recommended core curriculum will limit the instructional experiences of students to traditional academic subjects, severely restrict the number of dimensions of ability deemed legitimate within the school, and curtail student choice in constructing a program of study. Students with limited ability in traditional academic subjects may have to face repeated failure with little opportunity to engage in the broad range of activities valued in adult society that might afford them some success and encourage them to redouble their efforts to master academic content.[86] One major result of the full implementation of the New Basics could be the clarification of the distribution of ability in these basics, leaving some students only the choice of dealing with constant failure or dropping out of school.

The impact of increasing time demands on students may also have an adverse impact on potential dropouts. Schools can demand more time of students by lengthening the school day and by assigning more homework, which raises the time required of students out of the school setting. However, because time is a fixed commodity, such increased time demands might create conflicts for some students between the time needed for school commitments and the time needed for commitments to families and jobs.

For most students, time does not appear to be that scarce a resource. One recent national survey showed that the average high school student spent more time watching television per *day* than doing homework per *week*. But here we are concerned with potential dropouts, who are quite different from the average student. One of the features of high school dropouts is that they have laid claim to adult status.[87] That is, they take on the attitudes and roles of adults while still in high school. A central role defining adulthood is the work role. As we noted earlier, both the rate and the intensity of employment among adolescents are surprisingly high.

Of course, time spent working is time taken away from studying, both in school and out.[88] Steinberg, Greenberger, Garduque, and McAuliffe have found that first-time high school workers spend less time on homework than nonworkers.[89] They also skip school more often and receive lower grades. D'Amico has found that extensive levels of work involvement among high school students result in fewer hours of study time.[90] Moreover, for some race/sex groups in his study, high levels of work involvement have direct effects on dropping out, a finding corroborated by Pallas.[91]

If the amount of time required for school work is increased, even modest levels of work involvement may have negative consequences for educational performance and persistence, *ceteris paribus*. A great deal would depend on how youngsters' propensity to work might respond to increased time demands. Some youngsters might reduce their work involvement, but those who are working to help support their families, for instance, are unlikely to stop in response to increased school demands.

Greater demands for time in school and on homework also create conflicts with extracurricular activities. Participation in extracurricular activities has been shown to have a variety of desirable effects on the academic progress of students by raising educational expectations and grades,[92] lowering delinquency,[93] and directly affecting persistence in school.[94] Participation in extracurricular activities builds a normative attachment to the school and also provides additional avenues for success for students who do not perform well in the classroom. It is precisely such students who are at greatest risk of dropping out. Reduced participation in extracurricular activities due to increased school time may lead to greater student alienation and may deprive the school of the only holding power it has for those high-risk students.

Raising achievement standards may present special problems for potential dropouts. Compared with high school graduates, dropouts are lower in socioeconomic background, academic aptitude, and reading skills. They have higher rates of absenteeism and truancy and poorer personal-social adjustment.[95] Furthermore, research has established that such dropout behavior is predictable in the elementary school years, with frequent absenteeism and academic failure being the most visible signs.[96] Numerous studies indicate that the withdrawal of students from school is often a response to goal failure experienced primarily in the academic and social context of the school.[97]

A number of studies[98] have noted the connection between unsatisfactory student experiences with the school authority system, which lead inevitably to a failure to attain goals, and student withdrawal from school. Spady has identified features of the system for evaluating student performance in school that condemn certain students (i.e., the very students in our population at risk) to inevitable failure.[99] A study of four suburban high schools by Natriello has found that when students perceive school performance standards as unattainable, they are more likely to become disengaged from high school.[100] Evidence of this disengagement takes the forms of apathy, participation in negative activities, and absenteeism — all precursors of dropping out.

Additional insight into the potentially adverse effects on at-risk students of tightening academic performance standards comes from consideration of the impact of minimum competency testing (MCT) programs adopted in many states in recent years. As noted by Labaree, because school systems have continued to be criticized for "social promotion" of students in the past two decades, they more recently have come to rely heavily on competency testing in their efforts to increase academic standards: "Standardized achievement tests — norm-referenced or criterion-referenced — are typically employed to determine whether or not a student meets the minimum requirements for promotion from one grade to another or for high school graduation."[101]

The extent of the concern over low academic standards in American schools and of the view that major educational reforms are necessary to reverse the deterioration can be measured by the fact that some form of MCT now exists in a large majority of states.[102] The MCT movement has generated a major ground swell of debate and controversy about its antecedents, operations, and consequences for both public and private education in America.[103] The impact of MCT programs on socially and economically disadvantaged students, minority students, and at-risk students such as potential dropouts is a major controversy surrounding such programs. Both Jaeger and Linn, Madaus, and Pedulla show that black students fail the tests in substantially higher proportions than do whites, and the latter authors conclude that "At this point in our history minimum competency testing requirements clearly have an adverse disproportionate impact on black students."[104]

Neill aptly expresses the concern over the effects of MCT programs on at-risk students: "Because minimum competency standards are so new, it is not known if they will result in a rise in the number of students enrolled below modal grade level or a rise in the number of students who drop out because they fail to pass minimum competency tests. Both of these predictions have been heard."[105]

In the absence of any systematic evaluative studies of the effects of MCT programs on at-risk students, Jaeger's conclusion would appear to remain applicable: "In predicting the consequences of competency testing for students and teachers, we must be content for the moment, with speculation rather than evidence."[106]

Although specific evidence on the adverse effects of MCT on likely school-leavers is currently unavailable, the results that show that failure rates on competency tests are much higher for economically disadvantaged students and those from minority racial/ethnic backgrounds are relevant since these sociodemographic groups are known to have disproportionately high rates of truancy, dropping out, and school discipline problems. However, we should note that these adverse effects on at-risk students will likely be mitigated if state and local education agencies conform to the following prediction by Eckland: "More than likely, however, most states probably will find mechanisms by which to pass all but a minority of their students, perhaps all but 2, 3, or 4 percent. As some districts are finding, one way to do this is to remove from the pool of students who are required to take the examinations those who are certified as 'mentally handicapped.' Depending on how liberally this is defined, this exemption could resolve part of the problem for certain groups."[107]

The implementation of the recently recommended reforms may not bring excellence in education for all students. If academic standards are raised and students are not provided with substantial additional help to attain them, it seems reasonable to expect that at-risk students — those socially and academically disadvantaged — will be more likely than ever to experience frustration and failure. The result for these students may not be notable increases in cognitive achievement but rather notable increases in absenteeism, truancy, school-related behavior problems, and dropping out. Without substantial assistance for these students the higher standards of the reform commissions will fail to break the strong "links in a long chain of interconnected problems."[108]

Of course the ultimate negative consequences of raising standards without providing additional help to students lie in the economic and cognitive costs of dropping out. Levin's monograph is the best information on the economic costs of dropping out, but unfortunately it is quite dated.[109] We cannot update the many calculations that Levin carried out, but we can provide an indirect estimate of the magnitude of the economic costs of dropping out. Our approach is to calculate the cost of dropping out for an individual and aggregate to the national level.

We first compare the estimated lifetime earnings for high school graduates and dropouts. According to the Bureau of the Census, a male who completes fewer than 12 years of school can expect to earn $601,000 in his working years between 18 and 65. In contrast, a man completing exactly 12 years of school can expect to earn $861,000 over the same period. The difference in the lifetime earnings for male dropouts and terminal high school graduates is thus $260,000.[110]

For females, the estimated lifetime earnings of high school dropouts is $211,000, whereas for terminal high school graduates it is $381,000. Hence the difference between lifetime earnings for female dropouts and graduates in $170,000. Since the number of male and female high school dropouts is quite similar, we can "split the difference" between the male figure of $260,000 and the female figure of $170,000 to obtain an average difference in lifetime earnings between high school dropouts and terminal high school graduates of $215,000.

Of course, not all of this difference in lifetime earnings should be attributed to the effects of dropping out. Some portion of this difference is due to factors common to both the dropout process and earnings determination. The most obvious of these factors are ability and socioeconomic background. There are many studies of the extent of bias[111] in estimated rates of return to educational investments due to omitting ability and other relevant factors from the estimation, including those of Griffin, Olneck, and Taubman.[112] Although the estimates of bias vary somewhat across studies, they hover around 50 percent. That is, about one-half of the difference in lifetime earnings between dropouts and graduates is due to differences in ability and other factors between the dropouts and graduates, and about one-half is due to the effects of dropping out. Hence, for an individual dropout, we estimate the economic cost of dropping out to be $107,500 in foregone lifetime earnings.

This seems like a large amount of money, and it becomes a great deal larger when it is summed over the number of dropouts. Of the 3,800,000 high school sophomores enrolled in the spring of 1980, 13.6 percent, or about 516,000, dropped out by the spring of 1982. For this one cohort of youth alone, then, the estimated lifetime cost of dropping out in terms of foregone earnings is $516,000 \times \$107,500 = \$55,470,000,000$ — more than 55 billion dollars. If we take this figure at face value, Levin's earlier conclusion still stands: the national cost of keeping students in school can scarcely approach the cost to the nation of them dropping out.[113]

There are other national costs associated with the high school dropout problem. An especially timely concern is the loss of cognitive skills, which is documented extensively in the reports discussed earlier. It has long been recognized that high school graduates outperform dropouts on tests of cognitive performance. Recent evidence suggests that the gap between dropouts and graduates *widens* after youngsters drop out. Alexander, Natriello, and Pallas showed that, all other things being equal, students who stay in school improve their test performance more than students who drop out.[114] The size of the effect, one-tenth of a standard deviation, represents a shift from the fiftieth percentile to the fifty-third percentile of a normal test score distribution. These findings show up on tests that are not specific to the details of the average high school curriculum but rather are broadly applicable. Since the tests are not especially sensitive to the content of high school courses, these effects are impressive in spite of their apparent modest size. For this and other reasons, it is likely that the estimate of Alexander, Natriello, and Pallas of the cognitive consequences of dropping out is a conservative one. In all probability, the cognitive costs of dropping out are even larger than they claim.[115]

We have seen that the cognitive costs associated with dropping out are quite large. Many of these costs may increase as a result of the school reform recommendations. There are, however, characteristics of school organization that might be manipulated to minimize these deleterious effects.

ALTERABLE CHARACTERISTICS OF SCHOOLS
TO MINIMIZE ADVERSE EFFECTS OF SCHOOL REFORM
ON STUDENTS AT RISK

One of the significant trends in educational research and development in the past 15 years has been the search for alterable or manipulable variables of schools and their members that are modifiable through direct intervention by the participants themselves, by administrators, or by researchers.[116] Bloom notes that "perhaps the most important methodological change [in educational research] is the movement from what I have termed stable or static variables to variables that are alterable either before the teaching and learning processes or as part of these processes."[117]

This reorientation of educational research is useful for identifying school characteristics subject to change in order to cushion the adverse effects of proposed educational reform on the population of students at risk. It is to this body of literature that we now turn for suggestions. An important segment of this research is social-ecological in nature; that is, it examines naturally occurring variations in *rates* of school behaviors[118] and relates them to the communities in which the schools are located and to a broad range of school composition and social organizational characteristics — including size, staffing and resources, student body composition, governance and administration, sanctioning practices, race relations, student beliefs and attitudes, and grading practices.[119]

The segment of the ecological literature most relevant to our concerns has to do with studies of deviant behavior such as school discipline problems and disorder (e.g., victimization of students and teachers and vandalism), absenteeism, truancy, and dropping out. One of the exemplary research and development efforts in this area, conducted on both junior and senior high schools, has been done by G. D. Gottfredson and colleagues over the past five years.[120] Not surprisingly, they find that schools with high dropout and truancy rates also have high rates of student disorder and discipline problems. These schools can be summarily classified in terms of two dimensions. The first has been labeled "urban social disorganization," which describes the schools as being concentrated in large cities, being large in size, having a "high proportion of minority students; measured by such community characteristics as high unemployment, high crime, much poverty and unemployment, and many female-headed households."[121]

The second significant dimension or cluster of characteristics of such schools has to do with the lack of soundness of the schools' administration and is defined as involving poor teacher-administration cooperation, teachers who emphasize the maintenance of control in classes rather than instructional objectives, teachers who employ ambiguous sanctions (e.g., lowering grades as a disciplinary practice or ignoring the misbehavior), perceptions by students that rules are not clear or fair, and students who do not believe in conventional social rules.

It should be noted that these ecological results on student body characteristics and behaviors are highly consistent with (1) the profile of the dropout based on individual-level analyses described earlier, (2) related research on delinquency, school disorders, and truancy,[122] and (3) the literature on alternative schools as a potentially useful educational innovation to combat school disorders, truancy, and related deviant behaviors.[123]

Of all the alterable characteristics of schools discussed in these different streams of literature, size of school is the one most emphasized. Researchers and practitioners are practically unanimous in asserting its importance. This is not surprising given the fact that size is conceptualized as a basic structural feature of social groups[124] and has been viewed "as the most important condition affecting the structure of organizations."[125] Small schools of 300–400 students with a low student-adult ratio are viewed as having fewer disorders,[126] higher achievement,[127] higher rates of student participation in extracurricular activities,[128] and feelings of satisfaction with school life.[129] Most analysts interpret these relationships in terms of differences in interactive characteristics between small and large schools, with the former being more manageable.[130] Specifically, small schools are more personalized or less anonymous, have a more homogeneous student body, have more flexible schedules, and have smaller classes. In fact, low student-adult ratios are important in making feasible other manipulable characteristics of schools believed to be useful in counteracting deviant behavior.

A second alterable characteristic of the school, closely linked to size, is the structure and content of the curriculum. Specifically, an individualized curriculum and instructional approach is crucial because psychologically disengaged students such as potential dropouts have substantial deficits in aptitude and achievement. Individualized learning approaches with the course content and mode and pace of presentation tailored to the individual student's aptitude and interests (to the extent possible) are of major importance to prevent the sense of academic failure and low self-esteem characteristic of school delinquents, truants, and dropouts — feelings that will be even more pronounced as standards are raised. Some dropout and delinquency programs have shown that self-designed and self-paced curricula that integrate vocational and academic subjects with work experience are promising because they enable the disaffected student to acquire salable skills and to perceive that his or her schooling is relevant to the workplace.[131]

A third modifiable feature of schools that appears to be useful in combating deviance may be labeled broadly as "climate,"[132] especially that component of school environment that relates to governance.[133] Climate encompasses a large number of potentially manipulable factors such as reward systems, clarity and consistency of rules and expectations governing social behavior, and degree of normative pressure in the school environment toward educational goals such as high achievement and intellectualism.

The concept that perhaps appears most frequently in the relevant literature on climate is governance. Several researchers have emphasized clear rules and their consistent enforcement as essential to maintaining an orderly environment, which, in turn, is crucial to high academic achievement.[134] G. D. Gottfredson states the consensus on this point succinctly: "The clearer and more explicit the school's rules, and the more firmly and fairly they are enforced, the less disorder that the school experiences."[135]

Another alterable component of school climate is the system of academic rewards.[136] Learning models applied to student achievement and social behavior typically involve the implicit or explicit premise that in order to generate students' commitment to the school and to motivate them to achieve, the system of rewards must be attainable and contingent on their effort and proficiency. Since potential dropouts and students with behavior problems or more serious conduct disorders have typically obtained poor academic grades, they likely discount the validity or legitimacy of traditional academic evaluation systems.[137] Thus, researchers and practitioners who work with such students have found it useful to employ a variety of alternative, detailed reward systems such as (1) learning contracts that specify both effort and proficiency requirements, (2) token economies, and (3) grading systems that base evaluation on individual effort and progress.[138]

The final modifiable component of school climate that we discuss here is the degree of environmental press or normative emphasis on academic excellence by students, teachers, and administrators.[139] Stated differently, at both the institutional and classroom levels, schools vary in the extent to which their student bodies and faculties provide support for achievement and intellectualism, and such variation has been found to be related systematically to levels of student achievement and motivation.[140]

Moving from the distal level of the school to the more proximate levels of the classroom and peer groups as a conceptualization of normative influence, the following statements capture the current views of researchers and practitioners concerning the importance of school climate to effective schooling: "A 'work and learning' orientation in the classroom can provide a context in which efforts to attain educational goals make sense to students. Individualized learning approaches and rewards contingent on proficiency are likely to require a context in which academic achievement remains valued, if genuine academic success is to be experienced";[141] "Without a clear orientation to work and learning in the classroom, even competent and caring teachers are unlikely to succeed in increasing academic achievement, reducing official delinquency, or affecting school dropout rates of their students";[142] and

"Teachers should structure their classes so that students' attention and effort are clearly focused on working to develop cognitive skills and to attain educational goals."[143] These three alterable characteristics of schools, which are viewed as especially promising in affecting the relevant performances and behaviors of at-risk students, are not exhaustive of those appearing in the literature.[144] Others of potential significance, but which some researchers believe are less firmly grounded in solid evidence, include student and parental involvement in governance or decision-making of the school,[145] peer counseling and/or tutoring,[146] and physical location of the treatment program in the traditional school setting versus in a physically distinct setting.[147]

In summary, the research and perspectives we have presented here suggest that at-risk students are likely to be adversely influenced by raising academic standards in accordance with recommendations of the various reform commissions. However, these deleterious effects can be counteracted or lessened by modifications in a variety of school organizational characteristics that recent research and development efforts have shown are related to the affective and cognitive development of students, including at-risk students. Under certain conditions the higher standards suggested by the reform commissions would seem to promise improved learning outcomes for all students. However, these conditions are not well understood by either researchers or practitioners. A greater understanding can only emerge from practical policy experimentation coupled with systematic analysis of the results, analysis that takes explicit account of the effects of policy reforms on students at risk.

STRATEGIES OF SCHOOL REFORM TO AID STUDENTS AT RISK

As mentioned above, a number of the alterable organizational characteristics of secondary schools that show promise in aiding at-risk students have emerged from research in the past decade on alternative educational programs. Much of the impetus for instituting a variety of schooling options came from widespread concern about discipline problems and victimization in American secondary schools. Alternative education programs or schools[148] are the "most visible manifestation"[149] of this movement for varied learning options.[150] As noted by Gold and Mann, there is no commonly agreed on definition of alternative schools, and they conclude that "about all that alternative schools have in common is that their programs are somehow different from the curriculum followed by the large majority of the community's students."[151]

The following definition of an alternative education program by the U.S. Department of Justice is the most comprehensive and specific that we have discovered: "An education program that embraces subject matter and/or teaching methodology that is not generally offered to students of the same age or grade level in traditional school settings, which offers a range of educational options and includes the student as an integral part of the planning team. The term includes the use of program methods and materials that facilitate student success and are relevant to the students' educational needs and interests as indicated by the student and facilitates positive growth and development in both [sic] academic, vocation, and social skills."[152] As this definition implies, alternative programs are not restricted to students with behavior problems and/or academic deficiencies; they also exist for high-achieving and even gifted students.[153] They exist for a variety of students who do not respond well to the academic program and social environment of the traditional school. However, our review of the literature suggests that alternative schools are more likely to be populated by at-risk or problem students than any other types.

The literature, both descriptive and analytical, on alternative schools is diverse: "There is a sizable literature which either extolls their virtues or denigrates their character."[154] Furthermore, it should be emphasized that much of the evaluative information on the effectiveness of alternative schools is anecdotal and/or testimonial rather than systematic scientific evidence,[155] a problem to which we return below.

Despite the lack of agreement about the efficacy of alternative schools, the relevant literature constitutes one of the most important sources of information on how to educate at-risk students, especially as a source of ideas on alterable characteristics of schools, whether they be traditional or alternative. From our review of this literature, we have selected one of the major efforts at designing, implementing, and systematically evaluating a large-scale alternative schools program at the secondary level that clearly reveals the relevance of modifiable characteristics of school organization to at-risk students. The program we review was sponsored by the Office of Juvenile Justice and Delinquency Prevention (OJJDP) of the U.S. Department of Justice.[156] Gottfredson and colleagues[157] had responsibility for the national evaluation of this ambitious effort, which is a demonstration program designed primarily to "develop transferable knowledge about approaches to reducing youth crime and victimization in schools" in seventeen sites scattered throughout the continental United States, Puerto Rico, and the Virgin Islands.[158] Secondary goals of the program include a reduction in suspensions and dropouts, increased attendance, and increased academic performance.

The School Action Effectiveness Study (SAES), G. D. Gottfredson and his colleagues' evaluation of OJJDP's Alternative Education Program (AEP), proceeds from the premise that organizational theory is a useful guide to change in-school policies, and that implementer-researcher collaboration in action research will advance both organizational theory and practice. These researchers designed SAES to strengthen the programs being conducted in the AEP, to evaluate them systematically, and to generate "transferable knowledge about delinquency prevention."[159] The approach that they employed in achieving these tasks is the Program Development Evaluation model (PDE), which has evolved from their experiences in action research[160] to create and evaluate change in school environments.[161] The PDE model involves program design, implementation, management, accountability, and evaluation.

Of the various sites in which SAES and PDE have been utilized by the research team, Project PATHE in Charleston, South Carolina, which operated in seven secondary schools between 1980 and 1983, provides a prototypical example of an alternative education program that has considerable potential in preventing school delinquency by enhancing student self-esteem, attachment to school, and participation in school activities. Project PATHE was designed to permit a comparison of the relative efficacy of two approaches, organizational change and individual treatment, in reducing school disruption and related deviant behaviors while simultaneously enhancing academic, affective, and career outcomes.[162]

Because a true experimental design was employed, the evaluation team was able to assess accurately the separate effects of the organizational change component and the individual treatment method. Project PATHE involved altering the school management and governance procedures at the school level while simultaneously providing intensive treatment to a target sample of students identified as being in special need of academic and affective assistance. Space limitations permit only a very brief description of each of these two approaches.[163] The organizational change approach attempted to establish and maintain a structure "to facilitate shared decision making among community agencies, students, teachers, school administrators, and parents in the management of its schools."[164] Five improvement teams from these groups were recruited and trained for each school by project staff to plan and implement change. Project managers formulated specific performance standards for each team and carefully monitored their activities while providing technical assistance. Policy review and revision staff produced outcomes such as revised curriculum guides, resource rooms, in-service training for school staff, and a specific uniform discipline system.

The individual treatment component of the project designed, implemented, and monitored an intensive program of academic and counseling services for students who had low achievement, poor attendance records, and discipline problems. Program specialists developed specific treatment objectives for each student and applied an individually prescribed program of academic tutoring and psychological counseling.

Evaluation of outcomes in PATHE revealed that the organizational change component of the project was more effective in achieving its goals than was the component that delivered direct services to individual students. The former component showed considerable promise in that the results "revealed persuasive evidence that the program succeeded at decreasing school disruption" based on statistical comparisons of experimental and control schools.[165] On the other hand, the direct-service component to individual students appeared to be ineffective with older students and only marginally effective with young students. These age differences are likely accounted for by the finding that the services were more intensively implemented in the middle schools than in the high schools, suggesting that the individual treatment approach "has potential."[166]

These results and those from other sites in the AEP lend credibility to the following conclusion concerning organizational change in schools to aid at-risk students: "There is every scientific reason to expect that theory-guided prevention efforts that address causes of youth crime in the schools can be effective, but that these interventions must be carefully and thoroughly implemented and subjected to much more careful evaluation than have past efforts."[167]

Some programs that utilize an individual-level treatment modality in school settings for different types of more serious behavior disorders such as "emotionally disturbed" or "serious delinquents" have shown promising results. As noted by Quay and Allen, students suffering from these types of disorders "have, among their other behavioral characteristics, most of the characteristics of dropouts."[168] In an informative overview of this research, Quay argues persuasively that the myriad forms of such behavior problems can be reduced parsimoniously to four basic constellations or types: conduct disorder, personality disorder, inadequacy-immaturity, and socialized delinquency. After reviewing the antecedents of these four types he discusses a variety of treatment modalities and concludes that in recent years "there has accumulated an impressive body of knowledge indicating that the systematic use of techniques of behavior modification in the school setting can drastically reduce deviant behavior, while at the same time increasing the acquisition of prosocial behavior and academic skills in all four subgroups."[169] Quay emphasizes that the modification techniques to be employed require a precise evaluation of the behavior to be changed, organization of the classroom or other educational setting to minimize disruptive behavior, and the use of contingency reward systems by teachers, parents, and significant others.

There are numerous psychologically oriented approaches other than behavior modification for treating the types of "acting-out" emotional disturbances in school described by Quay,[170] as well as other types of emotional disorders such as school phobia.[171] Since these approaches are so diverse and typically have not been evaluated systematically, Gold's conclusion seems valid: "Nevertheless, we know very little about what really works, and we suspect, from what careful research has been done, that very few methods have worked at all."[172] It is our hunch that behavior modification techniques are one of the modalities showing most promise.

AN AGENDA FOR EDUCATIONAL RESEARCH AND PRACTICE

We have suggested that the reform recommendations of the recent commissions for more challenging content, time, and achievement standards may have both positive and negative effects. Moreover, we have argued that some students will profit from the more challenging standards, whereas others may suffer under them. Whereas some students will find that the new core curriculum, increased time demands, and higher achievement requirements enhance their motivation and performance, others will suffer from being at the bottom of a more pronounced stratification system, from being forced to choose between devoting more time to school work or to their other pressing responsibilities, and from being subject to unattainable standards. In particular, students who are potential dropouts may suffer appreciably under the new standards unless appropriate measures are taken to provide them with additional learning resources to meet the new challenges that they will confront.

But the problems of at-risk students unable to meet the new standards may extend well beyond this group. In the face of increasing numbers of students from certain economic and ethnic groups being pushed out of school in greater numbers, the deep American commitment to equity may prompt a new round of lowering of standards. As we have noted, there is evidence of such a leveling in the MCT reforms,[173] and there is no reason to expect a different outcome for the latest round of reforms. Thus, not only the survival of at-risk students, but also the very survival of higher standards may hinge on our capacity to assist such students to achieve at the new higher levels.

The dilemma for educational policy makers and practitioners will be to devise ways to direct additional learning resources effectively and efficiently to those students who need them. Our review of alterable characteristics of schools that seem to be associated with successful learning experiences for students at risk suggests a variety of organizational characteristics that probably condition the extent to which the needs of students at risk can be identified and learning resources targeted to meet those needs. These are some of the options open to educational practitioners as they confront the educational reforms that are resulting from the studies and reports. Yet the commissions and study groups are often silent on the issue of providing additional support to students being challenged by the new standards. Unless the means of delivering such support are devised and implemented, the reforms may produce either of two quite unsatisfactory results: an improvement in aggregate measures of student performance chiefly attributable to the increasing selectivity of American schools (i.e., an increase in the dropout rate), or a relaxation of the standards as they are implemented by educators who must confront firsthand the negative consequences of such reforms—a pattern emerging in discussions of the effects of the MCT movement. The challenge for educational practitioners and researchers lies not in raising standards, for that has been done and is being done for them in the majority of states.[174] Rather the challenge lies in implementing these new reforms, delivering educational resources to students, and monitoring the impact of these more challenging standards and enhanced resources.

Moreover, the state of present knowledge on these issues suggests that much experimentation is in order. Despite the tone of some of the recent reports, it is not clear how to raise standards for uniformly good effect. Fortuitously, the various states are enacting different types of educational standards.[175] In addition, different school districts and schools will implement these standards in different ways. Many of them will not redirect efforts to deliver additional learning resources along with the more challenging standards, but many will. These new educational policies and their local implementation should be studied by researchers and practitioners alike. They should be evaluated on a range of criteria, some of which should explicitly consider the dual concerns for excellence and equity.

Although researchers and practitioners will, no doubt, mount a variety of investigations and programs in the wake of the reform recommendations, our analysis suggests at least four specific strategies that might be profitably pursued in tracking the effects of the higher standards and insuring their full implementation.

1. Monitor the Impact of the New Standards on Potential Dropouts at the Building and District Level

Most educational interventions are not evaluated at all, and those that are typically are not evaluated properly.[176] Program evaluation is expensive, yet it is essential for judging the efficacy of changing standards for performance. We believe it imperative that federal funding for education include sufficient resources both for the evaluation of the consequences of changing standards for performance and for more basic research on the effects of school organization on educational outcomes. Federal oversight of program evaluation is the most efficient way of assuring proper dissemination of information regarding effective programs.

It is difficult to collect reliable information on students who leave high school prior to graduation, and there is considerable variation from school to school and district to district in the methods of collecting and tabulating data on the dropout problem.[177] Such students often leave abruptly without warning. However, increased attention must be devoted to the collection of such data at the district and school-building level if we are truly to understand the dropout problem. Moreover, such information should be a key part of any assessment of the new reforms.

Although we cannot anticipate the needs for monitoring the great variety of educational reforms and implementations, we can present one fairly straightforward general model for evaluating the outcomes of these reforms that explicitly responds to both excellence and equity concerns. We refer to this approach as the "full enrollment model" of assessing educational outcomes.

If the assessment of the current wave of reforms is anything like the assessment of past efforts, we might expect a great deal of attention to be focused on various outcome measures. Although a great many factors can influence such measures quite apart from the policy reforms themselves, one in particular might be predicted. We might expect that once the more challenging standards are in place, aggregate measures of student performance will rise.[178] Practitioners and policy makers will, of course, be tempted to credit their reform efforts for the improvement. However, given our analysis of the potential impact of these reform efforts on likely dropouts, we would be more prone to credit the improvement to the greater selectivity of schools. For this reason we believe that aggregate measures of student performance should be based on a "full enrollment model" rather than on a "survivor model" as is typically done at present. Under this full enrollment model, aggregate performance measures would include scores for students who have dropped out of school. Scores for dropouts might be estimated on the basis of their earlier test scores and background characteristics. In any case, the likely effect of employing such a model wuld be to reduce the aggregate scores by making them reflective of both excellence and equity concerns. In this way we might judge the true effects of the reform efforts.

2. Include School Characteristics Associated with Successful Education of At Risk Students in Program Development and Research Efforts

The limited research on programs for at-risk students suggests that certain school characteristics are associated with successful dropout prevention programs. A cluster of such school organizational characteristics seems particularly worthy of further adoption and evaluation.

First, schools that are more responsive to student performance and behavior appear to be more successful in holding students in school. If they are to conform to commonly held expectations for performance and behavior, students, particularly at-risk students, may need to be in learning environments that provide timely reactions to both their academic performance and social behavior. Many at-risk students live in turbulent family and community environments in which the reactions to their behavior and the claims on their time are pressing and immediate. When schools are less responsive than the outside environments, students may become less engaged in school and more involved in activities that compete with the school for their time and attention.

One common method for increasing the responsiveness of the school to student performance and behavior is through greater individualization of curricular and instructional approaches. Schools and programs that tailor course content and the mode and pace of instruction to the aptitude and interests of individual students appear to be more successful in retaining at-risk students. Although the implementation of higher uniform standards as part of the latest wave of educational reforms, particularly the use of standardized tests of student achievement, complicates the management of individually oriented educational approaches, the past success of programs that rely heavily on individualization suggests that the additional effort necessary to manage individualized programs for higher overall standards may well be worthwhile.

Another aspect of school organization associated with greater retention of at-risk students involves a learning climate characterized by clear and fair rules and rewards based on the effort and progress of individual students. When rules are clear and conform to norms of fairness understood and accepted by students, they realize that their behavior in school will promote certain responses from school authorities. Similarly, when school rewards are based on individual effort and progress or student academic growth, students perceive clear effects from their efforts. This is particularly the case for at-risk students who seldom share in the school rewards tied to universalistic criteria and uniform standards of achievement.

The research literature suggests that these school organizational factors might be especially promising for dealing effectively with the high school dropout problem. There is, however, no systematic body of research that is conclusive. Nor have these factors been evaluated rigorously in the context of programmatic approaches to dropout prevention. For these reasons, we call for the inclusion of these promising avenues for reform in program development and evaluation efforts.

3. Provide Students Educational Services with Flexible Time Options

Potential dropouts appear to be subject to severe time constraints that will only be made more intense by the implementation of the additional time demands recommended by the reform commissions. Moreover, requiring higher achievement levels only further aggravates the problem, since these students are not likely to be in a position to devote the additional time that they will need to perform at the higher levels.

Since the outside time demands placed upon these students by economic and family conditions probably cannot be alleviated without major new social welfare initiatives that are unlikely to arise in the near future, it is up to the educational system to modify the time demands placed on these students if we want them to continue in school. This suggests educational options that are less concentrated and of longer duration. For example, it may be possible for many potential dropouts to achieve higher standards by participating in high school less intensively, perhaps spread out over five years instead of four.

This should be a planned sequence without the stigma that is now attached to failing to graduate in the customary four years of high school. Such a plan might permit students to work while they complete their high school education in order that they will not have to defer employment and its economic benefits until the end of their high school careers.

4. Maintain High Standards for All Students

Finally, we must continue to present challenging standards to secondary school students, particularly at-risk students, if we wish them to attach sufficient value to schooling to stay until graduation. Although we have questioned the practical effects of some of the specific types of standards recommended by the recent reform commissions, higher standards should increase the value of schooling for all students, if such standards can be placed within their reach and are not simply used as sorting and screening devices. There is growing evidence that students of all ability levels respond positively to more challenging standards when they have a chance to achieve them. It would be a terrible waste if the admirable goals put forth by the school reform commissions were defeated by the inappropriate and insufficient means suggested for achieving them.

Notes

1   For example, see E. L. Boyer, *High School: A Report on Secondary Education in America* (Washington, D.C.: Carnegie Foundation, 1983); J. I. Goodlad, *A Place Called School: Prospects for the Future* (New York: McGraw-Hill, 1983); National Commission on Excellence in Education, *A Nation at Risk: The Imperative for Educational Reform* (Washington, D.C.: Government Printing Office, 1983); National Science Board Commission on Precollege Education in Mathematics, Science, and Technology, *Educating Americans for the 21st Century* (Washington, D.C.: National Science Foundation, 1983); P. E. Peterson, *Making the Grade: Report of the Twentieth-Century Fund Task Force on Federal Elementary and Secondary Education Policy* (New York: Twentieth Century Fund, 1983); and Study Group on the Conditions of Excellence in Higher Education, *Involvement in Learning: Realizing the Potential of American Higher Education* (Washington, D.C.: National Institute of Education, 1984).

2   U.S. Department of Education, *The Nation Responds: Recent Efforts to Improve Education* (Washington, D.C.: Government Printing Office, 1984); S. Walton, "States' Reform Effort to Increase as Focus of Issues Shifts," *Education Week* 3 (December 7, 1983): 5–17.

3   H. Howe, "Giving Equity a Chance in the Excellence Game," Martin Buskin Memorial Lecture (Washington, D.C.: Education Writers Association, 1984); C. H. Edson, "Risking the Nation: Historical Dimensions on Survival and Educational Reform," *Issues in Education* 1 (1984): 171–84; L. C. Stedman and M. S. Smith, "Recent Reform Proposals for American Education," *Contemporary Education Review* 2 (1983): 85–104; Business Advisory Commission of the Education Commission of the States, "Reconnecting Youth: The Next Stage of Reform" (Denver: Cited in *Chronicle of Higher Education,* August 7, 1985): 14.

4   L. Steinberg, P. L. Blinde, and K. S. Chan, "Dropping out among Language Minority Youth," *Review of Educational Research* 54 (1984): 113–32.

5   In a provocative background paper for the National Commission on Excellence in Education, Alexander Astin confronts this issue directly: "A belief widely held among contemporary educators is that the twin goals of excellence and equity in American education are

inherently incompatible, and that the price of expanding opportunities is necessarily a reduction in quality" ("Excellence and Equity in American Education" [Paper prepared for the National Commission on Excellence in Education, Higher Education Research Institute, Inc., University of California, Los Angeles, 1982], p. 1). He develops the thesis that *the apparent* conflict between the two ideals is the consequence of an inadequate conceptualization of excellence by researchers and educators, and he argues for the use of a "value-added" approach to understanding excellence: "In its simplest terms, the value-added conception of excellence focuses on *changes* in the student from the beginning to the end of an educational program. The most excellent program, in this view, is one that facilitates the greatest learning or growth. Clearly, to know how excellent a program is in value-added terms requires some form of repeated assessment, whereby the knowledge and competence of the student is [*sic*] assessed initially at the beginning of the program and again at the completion of the program. An excellent school or college is thus one that provides substantial improvements in competency or achievement from the beginning to the end of the program" (pp. 14–15). Astin emphasizes that such an approach moves us away from a preoccupation with "resources" (e.g., quality of teachers, quality of students, physical plant, and fiscal resources) and "reputation" as measures of excellence: "As long as we cling to traditional notions of excellence based on institutional reputations or on simplistic measures of institutional resources, conflicts between excellence and equity are inevitable" (p. 26). Instead, he contends using the value-added approach focuses attention on the effective utilization of resources and the monitoring of student development over time. B. S. Bloom, in his conceptualization of mastery learning, offers an educational perspective compatible with that of Astin (*Human Characteristics and School Learning* [New York: McGraw-Hill, 1976]). As noted by D. F. Labaree, "He [Bloom] sees no contradiction between equality and excellence because he attributes the wide variations in student performance to instructional failure—the failure to focus on each student's areas of individual need—rather than the ability to learn" ("Setting the Standard: Alternative Policies for Student Promotion," *Harvard Educational Review* 54 [1984]: 87). See also J. S. Coleman, "Quality and Inequality in American Education: Public and Catholic Schools," *Phi Delta Kappan* 63 (1981): 159–64, and "Inequality in Education: Evidence on Equality and Excellence" (Paper presented at the Eighth Goucher College Conference, Baltimore, 1985); C. Finn, "The Futile Quest for No-Fault Excellence in Education," *Education Week* (November 23, 1983); pp. 3, 19, 24; J. W. Gardner, *Excellence: Can We Be Equal and Excellent Too?* (New York: Harper & Bros., 1961).

6   Contrast, for example, the positions of the National Commission on Excellence in Education, *A Nation at Risk: The Imperative for Educational Reform,* and Howe, "Giving Equity a Chance in the Equity Game."

7   R. V. Rosen, ". . .'for the short and long term'. . . ," *Harvard Educational Review* 54 (1984): 23–28.

8   See J. Spring, *American Education: An Introduction to Social and Political Aspects* (New York: Longman, 1982).

9   A. P. Parelius and R. J. Parelius, *The Sociology of Education* (Englewood Cliffs, N.J.: Prentice Hall, 1978).

10   A. P. Turnbull and J. Blacher-Dixon, "Preschool Mainstreaming: An Empirical and Conceptual Review," in *Mainstreaming of Children in Schools: Research and Programmatic Issues,* ed. P. S. Strain and M. M. Kerr (New York: Academic Press, 1981), pp. 71–100.

11   F. M. Wirt and M. W. Kirst, *Schools in Conflict* (Berkeley: McCutchan, 1982).

12   For reviews of this perspective, see J. S. Coleman, "Quality and Inequality in American Education: Public and Catholic Schools," 159–64; J. Fennessey and E. L. McDill, "Values in Tension: Achievement, Equity, and Pluralism," in *Values, Inquiry, and Education,* ed. H. D. Gideonse, R. Koff, and J. J. Schwab (Los Angeles: Center for the Study of Evaluation, University of California, 1980); P. E. Peterson, *Making the Grade,* pp. 30–35; D. Ravitch, "The Debate about Standards: Where Do We Go from Here?" *American Educator* 5 (1981): 14–19; and D. Tyack and E. Hansot, "Conflict and Consensus in American Public Education," *Daedalus* 110 (1981): 1–25.

13   L. Shephard, "Technical Issues in Minimum Competency Testing," in *Review of Research in Education*, vol. 8, ed. D. C. Berliner (Washington, D.C.: American Educational Research Association, 1980), pp. 30–82.

14   For example, Peterson in his lengthy background paper to *Making the Grade* (p. 160) makes the following observation: "Given the role that the federal government must play in ensuring equal educational opportunity, this recent trend [compensatory education and programs for the handicapped receiving a larger percentage of the Department of Education's elementary — and secondary — school program budget in 1982 than it did in 1976] should not, under the circumstances, be criticized. But there is also need for an explicit expression of federal attention to issues of educational quality. By almost exclusively focusing on equal opportunity, the Department of Education has implied that education quality is unimportant, as though, if access to schools is given equally to everyone, learning will take care of itself."

15   Rosen, ". . .'for the short and long term'. . . ," p. 23.

16   Education Commission of the States, *A Summary of Major Reports on Education* (Denver: Education Commission of the States, 1983), p. 2.

17   Stedman and Smith, "Recent Reform Proposals for American Education." In a similar vein, Peterson notes, "Just as Sputnik inspired concern for the quality of American education in the 1950's, so Japanese technology and vigorous competition from other foreign countries have awakened public interest in education as the means to enhance national productivity" (*Making the Grade*, p. 161).

18   Howe, "Giving Equity a Chance in the Excellence Game," pp. 7–8. Stedman and Smith, in a broader critique of this issue, state that "even though the rhetoric is egalitarian, the analysis and recommendations [of the four commission reports reviewed] failed to address the needs of the poor, the minorities, and inner city youth" ("Recent Reform Proposals for American Education," p. 95). In a provocative critique of the Excellence Commission report, Edson compares it in historical context to the Committee of Ten report sponsored by the NEA and chaired by President Charles Eliot of Harvard (National Educational Association, Report of the Committee on Secondary School Studies, U.S. Bureau of Education, Bulletin No. 205 [Washington, D.C.: Government Printing Office, 1893]). Edson concludes that both reports are "elitist" and preoccupied with school reform "tailored to the college bound" and wonders whether current educational reformers are adopting a "nineteenth-century philosophy of social Darwinism to guide our search for solutions to educational problems" ("Risking the Nation: Historical Dimensions of Survival and Educational Reform," pp. 171–72).

19   Howe notes: "It is absolutely astounding to me that so many intelligent people could look for so long at American schools and say so little about this problem. John Goodlad says (page 285), 'The quality of an educational institution must be judged on its holding power, not just on assessments of its graduates . . .' Their recommendations [the national groups issuing reports] for more homework, more demanding courses, longer school hours, and more tests are likely to be implemented in ways that will further increase dropouts, although some schools may be skillful enough to avoid this hazard" ("Giving Equity a Chance in the Excellence Game," pp. 8–9).

20   Stedman and Smith, "Recent Reform Proposals for American Education," p. 95.

21   Edson, "Risking the Nation: Historical Dimensions on Survival and Educational Reform," p. 181.

22   S. B. Neill, *Keeping Students in School: Problems and Solutions.* AASA Critical Issues Report (Arlington, Va.: American Association of School Administrators, 1979).

23   H. Levin, *The Costs to the Nation of Inadequate Education,* Report to the Select Committee on Equal Educational Opportunity, U.S. Senate (Washington, D.C.: Government Printing Office, 1972).

24   J. Meyer, C. Chase-Dunn, and J. Inverarity point out that attendance records are unreliable for two reasons. First, not only do teachers and students tend to protect students from the negative consequences of being listed as absent, but school records may also systematically exaggerate attendance in order to protect the school's resources, which are based on measures of

average daily attendance. As a result of these two factors, "Many students who make only an occasional or brief entry into the school may be continuously listed as present . . ." (*The Expansion of the Autonomy of Youth: Responses of the Secondary School to the Problems of Order in the 1960's* [Stanford, Calif.: The Laboratory for Social Research, Stanford University, 1971], p. 131). Indeed, Neill notes that a team of auditors from the office of the California State Auditor General found that physical counts of students in classrooms showed actual attendance substantially below that reported by school districts for the allocation of state funds. Second, the actual number of dropouts often exceeds the official count as a result of the data collection process. For example, Neill reports that data from Washington State admittedly underestimate the dropout rate, since students who fail to return to school after the summer are not included in the count (*Keeping Students in School: Problems and Solutions*). Additional insights into the problems of collecting statistics on school attendance are provided by C. Cooke, A. Ginsberg, and M. Smith, "The Sorry State of Education Statistics," *Basic Education* 29 (1985): 3 – 8; F. Hammack, "Large School Systems' Dropout Reports: An Analysis of Definitions, Procedures, and Findings," in this volume; and G. Morrow, "Standardizing Practice in the Analysis of School Dropouts," in this volume.

25   U.S. Department of Commerce, Bureau of the Census, *School Enrollment—Social and Economic Characteristics of Students: October 1981* (Advance Report), Current Population Reports, Series P-20, no. 373 (Washington, D.C.: Government Printing Office, 1982).

26   For example, a study by the Rhode Island Department of Education reported by Neill showed that 8 out of 10 dropouts were in grades 9, 10, or 11 when they left school (*Keeping Students in School: Problems and Solutions*).

27   J. L. Kaplan and E. D. Luck, "The Dropout Phenomenon as a Social Problem," *Educational Forum* 47 (1977): 41 – 56.

28   As Neill notes: "Students who fall behind their classmates drop out more readily than those who do not. They may, for example, be two or more years below grade level in reading and math. Or they may fail one or more grades. In either case, they are more apt to drop out than other students" (*Keeping Students in School: Problems and Solutions*, p. 31). Neill points out that since 1950, schools have changed their philosophy about the wisdom of retaining students who failed to meet academic standards. This trend was met with charges of "social promotion," which together with other charges, led to the minimum competency testing movement and the current calls for raising standards. Nonetheless, the association between students being retained at a grade level and dropping out suggests that there may be some negative consequences of tightening promotion policies.

29   A. M. Pallas, *The Determinants of High School Dropout* (Unpublished Doctoral Dissertation, Department of Sociology, Johns Hopkins University, 1984.)

30   S. S. Peng, R. T. Takai, and W. B. Fetters, "High School Dropouts: Preliminary Results from the High School and Beyond Survey" (Paper presented at the annual meeting of the American Educational Research Association, Montreal, 1983); R. W. Rumberger, "Dropping Out of High School: The Influence of Race, Sex, and Family Background," *American Educational Research Journal* 20 (1983): 199 – 220.

31   F. F. Furstenberg, Jr., *Unplanned Parenthood: The Social Consequences of Teenage Childbearing* (New York: Free Press, 1976).

32   Neill, *Keeping Students in School: Problems and Solutions*, p. 32.

33   Peng, Takai, and Fetters, "High School Dropouts: Preliminary Results from the High School and Beyond Survey." The costs to support teenage mothers who do not complete high school are substantial. For example, Neill reports that "in 1975, teenage mothers accounted for approximately $4.65 billion in payments for AFDC (Aid for Dependent Children). Approximately 60 percent of all teenage mothers were ending up on welfare, accounting for about one-half of the national welfare bill. In 1976, 31 percent of the teenage mothers and former teenage mothers age 14 – 30 on the AFDC rolls had failed to complete high school. By way of

contrast, only 11 percent of the teenage mothers and former teenage mothers who had completed high school were receiving AFDC" (*Keeping Students in School: Problems and Solutions*, p. 33).

34   Peng, Takai, and Fetters, "High School Dropouts: Preliminary Results from the High School and Beyond Survey."

35   Peng, Takai, and Fetters, "High School Dropouts: Preliminary Results from the High School and Beyond Survey"; Rumberger, "Dropping Out of High School: The Influence of Race, Sex, and Family Background."

36   R. Michael and N. B. Tuma, "Youth Employment: Does Life Begin at 16?" (Paper presented at the annual meeting of the Population Association of America, Pittsburgh, 1983).

37   Center for Human Resource Research, *The National Longitudinal Survey Handbook* (Columbus: Ohio State University, 1984).

38   R. D'Amico, "Does Employment During High School Impair Economic Progress?" *Sociology of Education* 57 (1984): 152–64.

39   Education Commission of the States, *A Summary of Major Reports on Education;* J. L. Griesemer and C. Butler, *Education under Study: An Analysis of Recent Major Reports on Education* (Chelmsford, Mass.: Northeast Regional Exchange, 1983).

40   National Commission on Excellence in Education, *A Nation at Risk: The Imperative for Educational Reform;* C. H. Edson, "Risking the Nation: Historical Dimensions on Survival and Educational Reform."

41   National Science Board Commission on Precollege Education in Mathematics, Science, and Technology, *Educating Americans for the 21st Century;* Task Force on Education for Economic Growth, *Action for Excellence: A Comprehensive Plan to Improve Our Nation's Schools* (Denver: Education Commission of the States, 1983).

42   Boyer, *High School: A Report on Secondary Education in America.*

43   U.S. Department of Education, *The Nation Responds: Recent Efforts to Improve Education.*

44   National Commission on Excellence in Education, *A Nation At Risk: The Imperative for Educational Reform;* Task Force on Education for Economic Growth, *Action for Excellence: A Comprehensive Plan to Improve Our Nation's Schools;* National Science Board Commission on Precollege Education in Mathematics, Science, and Technology, *Educating Americans for the 21st Century.*

45   National Commission on Excellence in Education, *A Nation At Risk: The Imperative for Educational Reform;* Task Force on Education for Economic Growth, *Action for Excellence: A Comprehensive Plan to Improve Our Nation's Schools.*

46   National Commission on Excellence in Education, *A Nation At Risk: The Imperative for Educational Reform;* Task Force on Education for Economic Growth, *Action for Excellence: A Comprehensive Plan to Improve Our Nation's Schools.*

47   Goodlad, *A Place Called School: Prospects for the Future.*

48   National Commission on Excellence in Education, *A Nation At Risk: The Imperative for Educational Reform;* Task Force on Education for Economic Growth, *Action for Excellence: A Comprehensive Plan to Improve Our Nation's Schools.*

49   National Commission on Excellence in Education, *A Nation At Risk: The Imperative for Educational Reform;* Task Force on Education for Economic Growth, *Action for Excellence: A Comprehensive Plan to Improve Our Nation's Schools.* S. M. Dornbusch reports that students in the high schools in his San Francisco study received passing grades simply for attending class ("To Try or Not to Try," *Stanford Magazine* 2 [1974]: 50–54).

50   National Commission on Excellence in Education, *A Nation At Risk: The Imperative for Educational Reform;* Task Force on Education for Economic Growth, *Action for Excellence: A Comprehensive Plan to Improve Our Nation's Schools;* National Science Board Commission on Precollege Education in Mathematics, Science, and Technology, *Educating Americans for the 21st Century.*

51   Boyer, *High School: A Report on Secondary Education in America.*

52   National Commission on Excellence in Education, *A Nation At Risk: The Imperative for Educational Reform.*

53   Task Force on Education for Economic Growth, *Action for Excellence: A Comprehensive Plan to Improve Our Nation's Schools.*

54   This assumption receives support from the work of G. Natriello and S. M. Dornbusch, which shows that students, particularly minority students, are only infrequently exposed to challenging standards in secondary school (*Teacher Evaluative Standards and Student Effort* [New York: Longman, 1984]).

55   K. L. Alexander and E. L. McDill, "Selection and Allocation Within Schools: Some Causes and Consequences of Curriculum Placement," *American Sociological Review* 41 (1976): 963–80; K. L. Alexander, M. A. Cook, and E. L. McDill, "Curriculum Tracking and Educational Stratification," *American Sociological Review* 43 (1978): 47–66; K. L. Alexander and M. A. Cook, "Curricula and Coursework: Surprise Ending to a Familiar Story," *American Sociological Review* 47 (1982): 626–40; and K. L. Alexander and A. M. Pallas, "Curriculum Reform and School Performance: An Evaluation of the 'New Basics,'" *American Journal of Education* 92 (1984): 391–420.

56   Alexander and Pallas, "Curriculum Reform and School Performance: An Evaluation of the 'New Basics.'"

57   Alexander and McDill, "Selection and Allocation Within Schools: Some Causes and Consequences of Curriculum Placement"; Alexander, Cook, and McDill, "Curriculum Tracking and Educational Stratification."

58   Alexander and Cook, "Curricula and Coursework: Surprise Ending to a Familiar Story."

59   Alexander and Pallas, "Curriculum Reform and School Performance: An Evaluation of the 'New Basics,'" p. 393.

60   Alexander and Pallas, "Curriculum Reform and School Performance: An Evaluation of the 'New Basics.'"

61   T. Hilton, *A Study of Intellectual Growth and Vocational Development,* Final Report (grant no. OEG-1-6-061830-0650) to U.S. Department of Health, Education, and Welfare, Office of Education (Princeton, N.J.: Bureau of Research, Educational Testing Service, 1971).

62   Alexander and Pallas are cautious in interpreting these results, noting that "these differences at the lower end are not large, though, and we would not want to make too much of them. They could, for example, be an artifact of the linearity constraint built into our regression approach; assuming nonparallel GPA slopes for the two groups (core completers and noncompleters), the lines of necessity must cross someplace. On the other hand, they could also have a substantive basis, perhaps reflecting the price one pays for being out of place in an especially competitive environment. Whether artifact or finding, however, the shortfall observed for low-performing core completers generally is quite small" (Curriculum Reform and School Performance: An Evaluation of the 'New Basics,'" p. 411).

63   National Commission on Excellence in Education, *A Nation At Risk: The Imperative for Educational Reform.*

64   In "A Model for School Learning," J. Carroll calls attention to the importance of time by arguing that the degree of learning is a function of the quotient of the time actually spent over the time needed (*Teachers College Record* 64 [1963]: 723–33). B. S. Bloom argues that when time and help are provided to slower students, and these students are motivated to use the time and help available, 90 percent or more finally reach the learning criteria ("Time and Learning," *American Psychologist* 29 [1974]: 682–88, and *Human Characteristics and School Learning*). D. E. Wiley and D. E. Wiley and A. Harnischfeger argue that student achievement is directly determined by the time needed to learn a task and the time actually spent on the task; the effects of all other factors are mediated through these two variables (D. E. Wiley, "Another Hour, Another Day: Quantity of Schooling, a Potent Path for Policy," in *Schooling and Achievement in American Society,* ed. W. J. Sewell, R. M. Hauser, and D. L. Featherman [New York: Academic Press,

1967]; and D. E. Wiley and A. Harnischfeger, "Explosion of a Myth: Quantity of Schooling and Exposure to Instruction, Major Educational Vehicles," *Educational Researcher* 3 [1974]: 7–12).

65   N. L. Karweit, "Time-On-Task Reconsidered: A Synthesis of Research on Time and Learning," *Educational Leadership* 41 (1984): 33–35.

66   N. L. Karweit, "Time-On-Task: A Research Review," Report no. 332. (Baltimore: Center for the Social Organization of Schools, Johns Hopkins University, 1983); Karweit, "Time-On-Task Reconsidered: A Synthesis of Research on Time and Learning."

67   J. S. Coleman, T. Hoffer, and S. Kilgore, *High School Achievement: Public, Catholic and Private Schools Compared* (New York: Basic Books, 1982).

68   S. S. Peng, W. B. Fetters, and A. J. Kolstad, *High School and Beyond: A National Longitudinal Study for the 1980's: A Capsule Description of High School Students* (Washington, D.C.: National Center for Education Statistics, 1981).

69   T. Z. Keith, "Time Spent on Homework and High School Grades: A Large-Sample Path Analysis," *Journal of Educational Psychology* 74 (1982): 248–53.

70   R. A. Paschal, T. Weinstein, and H. J. Walberg, "The Effects of Homework on Learning: A Quantitative Synthesis" (Paper presented at the annual meeting of the American Educational Research Association, Montreal, 1983.)

71   Keith, "Time Spent on Homework and High School Grades: A Large-Sample Path Analysis," p. 251.

72   G. Natriello and E. L. McDill, "Performance Standards, Student Effort on Homework and Academic Achievement," *Sociology of Education* (forthcoming).

73   J. E. Brophy and C. M. Evertson, *Student Characteristics and Teaching* (New York: Longman, 1981).

74   R. Rosenthal and L. Jacobson, *Pygmalion in the Classroom* (New York: Holt, Rinehart & Winston, 1968).

75   J. E. Brophy and T. L. Good, in *Teacher-Student Relationships: Causes and Consequences* (New York: Holt, Rinehart & Winston, 1974), present a review of the early work in this tradition, including the controversy surrounding the original study, while H. M. Cooper and T. L. Good review the most recent work in *Pygmalion Grows Up: Studies in the Expectation Communication Process* (New York: Longman, 1983).

76   W. Beez, "Influence of Biased Psychological Reports on Teacher Behavior and Pupil Performance," in *Proceedings of the 76th Annual Convention of the American Psychological Association* 3 (Washington, D.C.: American Psychological Association, 1968): 605–6; S. Kester and G. Letchworth, "Communication of Teacher Expectations and Their Effects on Achievement and Attitudes of Secondary School Students," *Journal of Educational Psychology* 66 (1972): 51–55; J. E. Brophy and T. Good, "Teachers' Communication of Differential Expectations for Children's Classroom Performance: Some Behavioral Data," *Journal of Educational Psychology* 61 (1970): 365–74.

77   Brophy and Evertson, *Student Characteristics and Teaching.*

78   Natriello and Dornbusch, *Teacher Evaluative Standards and Student Effort.*

79   Natriello and Dornbusch note the low standards found in the high schools in their studies and suggest a variety of strategies that might be employed by administrators, teachers, and parents interested in raising standards for student performance and behavior in school. These include presenting more challenging standards along with more support for students in the classroom, paying more attention to the evaluation of teachers, and helping parents to translate student interest in school into effort on school tasks (*Teacher Evaluative Standards and Student Effort*).

80   Natriello and Dornbusch, *Teacher Evaluative Standards and Student Effort.*

81   Natriello and Dornbusch, *Teacher Evaluative Standards and Student Effort*, p. 106.

82   Natriello and Dornbusch argue that unless students are provided with additional help and support when they are challenged by higher standards, there is little reason to expect their performance to improve. Such help may take a variety of forms, including support and encouragement to accompany the more frequent negative evaluations likely to accompany higher

standards and special tutoring and attention to enable students to reach higher levels of performance (*Teacher Evaluative Standards and Student Effort*).

83   Alexander and Pallas, "Curriculum Reform and School Performance: An Evaluation of the 'New Basics.' "

84   S. J. Rosenholtz and B. Wilson, "The Effect of Classroom Structure on Shared Perceptions of Ability," *American Educational Research Journal* 17 (1980): 75–82; C. Simpson, "Classroom Structure and the Organization of Ability," *Sociology of Education* 54 (1981): 120–32; S. J. Rosenholtz and S. H. Rosenholtz, "Classroom Organization and the Perception of Ability," *Sociology of Education* 54 (1981): 132–40. For a thorough review of this and related literature on "ability formation," see S. J. Rosenholtz and C. Simpson, "The Formation of Ability: Developmental Trend or Social Construction?" *Review of Educational Research* 54 (1984): 31–64.

85   Rosenholtz and Rosenholtz, "Classroom Organization and the Perception of Ability."

86   R. L. Crain, *The Quality of American High School Graduates: What Personnel Officers Say and Do about It,* Report no. 354 (Baltimore: Center for the Social Organization of Schools, Johns Hopkins University, 1984).

87   A. L. Stinchcombe, *Rebellion in a High School* (Berkeley: Quadrangle Books, 1964); T. Hirschi, *Causes of Delinquency* (Berkeley: University of California Press, 1969).

88   D'Amico, "Does Employment During High School Impair Economic Progress?"

89   L. Steinberg, E. Greenberger, L. Garduque, and S. M. McAuliffe, "High School Students in the Labor Force: Some Costs and Benefits to Schooling and Learning," *Educational Evaluation and Policy Analysis* 4 (1982): 363–72.

90   D'Amico, "Does Employment During High School Impair Economic Progress?"

91   Pallas, *The Determinants of High School Dropout.*

92   E. Spreitzer and M. D. Pugh, "Interscholastic Athletics and Educational Expectations," *Sociology of Education* 46 (1973): 182–91.

93   D. Landers and D. Landers, "Socialization via Interscholastic Athletics: Its Effects on Delinquency," *Sociology of Education* 51 (1978): 299–303.

94   L. B. Otto and D. F. Alwin, "Athletics, Aspirations and Attainments," *Sociology of Education* 42 (1977): 102–13.

95   Neill, *Keeping Students in School: Problems and Solutions;* H. C. Quay and L. B. Allen, "Truants and Dropouts," in *Encyclopedia of Educational Research*, vol. 5, 5th ed., ed. H. E. Mitzel (New York: Free Press, 1982), pp. 1958–62; L. N. Robins and K. S. Ratcliff, "The Long-Term Outcome of Truancy," in *Out of School: Modern Perspectives in Truancy and School Refusal*, ed. L. Hersov and I. Berg (New York: John Wiley, 1980), pp. 65–83.

96   A. L. Stroup and L. N. Robins, "Research Notes: Elementary School Predictors of High School Dropout Among Black Males," *Sociology of Education* 45 (1972): 212–22; D. Schreiber, ed. *Profile of the School Dropout* (New York: Random House, 1967); N. E. Silberberg and M. C. Silberberg, "School Achievement and Delinquency," *Review of Educational Research* 41 (1971): 17–34; J. L. Kaplan and E. D. Luck, "The Dropout Phenomenon as a Social Problem," *Educational Forum* 47 (1977): 41–56.

97   D. S. Elliott, "Delinquency and School Dropout," in *Crime in Society,* ed. L. Savitz and N. Johnston (New York: John Wiley, 1978), pp. 453–69; M. Gold and D. W. Mann, *Expelled to a Friendlier Place: A Study of Effective Alternative Schools* (Ann Arbor: University of Michigan Press, 1984).

98   J. M. McPartland and E. L. McDill, "Research on Crime in Schools," in *Violence in Schools: Perspectives, Programs, and Positions,* ed. J. M. McPartland and E. L. McDill (Lexington, Mass.: D. C. Heath, 1977), pp. 3–33; W. Spady, "The Authority System of the School and Student Unrest: A Theoretical Exploration," in *Uses of the Sociology of Education,* ed. C. W. Gordon (Chicago: University of Chicago Press, 1974), pp. 36–77; G. Natriello, *Organizational Evaluation Systems and Student Disengagement in Secondary Schools,* Final report to the National Institute of Education (St. Louis: Washington University, 1982); Natriello and Dornbusch, *Teacher Evaluative Standards and Student Effort.*

99   Spady, "The Authority System of the School and Student Unrest: A Theoretical Exploration."

100   In *Organizational Evaluation Systems and Student Disengagement in Secondary Schools*, Natriello notes that standards can be unattainable because they are set too high for the ability level of students, because students are not provided the necessary resources or facilities to accomplish the task, or because the tasks themselves are too unpredictable. See also Natriello and Dornbusch, *Teacher Evaluative Standards and Student Effort.*

101   D. F. Labaree, "Setting the Standard: Alternative Policies for Student Promotion," *Harvard Educational Review* 54 (1984): 74.

102   R. M. Jaeger, "The Final Hurdle: Minimum Competency Achievement Testing," in *The Rise and Fall of National Test Scores*, ed. G. R. Austin and H. Garber (New York: Academic Press, 1982), pp. 223–46.

103   R. M. Jaeger and C. R. Tittle, "Prologue," in *Minimum Competency Achievement Testing: Motives, Models, Measures, and Consequences*, ed. R. M. Jaeger and C. R. Tittle (Berkeley: McCutchan, 1980), pp. v–xii; Phi Delta Kappan, "Minimum Competency Testing," *Phi Delta Kappan* 59 (1978): 585–625.

104   Jaeger, "The Final Hurdle: Minimum Competency Achievement Testing," p. 241; R. L. Linn, G. F. Madaus, and J. J. Pedulla, "Minimum Competency Testing: Cautions on the State of the Art," *American Journal of Education* 91 (1982): 15–19.

105   Neill, *Keeping Students in School: Problems and Solutions*, p. 32. Neill adds that "on the other hand, some educators argue that the standards will cause schools to identify 'problem' learners earlier in their school careers and to provide the remedial help that would enable them to catch up with their peers" (p. 32).

106   Jaeger, "The Final Hurdle: Minimum Competency Achievement Testing." Jaeger reiterated this conclusion to one of us (McDill) in a personal communication on October 1, 1984. We also contacted three prominent research and development organizations that devote major efforts to school evaluation practices. Their comments reinforced this conclusion.

107   B. K. Eckland, "Sociodemographic Implications of Minimum Competency Testing," in *Minimum Competency Achievement Testing: Motives, Models, Measures, and Consequences*, ed. R. M. Jaeger and C. R. Tittle, pp. 134.

108   Kaplan and Luck, "The Dropout Phenomenon as a Social Problem," p. 44.

109   Levin, *The Costs to the Nation of Inadequate Education.*

110   U.S. Department of Commerce, Bureau of the Census, *Lifetime Earnings Estimates for Men and Women in the United States: 1979* (Washington, D.C.: Government Printing Office, 1979).

111   An extreme version of the "bias" explanation is offered by J. G. Bachman, who argues that high school dropouts have a variety of personal and intellectual liabilities that both prevent completion of high school and impede labor market success ("Response to Levin," in H. Levin, *The Costs to the Nation of Inadequate Education*).

112   L. Griffin, "Specification Biases in Estimates of Socioeconomic Returns to Schooling," *Sociology of Education* 49 (1976): 121–39; M. Olneck, "The Effects of Education," in *Who Gets Ahead: The Determinants of Economic Success in America*, ed. C. Jencks et al (New York: Basic Books, 1979), pp. 159–90; P. Taubman, "Earnings, Education, Genetics, and Environment," *Journal of Human Resources* 11 (1976): 447–61.

113   Levin, *The Costs to the Nation of Inadequate Education.*

114   K. L. Alexander, G. Natriello, and A. M. Pallas, "For Whom the School Bell Tolls: The Impact of Dropping Out on Cognitive Performance," *American Sociological Review* 50 (1985): 409–20.

115   Alexander, Natriello, and Pallas, "For Whom the School Bell Tolls: The Impact of Dropping Out on Cognitive Performance."

116   B. S. Bloom, "The New Direction in Educational Research: Alterable Variables," *Phi Delta Kappan* 62 (1980): 382–85; J. L. Epstein, "School Environment and Student Friendships: Issues, Implications, and Interventions," in *Friends in School: Patterns of Selection and Influence in*

Secondary Schools, ed. J. L. Epstein and N. Karweit (New York: Academic Press, 1983), pp. 235–53.

117   Bloom, "The New Direction in Educational Research: Alterable Variables," p. 382. Bloom notes that one of the most important examples of this shift is in the area of research on teachers. He cogently argues that four decades of work on teacher characteristics (e.g., age, training, and teaching experience) have revealed that such attributes "have little to do with learning of their students." In contrast, more recent research in this area has shifted from qualities of teachers to qualities of teaching. Such a focus has been productive in that "it isolates those qualities of teaching which are alterable as a result of inservice education that provides teachers with feedback on what they are doing (or not doing) and what they can do to alter the situation" (p. 384).

118   Such outcome behaviors include academic performance and aspirations, victimization of teachers and students, vandalism, truancy, dropping out, and delinquency outside of school.

119   G. D. Gottfredson and D. C. Gottfredson, *Victimization in Six Hundred Schools: An Examination of the Roots of Disorder* (New York: Plenum Publishing Corp., in press).

120   G. D. Gottfredson, *The School Action Effectiveness Study: Interim Summary of the Alternative Education Evaluation* (Baltimore: Johns Hopkins University, 1983); G. D. Gottfredson, "A Theory-Ridden Approach to Program Evaluation: A Method for Stimulating Researcher-Implementer Collaboration," *American Psychologist* 39 (1984): 1101–12; G. D. Gottfredson, "Response of Gary D. Gottfredson," in *Discipline in the Public Scools: Educator Responses to the Reagan Administration Policies* (Arlington, Va.: Education Research Service, School Research Forum, 1984); G. D. Gottfredson and D. C. Gottfredson, *Victimization in Six Hundred Schools: An Examination of the Roots of Disorder;* D. C. Gottfredson, "Environmental Change Strategies to Prevent School Disruption," Paper presented at the annual meeting of the American Psychological Association, Toronto, 1984; D. C. Gottfredson, *Implementing A Theory in a Large-Scale Educational Intervention* (Baltimore: Johns Hopkins University, Center for the Social Organization of Schools, 1984); M. D. Wiatrowski, G. D. Gottfredson, and M. Roberts, "Understanding School Behavior Disruption: Classifying School Environments," *Environment and Behavior* 15 (1983): 53–76.

121   G. D. Gottfredson, "Response of Gary D. Gottfredson," p. 74.

122   K. Polk and W. E. Schafer, eds., *Schools and Delinquency* (Englewood Cliffs, N.J.: Prentice-Hall, 1972); G. Spivack and M. Swift, "The Classroom Behavior of Children: A Critical Review of Teacher-Administrator Rating Scales," *Journal of Special Education* 7 (1973): 55–89; McPartland and McDill, "Research on Crime in Schools."

123   For example, Neill, *Keeping Students in School: Problems and Solutions;* E. Foley, "Alternative Schools: New Findings," *Social Policy* 13 (1983): 44–46; U.S. Department of Justice, Office of Juvenile Justice and Delinquency Prevention, *Program Announcement: Prevention of Delinquency through Alternative Education* (Washington, D.C.: Government Printing Office, 1980), appendix 3.

124   D. L. Morgan and D. E. Alwin, "When Less is More: School Size and Student Social Participation," *Social Psychological Quarterly* 43 (1980): 241–52.

125   P. Blau and R. Shoenherr, *The Structure of Organizations* (New York: Basic Books, 1971), p. 57.

126   H. Levin, "Reclaiming Urban Schools: A Modest Proposal," *IFG Policy Perspectives* vol. 4, no. 1 (1983).

127   T. A. Diprete, *Discipline and Order in American High Schools.* Report prepared for the National Center for Education Statistics (Washington, D.C.: Government Printing Office, 1982); G. D. Gottfredson, "Response of Gary D. Gottfredson"; McPartland and McDill, "Research on Crime in Schools"; U.S. Department of Justice, *Program Announcement: Prevention of Delinquency through Alternative Education,* appendix 3; Levin, *Reclaiming Urban Schools: A Modest Proposal.*

128   R. G. Barker and R. V. Gump, *Big School, Small School: High School Size and Student Behavior* (Stanford, Calif.: Stanford University Press, 1964); Morgan and Alwin, "When Less is

More: School Size and Student Social Participation."

129   Barker and Gump, *Big School, Small School: High School Size and Student Behavior.*

130   D. L. Duke and W. Seidman, "School Organization and Student Behavior: A Review" (Unpublished paper, Stanford University, 1981), p. 8.

131   L. S. Lotto, "The Holding Power of Vocational Curricula: Characteristics of Effective Dropout Prevention Programs," *Journal of Vocational Education Research* 7 (1982); 39–48.

132   "Organizational climate is a term to describe and summarize the patterns of expectations and incentive values that impinge on and are created by a group of people that live or work together. Organizational climate is assumed here to be a property of work environments that can be perceived directly or indirectly by the people who live and work in these environments. . . . Organizational climate molds and shapes the motivation and behavior of every member of a work group through its effect on each member's perception of what is expected of him, and what he will 'get' for doing a job in a particular way" (G. Litwin, "The Influence of Organizational Climate on Human Motivation [Paper presented to the Conference on Organizational Climate, Dearborn, Mich., 1966]; quoted in A. S. Alschuler, "How to Increase Motivation through Climate and Structure," Working Paper no. 8 in Achievement Motivation Development Projects [Cambridge, Mass.: Graduate School of Education, Harvard University, 1968], p. 5, and E. L. McDill and L. C. Rigsby, *Structure and Process in Secondary Schools: The Academic Impact of Educational Climates* [Baltimore: Johns Hopkins University Press, 1973], p. 125).

133   G. D. Gottfredson, "Response of Gary D. Gottfredson."

134   For example, J. S. Coleman states that "the evidence from these data — and from other recent studies — is that *stronger academic demands and disciplinary standards produce better achievement*" ("Quality and Inequality in American Education: Public and Catholic Schools," *Phi Delta Kappan* 63 [1981], p. 163). See also, J. S. Coleman, T. Hoffer, and S. Kilgore, *High School Achievement: Public, Catholic and Private Schools Compared* (New York: Basic Books, 1982).

135   G. D. Gottfredson, "Response of Gary D. Gottfredson," p. 76.

136   McPartland and McDill, relying on evidence from four different empirical analyses, state that "while the main sources of most serious offenses [in schools] almost certainly lie in features of the broad society, we feel that schools can aggravate the problem or reduce it according to the way they organize themselves to dispense costs, rewards, and access to individual students" ("Research on Crime in Schools," p. 22).

137   U.S. Department of Justice, *Program Announcement: Prevention of Delinquency through Alternative Education,* appendix 3, pp. 6–7.

138   H. L. Cohen and J. Filipczak, *A New Learning Environment* (San Francisco: Jossey-Bass, 1971); McPartland and McDill, "Research on Crime in Schools"; U.S. Department of Justice, *Program Announcement: Prevention of Delinquency through Alternative Education,* appendix 3. In a related vein, researchers and practitioners have frequently employed a variety of behavior modification techniques such as verbal reinforcement, token economies, and use of free time to reduce disruptive classroom behavior and to treat conduct disorders (H. C. Quay, "Behavior Disorders in the Classroom," *Journal of Research and Development in Education* 11 (1978): 8–17; U.S. Department of Justice, *Program Announcement: Prevention of Delinquency through Alternative Education,* appendix 3, p. 7).

139   A body of research is beginning to accumulate on the importance of leadership by administrators, especially the principal, to effective schools in terms of leadership role, change facilitator, and curriculum leader. For example, see A. Blumberg and W. Greenfield, *The Effective Principal: Perspectives in School Leadership* (Boston: Allyn and Bacon, 1980); S. T. Bossert, D. C. Dwyer, B. Rowan, and G. Lee, "The Instructional Management Role of the Principal," *Educational Administration Quarterly* 3 (1982): 34–64; and S. M. Stiegelbauer, "Leadership for Change: Principals' Actions Make a Difference in School Improvement Efforts," *Newsletter of the Research and Development Center for Teacher Education* (University of Texas at Austin) 2 (1984): 1, 2, 6. As director of school activities, the principal is viewed as playing a crucial part in establishing and maintaining the affective and intellectual tone of the institution.

140   K. L. Alexander, J. Fennessey, E. L. McDill, and R. J. D'Amico, "School SES Influences

—Composition or Context?" *Sociology of Education* 52 (1979): 222–37; McDill and Rigsby, *Structure and Process in Secondary Schools: The Academic Impact of Educational Climates.*

141   B. N. Odell, "Accelerating Entry into the Opportunity Structure: A Sociologically Based Treatment for Delinquent Youth," *Sociology and Social Research* 16 (1974): 312–17; D. A. Romig, *Justice for Our Children: An Examination of Juvenile Delinquency Rehabilitation Programs* (Lexington, Mass.: D. C. Heath, 1978).

142   W. E. Reckless and S. Dinitz. *Prevention of Juvenile Delinquency—an Experiment* (Columbus: Ohio State University Press, 1972).

143   U.S. Department of Justice, *Program Announcement: Prevention of Delinquency through Alternative Education,* appendix 3, p. 10.

144   U.S. Department of Justice, *Program Announcement: Prevention of Delinquency through Alternative Education,* appendix 3, p. 15.

145   R. Amenta, "What's Happening in Horizon High School?" *Phi Delta Kappan* 64 (1982): 204–5; Duke and Seidman, *School Organization and Student Behavior: A Review;* R. E. Maurer, "Dropout Prevention: An Intervention Model for Today's High Schools," *Phi Delta Kappan* 63 (1982): 470–71; U.S. Department of Justice, *Program Announcement: Prevention of Delinquency through Alternative Education.*

146   Odell, "Accelerating Entry into the Opportunity Structure: A Sociologically Based Treatment for Delinquent Youth"; Romig, *Justice for Our Children: An Examination of Juvenile Delinquency Rehabilitation Programs;* U.S. Department of Justice, *Program Announcement: Prevention of Delinquency through Alternative Education,* appendix 3.

147   I. Harris, C. Hedman, and M. Horning, "Success with High School Dropouts," *Educational Leadership* 40 (1983): 35–36; J. Robbins, S. Mills, and W. Clark, "Alternative Programs: Sometimes They Work, Sometimes They Don't," *NASSP Bulletin* 65 (1981): 48–56.

148   Since an alternative school is a physically distinct setting that houses an alternative program (either within the traditional school [i.e., a school-within-a-school] or in a separate building), we use the two terms interchangeably.

149   D. L. Duke and C. Perry, "Can Alternative Schools Succeed Where Benjamin Spock, Spiro Agnew, and B. F. Skinner Have Failed?" *Adolescence* 13 (1978): 375.

150   T. W. Deal and R. R. Nolan, "Alternative Schools: A Conceptual Map," *School Review* 87 (1978): 29.

151   Gold and Mann, *Expelled to A Friendlier Place: A Study of Effective Alternative Schools,* p. 4.

152   U.S. Department of Justice, *Program Announcement: Prevention of Delinquency through Alternative Education,* p. 11.

153   Gold and Mann, *Expelled to A Friendlier Place: A Study of Effective Alternative Schools,* p. 4; H. R. Johnson, "Alternative Schools: A Salvage Operation?" *Clearing House* 55 (1982): 316–18; Robbins, Mills, and Clark, "Alternative Programs: Sometimes They Work, Sometimes They Don't," pp. 48–56.

154   Deal and Nolan, "Alternative Schools: A Conceptual Map," p. 30.

155   Deal and Nolan, "Alternative Schools: A Conceptual Map"; U.S. Department of Justice, *Program Announcement: Prevention of Delinquency through Alternative Education,* appendix 3, p. 34.

156   U.S. Department of Justice, *Program Announcement: Prevention of Delinquency through Alternative Education.*

157   G. D. Gottfredson, *The School Action Effectiveness Study: Interim Summary of the Alternative Education Evaluation;* G. D. Gottfredson, "Response of Gary D. Gottfredson"; D. C. Gottfredson, "Environmental Change Strategies to Prevent School Disruption"; D. C. Gottfredson, *Implementing a Theory in a Large-Scale Educational Intervention;* G. D. Gottfredson, D. E. Rickert, Jr., D. C. Gottfredson, and N. Advani, "Standards for Program Development Evaluation Plans," *Psychological Documents,* in press.

158   G. D. Gottfredson, *The School Action Effectiveness Study: Interim Summary of the Alternative Education Evaluation,* p. 6.

159 G. D. Gottfredson, *The School Action Effectiveness Study: Interim Summary of the Alternative Education Evaluation*, p. 12.

160 K. Lewin, "Group Decision and Social Change," in *Readings in Social Psychology*, ed. T. M. Newcomb and E. L. Hartley (New York: Holt, Rinehart & Winston, 1947), pp. 330–44.

161 G. D. Gottfredson, "A Theory-ridden Approach to Program Evaluation: A Method for Stimulating Researcher-Implementer Collaboration."

162 G. D. Gottfredson, "A Theory-ridden Approach to Program Evaluation: A Method for Stimulating Researcher-Implementer Collaboration"; G. D. Gottfredson, "Response of Gary D. Gottfredson."

163 See D. C. Gottfredson, *Implementing a Theory in a Large-Scale Educational Intervention*, for an in-depth description of each approach.

164 D. C. Gottfredson, "Environmental Change Strategies to Prevent School Disruption," p. 3.

165 D. C. Gottfredson, *Implementing a Theory in a Large-Scale Educational Intervention*, p. 10.

166 D. C. Gottfredson, "Environmental Change Strategies to Prevent School Disruption," p. 11.

167 G. D. Gottfredson, *The School Action Effectiveness Study: Interim Summary of the Alternative Education Evaluation*, p. 5.

168 Quay and Allen, "Truants and Dropouts," p. 1961.

169 Quay, "Behavior Disorders in the Classroom," p. 13.

170 Quay, "Behavior Disorders in the Classroom," p. 13. For a listing of these different modalities, see M. Gold, "Delinquent Behavior in Adolescence," in *Handbook of Adolescent Psychology*, ed. J. Adelson (New York: John Wiley, 1980), pp. 517–18.

171 I. Berg, "School Refusal in Early Adolescence," in *Out of School: Modern Perspectives in Truancy and School Refusal*, ed. L. Hersov and I. Berg (New York: John Wiley, 1980), pp. 231–49; M. Lewis, "Psychotherapeutic Treatment in School Refusal," in *Out of School: Modern Perspectives in Truancy and School Refusal*, ed. L. Hersov and I. Berg (New York: John Wiley, 1980), pp. 252–65.

172 Gold, "Delinquent Behavior in Adolescence," p. 518.

173 Eckland, "Sociodemographic Implications of Minimum Competency Testing."

174 Walton, "States' Reform Effort to Increase as Focus of Issues Shifts."

175 Walton, "States' Reform Effort to Increase as Focus of Issues Shifts."

176 G. D. Gottfredson, "A Theory-ridden Approach to Program Evaluation: A Method for Stimulating Researcher-Implementer Collaboration."

177 F. Hammack, "Large School Systems' Dropout Reports: An Analysis of Definitions, Procedures, and Findings," in this volume; and G. Morrow, "Standardizing Practice in the Analysis of School Dropouts," in this volume.

178 Indeed, if we believe the current argument that the tiny increase in SAT scores is attributable to the work of the National Commission on Excellence in Education, such increases may even anticipate the reforms.

Raising Standards and Reducing Dropout Rates

STEPHEN F. HAMILTON
Cornell University

If we raise school standards as the current reports on education recommend, will we have to contend with an inevitable increase in dropout rates? Stephen Hamilton considers this problem and some potential remedies by examining the characteristics of school programs that seem to minimize the dropout rate. He also looks at secondary education in West Germany as a source of alternatives to increase the holding power of American secondary schools.

This article begins with the assumption that raising standards in secondary schools without making other organizational and instructional changes would increase the dropout rate because those students who now drop out would continue to do so and some additional proportion of marginal students or potential dropouts would move into the dropout category rather than increase their efforts sufficiently to graduate from high school. My aim, therefore, is to identify what changes might reduce dropout rates as standards are raised.

A review of research on successful dropout-prevention programs revealed four common characteristics: (1) They separate potential dropouts from other students; (2) they have strong vocational components; (3) they utilize out-of-classroom learning; and (4) they are intensive in the sense of being small, individualizing instruction, having low student-teacher ratios, and offering more counseling than ordinary schools. A brief examination of West German secondary schools, emphasizing the "dual system" of apprenticeship combined with part-time vocational schooling, helped to identify and elaborate on issues related to the first three characteristics.

Differentiation among students, although it appears to be an essential

This article was originally written for a project organized by the American Educational Research Association with funding from the National Institute of Education, U.S. Department of Education, entitled, "The Nation's Educational Issues: Research Contributions for Educational Improvement." The views expressed are my own. No endorsement from either of the sponsoring organizations should be inferred. Claire DeBoer assisted in the review of research on dropout prevention programs. George Kaplan improved the style of an earlier draft.

component of successful dropout-prevention programs and of West German schools, is a troubling practice because research has demonstrated that it can harm the achievement and self-evaluations of students identified as slower. Nonetheless, such differentiation seems justifiable in the absence of large-scale societal and educational change when the basis is accurate and appropriate, the barriers created among groups of students are no greater than required for effective instruction, the process and implications of assignment to a lower group are understood by students and parents, and the probable consequences of assignment to a lower group are favorable. Research does not support the claim that vocational education at the secondary level trains young people for employment. However, the practical, real-life quality of vocational education is more comfortable and more effective for marginal students than is abstract academic education. Therefore, vocational education or manual training can serve as a vehicle for teaching academic skills and general rather than specific competence for employment.

The assumption found in recent secondary education reform proposals that the classroom is always the best environment for learning is not supported by research. Marginal students, in particular, who have not been successful in classrooms, need planned opportunities to learn in other settings.

ASSUMPTIONS AND DEFINITIONS

The purpose of this article is to synthesize research bearing on the implications of recent recommendations for the reform of secondary schools for potential dropouts, also referred to as marginal students. Dropouts will be defined as students who choose to leave school before graduating although they are intellectually capable of doing the work required for graduation. Excluded from this definition are those with such severe learning disabilities that they are unable to perform high school level work and those who are expelled or otherwise pushed out of school.

Two stipulations must be stated before proceeding. First, this article accepts the assumption that reducing the proportion of high school dropouts is a good idea, despite the complexities of the issue. Based on their longitudinal study of young men, Bachman, O'Malley, and Johnston argued that dropping out of school is not so much a cause of subsequent problems as a symptom of underlying personal attitudes and behaviors that render certain young people marginal both in school and in work. During the first few years out of school, male high school graduates and dropouts are hired for the same kinds of jobs; the difference is that graduates are twice as likely to be hired.[1] Elliott and Voss also employed a longitudinal study to demonstrate that, contrary to common expectations, dropping out of school actually reduced delinquent behavior. Dropping out, they claimed, reduces the conflicts and frustrations

that marginal students experience in school, thus reducing their delinquency.[2]

Eliminating dropping out altogether would not necessarily benefit marginal students. If all job applicants have high school diplomas, then having a
diploma ceases to confer an advantage on job applicants.[3] However, at the
individual level, it would be irresponsible to counsel a marginal student to
drop out because the diploma can confer advantages in comparison with
other competitors in the labor market and because not having the diploma
excludes some options for employment and further education. Moreover,
there are personal and societal benefits to learning that go beyond the accu-
mulation of human capital. Therefore, despite some reservations, I accept
for present purposes the assumption that reducing dropout rates would be
beneficial, especially considering that all of the recent reform proposals have
stressed that a high school diploma should be more than a certificate of
attendance.

The second stipulation is an assumption that the implementation of reform
proposals calling for higher standards would increase dropout rates unless
accompanied by other reforms in school organization and instructional practice. Demanding more of marginal students, whether in terms of examinations passed, courses taken, or time spent in school, is unlikely to encourage
them to remain in school. Therefore, I would predict that raising standards
without making other changes would push some marginal students over the
line without retaining current dropouts, thus producing a higher dropout
rate — hence the motivation to identify what some of those other changes
might be.

A final caveat is that although this article presents insights from educational research with respect to this issue, the reader should not infer that
educational research is sufficient to determine educational policy and practice. Research can contribute to what Cohen and Garet have termed the
dialogue of policymaking[4] and it can inform practitioners, but research results are never powerful enough to dictate policies and practices, nor can
research take into account all of the influences that can and should bear on
policy and practice.

In this article I review evaluation studies of dropout-prevention programs to
identify practices that seem to reduce dropping out. There follows a description of the West German secondary schools with special emphasis on the dual
system of apprenticeship combined with part-time vocational schooling, in
order to make the point that alternative structures for secondary schools
might reduce dropping out. Finally, I examine three issues raised by the
review of dropout-prevention programs and West German schools as they
relate to recent reform proposals and in the light of available research: differ-

entiation among students, vocational education, and learning outside of classrooms.

DROPOUT-PREVENTION PROGRAMS

A computer search of reports on dropout-prevention programs was conducted using the index compiled by ERIC (Educational Resources Information Center). The search yielded a surprisingly small number of reports and only a few offered both program descriptions and data indicating program effectiveness. More reports are available on programs for people who have already left school, but they are not reviewed here. The best-documented and most-informative programs will be described individually. Two previous reviews of programs will also be summarized. The conclusion of this section will extract common characteristics of effective dropout-prevention programs.

Introduction to the Allied Health Professions

This program placed high school students, beginning in their first semester, into hospital jobs, both as an orientation to health care occupations and as an incentive to remain in school. Students received academic credit and a small stipend for their work. Both project staff and regular high school staff provided special counseling to participants. Grade-point averages showed a modest advantage for participants compared with controls, and over the project's first two years only 2.6 percent of participants dropped out, compared with 8.9 percent of controls.[5]

Project MACK

An effort by McClymonds High School in Oakland, California, to reduce the dropout rate, increase attendance, and improve students' attitudes toward school, Project MACK was evaluated during the 1974–1975 school year. It featured work experience and career education along with basic academic subjects and strong support services, including guidance and counseling, a health program, and student activities. Compared with 1970 rates (i.e., before the program began), dropping out declined by the end of the 1974–1975 year from 16.9 to 6.2 percent. Class cutting and absenteeism also declined and test scores in reading and math improved.[6]

Career Intern Program

Since its development as a demonstration project in Philadelphia funded by the National Institute of Education, the Career Intern Program (CIP) has been adopted in many other locations, often with funding from the Youth

Employment and Demonstration Projects Act (YEDPA). CIP is an alternative high school that aims to help dropouts and potential dropouts earn a high school diploma and prepare for either employment or further education. Instruction is tied closely to employment demands. All academic courses are infused with career information. Work experience is an integral part of the main phase of the program, with students moving through two to four workplaces. Individual instruction, independent study, and counseling are part of the program. The program continues to serve students until they have enrolled in vocational or on-the-job training for six months or postsecondary education for a year. An evaluation study compared 286 CIP students with a control group chosen randomly from nonselected applicants. It showed that between January 1974 and December 1975, 67 percent of CIP students had either graduated or were still attending school, compared with 13 percent of those in the control group. A follow-up of 77 graduates in the fall of 1975 found 71 percent either employed or enrolled in postsecondary education but only 39 percent of the controls. Higher school enrollment among CIP graduates accounted for most of the difference.[7]

Youth Incentive Entitlement Pilot Projects

Based on research indicating that youth who fail to graduate from high school and fail to establish significant work experience are at greatest risk of persistent unemployment as adults, the Youth Incentive Entitlement Pilot Projects (YIEPP) sought to increase the likelihood of high school graduation and provide paid work experience to disadvantaged youth ages 16–19. The long-term goal was to improve their adult employment and earnings. The basic strategy was to provide employment, full-time during the summer and part-time during the school year, on the condition that participants either remain in or return to high school. In addition, YIEPP guaranteed employment to any eligible youth within the seventeen target communities. This was the "entitlement." Like other YEDPA programs, YIEPP's purpose was not only to provide services to the target population but to add to policymakers' knowledge of effective strategies for dealing with youth unemployment, hence the designation of pilot projects and the quite elaborate evaluation design.

As a dropout-prevention program, YIEPP was not spectacularly successful. School enrollment for the first year of operation (1978) was found to be 4.8 percent higher in the pilot sites than in comparable communities without the program. In 1979, the difference declined to 2.5 percent. These figures are modest, but the conservative nature of the evaluation design is at least partially responsible. This was not a comparison between participants and non-participants but between overall enrollment rates in entire communities. Therefore even small increments in enrollment represent large numbers of young people remaining in school, and the program was found to be even more effective in attracting dropouts back into school than in retaining potential dropouts. It also accomplished its other goals of providing paid work experience and demonstrating that labor force participation of disadvantaged youth is limited, for all practical purposes, solely by the availability of jobs.[8] YIEPP was reminiscent of the earlier Vocational Exploration in the Private Sector program in its basic strategy but more effective at reducing dropping out.[9] In general, federal youth employment programs have been more effective for older out-of-school youth than for high school students and either ineffective or modestly effective at reducing dropping out.[10]

Review of Effective Dropout-Prevention Programs

Lotto identified seventeen dropout-prevention programs emphasizing vocational education for which evidence of holding power has been collected. Most of the programs were found by contacting various funding agencies, thus revealing reports that have probably not been published. The author found three common characteristics in these programs. First, each utilized a variety of strategies rather than depending on only one approach, and these strategies were well integrated. Second, all of the programs removed potential dropouts from their ordinary schools and placed them in different kinds of environments. Third, the participants constituted a small population for which resources were narrowly targeted and concentrated.[11]

Wisconsin Programs for the Marginal High School Student

Wehlage and his colleagues at the University of Wisconsin – Madison have engaged for several years in research, staff training, and technical assistance to reduce dropping out of high schools. They described six exemplary programs for marginal students in Wisconsin high schools that were effective in terms of reducing truancy, increasing credits earned, and generating favorable testimony from students and educators. A list of characteristics of effective programs summarizes their findings. They found small size and autonomy to be uniform organizational features of the programs. Teachers accepted responsibility for their students' success and communicated to their students an expectation of success, defined in relation to the students' previous work rather than according to a uniform standard. Teachers combined expectations of success with caring for students, which was expressed by teachers' taking responsibilities beyond those normally associated with their role. The teacher culture was characterized by collegiality, with a counterpart supportive peer culture among students, often described as a family atmosphere. Curriculum and instruction in the programs emphasized individualization in cooperative group settings. Many classes emphasized real-life problem solving. Most important, according to the investigators, was a careful use of experiential learning to complement and motivate classroom learning.[12]

CHARACTERISTICS OF EFFECTIVE DROPOUT-PREVENTION PROGRAMS

The foregoing programs vary widely in scope; several took place in one school, while others were widespread, nationally funded efforts. However, they share some common features that raise important issues regarding the nature of schools and school programs that might reduce dropping out. One feature is the separation of potential dropouts from other students and their placement in programs that differ markedly from the ordinary high school experience. In some programs, potential dropouts are even combined with actual dropouts. A second shared characteristic is a strong vocational emphasis. Students learn practical, often job-related skills in school and apply academic learning to real-life situations. Third, usually but not always as part of the vocational emphasis, much learning occurs outside the classroom, often in connection with paid employment. Finally, all the programs are intensive, in the sense that they have low student/teacher ratios, individualized instruction, strong counseling components, and small size.

The first three characteristics identify the issues that will be examined in the light of research for their implications for improving secondary schools. The fourth characteristic, intensity, does not lend itself to such analysis because of its breadth and the many distinct practices defining it here. Further research on these practices would be valuable.

SECONDARY EDUCATION IN WEST GERMANY

A brief look at West Germany's secondary schools may help to clarify some of the issues raised thus far and to suggest some alternative approaches. However, those schools do not provide a model that could be adopted whole in the United States because the cultural values and institutional supports underlying them are different in this country.

Differentiation occurs early in West Germany and is quite strong. Beginning as early as fifth grade in some states (seventh in others), students whose parents want them to prepare for the university and whose performance indicates that they are able to do so are removed from the main school (*Hauptschule*) and sent to the university preparatory school (*Gymnasium*). This school continues through grade thirteen and offers a highly demanding arts and sciences curriculum. Students take at least two foreign languages, and graduates have the equivalent of the first year or two of college in the United States. When two or more *Gymnasien* are available, they specialize, for example, in mathematics and science or classics, and students choose which to attend on the basis of their interests and plans and the school's reputation.

Students of middle ability depart the *Hauptschule* at the beginning of grade five (or seven) for technical secondary schools (*Realschulen*), where they prepare for commercial and technical occupations, graduating after grade ten. Those students who do not qualify for or whose parents do not wish them to attend one of the more selective secondary schools remain in the *Hauptschule* through grade nine (in some cases, grade ten). Comprehensive schools (*Gesamtschulen*) have been established as an alternative, less differentiated structure in some locations, but they enroll only 16 percent of all students and half are simply the three traditional types of schools under the same roof.[13]

As in U.S. tracking systems, movement from one of these levels to another is possible, but almost always in a descending direction. A student who chooses to leave the *Gymnasium* after grade ten receives the equivalent of a *Realschule* completion certificate. Upward movement, when it occurs, often requires repetition of all grades not taken in the higher-level school; it therefore becomes daunting after a year or two.

Over the past two decades there has been a strong effort to add flexibility to this system. The principal result has been the expansion of an alternative route to the university, the second educational path (*der zweite Bildungsweg*). It is now possible to achieve university entrance through a combination of advanced trade training and attendance at an evening *Gymnasium*. University study must be in an area related to one's vocational training, and the number of people with sufficient stamina who can also afford to forgo full-time earnings as adults to take advantage of this possibility is quite small, but it does offer a second chance at least in principle. A variety of postsecondary vocational schools can also lead to what would be considered a college diploma in the United States, though it is clearly distinguished from a university degree in Germany.

Although full-time schooling may be completed for those in the *Hauptschule* by age fifteen and for *Realschule* pupils by age sixteen, schooling is compulsory through age eighteen. The gap is filled by an array of advanced full-time vocational schools but most notably by the dual system of part-time vocational schooling combined with apprenticeship. Half of the sixteen-to-eighteen-year-olds in West Germany are involved in this system. Participants include about half of those completing the main school and one-third of those completing the *Realschule*.[14] Apprenticeship rather than school constitutes the primary educational setting for West German youth not going on to the university.

The medieval image of a young man learning a trade while assisting a craftsman does not do justice to the West German apprenticeship system. Apprentices are trained in a wide range of occupations—more than 400 leading to over 20,000 more specialized occupations including male- and female-dominated occupations and nonmanual occupations.[15] It is nearly impossible to enter those occupations for which apprenticeship programs exist without completing an apprenticeship, which requires from two to three-and-a-half years and a passing examination grade.

Employers, educational authorities, and unions participate in planning apprenticeship programs. Apprentices and their parents sign contracts with employers, the terms of which have been determined by collective bargaining and are standard within each occupation. Apprentices receive modest stipends, normally in the range of $100–200 per month, and they are entitled to a paid vacation, which is typically four weeks. Apprentices who complete their training and pass the qualifying examination are certified to be skilled workers and are, by law, entitled to earn the wages determined by collective bargaining for their occupation.

This system has flaws. The most serious is a shortage of apprenticeship positions at a time when recession has caused a shortage of jobs while the youth population has peaked. But the system does provide a smooth and rewarding path from school to career for the majority of young people who do not enter higher education. More than half of all successful apprentices are employed by the firms in which they were trained two years after the completion of their training.[16] Most others find jobs as skilled workers in the same occupation. Those who change occupations retain the advantage of their training, not only as a fall-back possibility but as a powerful credential. Employers view successful apprentices as trainable and reliable workers and are willing to invest in further training to fit them to other skilled occupations. As a result, many young people establish themselves in well-paid careers with security and advancement possibilities between the ages of eighteen and twenty. (Males must complete fifteen months of military or alternative service, usually between apprenticeship and career entry.) The contrast with noncollege youth in the United States is stark. Here employers view young people as inherently irresponsible and seldom offer them career entry positions until they are in their early to mid-twenties (with the exception of females trained in clerical skills). The modal transition from school to career for noncollege males in the United States includes a floundering period of two or more years working at low-level jobs in the secondary labor market, interspersed with periods of unemployment.[17]

DIFFERENTIATION

West German schools differentiate very strongly and very early among students they consider to have varying abilities and divergent futures. Although this practice seems undemocratic because it severely limits the educational opportunities of a large proportion of young children, it has one great advantage over more weakly differentiated U.S. schools: The lowest track leads directly to remunerative and productive employment. Differentiation is also accomplished publicly with the clear understanding by parents and students of its implications. Ironically, German schools differentiate primarily at the school level. Within elementary school classrooms there is little of the sub-grouping by ability that is nearly universal in U.S. elementary schools. Within secondary schools, the curricular tracks that in fact strongly differentiate U.S. comprehensive high schools are unnecessary because students have already been sorted.

The dilemma raised by differentiation among students in schools is a persistent one, not only in education but in U.S. society more broadly. The subtitle of Gardner's well-known *Excellence: Can We Be Equal and Excellent Too?*[18] states it well. It is represented in the successful struggle to shatter the myth that segregated schools were separate but equal. The dilemma is not resolved by proposals for minimum competency tests or other attempts to raise standards for all students. If the tests and the more demanding courses can be passed by the weakest students, how can they possibly improve the education of the strongest? If a substantial portion of the weaker students fail the tests or courses, can we tolerate the increased dropout rate, especially considering that it will affect different races and classes unequally?

John Rawls's *Theory of Justice* helps to clarify the dilemma. Rawls addressed at some length the question of how inequalities can be justified in a democratic society. One of the principles he proposed is that inequalities may be justified if they benefit those who are at the lowest level.[19] High salaries for corporate executives, for example, might be justified if they contributed to economic productivity, which provided jobs for the least advantaged. In schools, differentiation can be justified if it results in more learning for those in the lowest group.

Research on grouping practices is not encouraging by this criterion. Rosenbaum[20] cited studies and previous reviews, notably one by the National Education Association,[21] yielding mixed results regarding the achievement effects of ability grouping. Some studies found gains in achievement overall, some losses; some demonstrated advantages for slower learners, others that grouping aided faster learners. Looking at the effects of grouping on students' self-evaluations, Rosenbaum found some of the same ambiguity of results but generally strong support for the claim that being labeled average or below average makes students think poorly of themselves. This finding was strongest in those studies that actually asked students how they felt about their group assignment and the group structure in their school[22] and in studies of curriculum grouping at the secondary level as compared with ability grouping. Rosenbaum concluded that the costs of grouping to the lowest students' achievement and feelings about themselves are not justified by the uncertain benefits of the practice. Good and Marshall reached a similar conclusion in their more recent review.[23]

In view of the costs of ability grouping to those in the lower groups, students should be treated as uniformly as is consistent with optimal learning.

But equality of opportunity, as Husén has pointed out, implies pluralism rather than uniformity,[24] and the circumstances surrounding differentiation at the secondary level are different from those at the elementary level. If elementary and middle schools could more nearly equalize students' performance, perhaps through mastery learning techniques as advocated by Bloom[25] and others, then secondary schools would not be forced to differentiate so much. Faced with some students capable of college-level work and others struggling to read at the third-grade level, secondary schools can hardly be blamed for creating inequality. More broadly, if differences in earnings and status among occupations in our society were less marked, then differences in school performance could be treated purely as a pedagogical issue. It is the association of school performance with subsequent income and prestige that renders differentiation invidious.

Although I am concerned about the negative consequences of grouping or tracking, I believe the differential treatment of potential dropouts can be justified under certain conditions, which are suggested by the material presented above on dropout-prevention programs and West German secondary schooling: (1) The basis for differentiation must be accurate and appropriate; (2) the strength of the differentiation must be no greater than required for effectiveness; (3) the process of differentiation must be understood by students and parents; and (4) the probable consequences of assignment to the lowest group must be favorable and acceptable to those students and their parents. These conditions might apply to dropout-prevention efforts as follows.

1. The bases for identifying potential dropouts should be past performance and clearly expressed attitudes. Tests of aptitude or achievement and the judgments of teachers and counselors are inadequate bases. The studies reviewed by Rosenbaum found inappropriate placements in ability groups when, for example, IQ tests were used to form reading groups, since reading ability is not identical to IQ. Teachers can sometimes substitute social class characteristics for hard evidence of ability, as Rist dramatically illustrated,[26] and counselors can do the same with older students, as Erickson showed.[27] McClelland argued in his critique of intelligence testing that what we want to know is what people are able to do, which is better indicated by performance on the task in question than by a score on a test of some abstract quality like intelligence.[28] Only students who are in fact performing poorly in school and who say they are actively considering dropping out should be placed in dropout-prevention programs. The West German process of differentiating students meets this criterion, although it occurs much sooner than most Americans would think necessary. The Germans use very few tests of ability and therefore do not have to deal with the bizarre category of overachievers, students whose achievement test scores and grades are higher than they should be able to achieve according to their ability test scores.

2.   Over the past decade, the principle has been established that disabled children should be mainstreamed, that is, taught in ordinary classrooms, to the extent that it optimizes their learning. Those struggling to establish this principle have been motivated in part by the same phenomenon noted by the research on ability grouping, namely, that labeling some students deficient and placing them in separate groups to remedy those deficiencies can have a negative effect on their learning and self-evaluations. Programs for potential dropouts should apply the same principle and minimize the barriers separating their students from ordinary students. Students in special programs should retain access to extracurricular activities and specialized courses in the regular school and the goal of the programs should be to move them back into the regular school if possible. With respect to this criterion, the West German system provides a bad example, since students are sent to entirely different schools for many years and movement from one to another is both difficult and rare. However, before feeling smug about the openness of our system, we should attend to Rosenbaum's finding that mobility within the comprehensive high school he studied was much more likely to be downward than upward,[29] a finding also reported in several other studies he reviewed.[30] According to Rist, this sorting process begins in the first year of school, persists from year to year, and may be based on social class rather than academic ability.[31]

3.   In order for students and parents to be able to make an informed choice to enter a special program, they must understand the selection criteria and the implications of placement in the program. That this condition is not always met in current tracking arrangements is indicated by research cited by Rosenbaum[32] indicating that many students in non-college preparatory tracks hope and plan to attend college.[33] The West German system seems fairer than ours with respect to this criterion. In part because the intergroup barriers are so strong and the consequences of assignment to one of the lower-level secondary schools are so great, parents and students are well aware of the implications of the placement. U.S. grouping practices, in contrast, are presented as short-term, and the opportunity for all high school graduates to attend college is so strongly emphasized that students and parents can be surprised, like many in Rosenbaum's study,[34] to discover that they have had their options limited by a succession of group assignments whose implications they did not understand.

4.   The final condition, the probable consequences of assignment to the lowest track, is also the most important. Unless a special program for potential dropouts actually reduces the likelihood of failing to graduate, then it cannot be justified, particularly in view of the possible negative effects of publicly identifying a student as a potential dropout. This commonsense criterion can be met at the aggregate level by demonstrating a lower dropout rate among participants or in a whole school, but at the individual level it is

impossible to prove that a specific student would have dropped out had it not been for the program. Ideally we should also ask a more difficult question: Is the graduate who participated in the program better off five years later, both financially and otherwise, than a comparable dropout?

The West German system is particularly instructive with regard to this condition. Although West German society is strongly stratified, and those engaged in the kinds of work for which the *Hauptschule* followed by vocational school and apprenticeship prepare them are near the bottom of the hierarchy (the bottom is occupied by the unemployed and the unskilled, who are predominantly foreign), the difference in income and prestige between the top and the bottom is not so great as in the United States. Skilled workers earn decent wages and are accorded respect for their skills. The most highly skilled have the chance to become masters, which confers upon them the right to establish their own business and to train apprentices, and gives them a high status in their community. The title *Meister*, though held by only a small minority of skilled workers, undergirds the status of all skilled workers.[35] In short, students in the lowest track are not viewed as failures but as people not particularly well suited to academic work. They have open to them a range of rewarding occupations and some opportunities for further education. Young people who leave full-time schooling at the age of fifteen can be highly skilled workers with secure, well-paid, and interesting jobs at the age of eighteen. Can anyone seriously argue that they would be better off spending three more years in the general track of a comprehensive high school and then being turned loose in the secondary labor market to seek jobs pumping gasoline and serving hamburgers?

THE PLACE OF VOCATIONAL EDUCATION

Vocational education in West Germany cannot be compared without qualifications to dropout-prevention programs in the United States since the German system accommodates large numbers of students, including a great many who would not be potential dropouts in the United States. Dropout-prevention programs, by definition, serve only those at greatest risk of dropping out, those who most desperately need some alternative to ordinary school. However, many of those programs include some vocational components, and U.S. vocational curricula are often viewed as legitimate alternatives for students who are ill at ease and unsuccessful with academic learning. It is thus appropriate in this context to review research on U.S. vocational education and compare it with the West German approach.

The most important point to make about vocational education in our secondary schools is that, with few exceptions, it does not educate students for vocations. Numerous studies and research reviews have concluded that vocational graduates have little if any advantage in the labor market when compared with graduates of the general or academic tracks.[36] The major exception is that young women who have learned typing and related office skills in high school are more likely to gain clerical and secretarial jobs. Overall, less than one-third of vocational graduates ever work in the occupation for which they were trained.[37]

This reflects poorly on the quality of the training provided in high school vocational programs, but it also reflects the realities of the youth labor market. Studies of employers' preferences with respect to young job applicants reveal first of all that many employers are reluctant to hire young people, especially young men, before they are at least twenty-one or twenty-two years old.[38] Moreover, the majority of employers say they are much more interested in prospective employees' basic academic skills, their interpersonal relations and communications skills, and their general work skills — such as ability to take supervision, punctuality, reliability, and trainability — than in their specific job training. Most of their skilled work, employers say, is either too specific to their firms to be taught anywhere else or it requires speed and precision in repetitive work that are not taught in vocational programs.[39]

Nevertheless, there is evidence that vocational education has a place in secondary schools because it creates what Berryman called a "niche" for students who might otherwise become discouraged and drop out.[40] Many studies have found that vocational students like their programs, especially in comparison with the regular academic programs from which they came.[41] Combs and Cooley found that dropouts were much more likely to come from the general curriculum than the vocational track.[42] It is difficult to say with certainty that vocational education prevents dropping out, given that the strongest predictions of dropping out found by Bachman, Green, and Wirtanen were personal and family characteristics that are unaffected by curriculum.[43] The higher dropout rate of general-track students may reflect preexisting differences rather than the impact of vocational education.

Vocational education in West Germany produces skilled workers ready for either immediate employment or more advanced education and training. In the United States, with some exceptions, vocational education is a less painful way for students who do not excel at academic work to earn a high school diploma.[44] It is, in a sense, a huge dropout-prevention program, and is sometimes touted as such. Although the dropout-prevention function of vocational education is not firmly established by research, the nearly universal presence of vocational components in successful dropout-prevention programs and the testimony of vocational students that they prefer vocational to academic classes strongly support the claim of its proponents that without vocational education many more students would drop out.

The place of vocational education remains a question, particularly in view of the current emphasis of the school reform movement on raising academic standards. Should vocational programs train young people for employment?

If so, standards must be raised in terms of the level of work-related skills actually taught. The West German comparison suggests that this would require much more training in work sites than is now done. It is simply not feasible for school shops to have the kind of equipment that modern industry uses or to expect the same level of technical expertise from a vocational teacher as from an active practitioner selected to train apprentices. Motivation is also more difficult in a school setting than on the job. Another direction might be to view vocational education as a vehicle for teaching academic knowledge and skills. For this purpose, the old term "manual training" might be resurrected, as suggested in *The Paideia Proposal*.[45] The goal then would not be teaching specific employment skills but giving practical, concrete application to academic instruction on the one hand and teaching generalizable employee virtues such as punctuality, orderliness, and precision on the other.

For many reasons, the second direction seems more feasible than the first. The United States conspicuously lacks the tradition of cooperation among schools, employers, and labor unions that stabilizes the West German apprenticeship system. Furthermore, as noted above, there is no evidence that employers want specifically trained job applicants and therefore no likelihood that they would assume the considerable costs of a formal apprenticeship program.

LEARNING OUT OF SCHOOL

The third issue raised by successful dropout-prevention programs and the West German dual system is the place or potential place of out-of-school learning in secondary education. Recent reform proposals read as though no other distinguished panels of experts had surveyed the problems of secondary schools lately and proffered their considered opinions regarding improvements. In a series of reports issued between 1973 and 1979, several such groups achieved remarkable agreement in recommending that high school students spend more of their learning time in the community and less in the classroom.[46] Although these groups addressed concerns that have faded from the political agenda of the 1980s, such as alienated youth and youth unemployment, those problems have not disappeared. In addition, some of the innovations that occurred along the lines recommended by these reports offer valuable lessons to contemporary reformers.

In the light of the recent reform proposals' emphases on improving basic academic skills and their explicit claims that this is best accomplished in classrooms, the first question to ask about programs that remove students from classrooms is whether they retard academic skills. The clearest answer to that question comes from evaluations of Experience Based Career Education (EBCE), a program sponsored by the National Institute of Education in which students may spend as much as 80 percent of their time for a full school year learning in work settings. The least favorable finding from those evaluations with regard to academic learning is that EBCE students learn no less, as measured by standardized tests, than comparable students spending full-time in classrooms.[47] In a recent meta-analysis of eighty external evaluations, Bucknam and Brand found the EBCE students gained more often than non-EBCE students on tests of academic knowledge as well as tests of life attitude skills and career-related skills.[48]

The finding of at least no harm to academic learning from out-of-classroom experiential learning programs is surprising on two counts. First, consistent with the concerns of the school reform panels of the 1970s, the programs aim primarily at noncognitive learning, toward enhancing the development or socialization of adolescents. That good experiential learning programs can have positive developmental effects has been demonstrated by Conrad and Hedin's large-scale evaluation study.[49] Second, the design of experiential learning programs fits poorly with the structure of standardized tests. Such tests seek to identify common areas of learning, but much of the academic learning that occurs via experience is idiosyncratic. It depends on the site, on the nature of the activity, and on the interests and choices of the individual student. A student serving as an intern in a county tax assessor's office, for example, might learn some applied mathematics and something about local government but be able to demonstrate neither on a standardized test. Even if a test were to tap this learning, it would show gains for only that student and not for classmates placed in a nursing home and a theater.[50]

There is, nonetheless, some empirical ground for optimism regarding the measurable contribution of experiential programs to academic learning. MacKenzie and White found that eighth and ninth graders participating in an active excursion retained geographical facts much better than those receiving either a passive excursion or no out-of-classroom instruction. All three groups received the same classroom instruction, and both excursion groups demonstrated slightly better learning immediately after the treatment.[51] Agnew added experiential components to high school courses in a variety of subjects without varying the total amount of instruction time and found that out-of-classroom activity improved students' performance on tests of subject matter.[52] Hamilton and Zeldin compared the attitudes toward and knowledge about local government of three groups of high school students: interns to county legislators, control groups of students waiting to enter the same intern programs, and comparison groups of students enrolled in civics courses teaching about local government. The interns showed greater gains in knowledge and attitudes than either of the other groups.[53] These studies not only demonstrate the potential of out-of-classroom educational programs, but also suggest the importance of integrating in-class instruction since all of them included both, as does EBCE.

The West German comparison is again instructive. The educational value of apprenticeship is unquestioned, although there are debates about its duration and content. Recent efforts to extend schooling at the expense of apprenticeship have not been notably successful, in large part because both employers and parents view school-based training as a second choice, a fallback activity in case an apprenticeship position cannot be found.[54]

The reliance of successful dropout-prevention programs on out-of-classroom learning, the effectiveness of experiential learning programs, and the example of the West German dual system all argue that the concentration of recent reform proposals on in-class instruction is unwarranted, particularly for marginal students. Out-of-classroom educational programs should be part of current efforts to improve secondary schools. Integrating classroom and experiential components should be high on the agenda of designers of such programs.

Experiential education also offers a strategy for coping with some of the dilemmas identified in connection with both differentiation and vocational education. Learning outside of the classroom breaks down some of the barriers between previously successful and unsuccessful students because new skills and new combinations of skills are called for. A group project may require many different skills, and some of the slower students will either already have them or acquire them more quickly than those who excel in the classroom. Many of those skills, in addition, will be related to vocations but can be acquired at least to the beginner's level without choosing and training for a specific vocation.

If standards are raised for high school graduation without addressing the special needs of marginal students, then fewer young people will graduate from high school. Although there are distinct dangers to identifying some students as marginal and separating them from others, the evidence reviewed above favors providing programs for students at risk of dropping out that are more intensive, include manual training, and involve learning outside of classrooms. The dangers of labeling potential dropouts could be avoided by making the same opportunities available to all students.

Notes

1 J. G. Bachman, P. M. O'Malley, and J. Johnston, *Adolescence to Adulthood: Change and Stability in the Lives of Young Men* (Ann Arbor, Mich.: Institute for Social Research, 1978).

2 D. S. Elliott and H. L. Voss, *Delinquency and Dropout* (Lexington, Mass.: Lexington Books, 1974).

3 I. Berg, *Education and Jobs: The Great Training Robbery* (Boston: Beacon Press, 1971).

4 D. K. Cohen and M. S. Garet, "Reforming Educational Policy with Applied Research," *Harvard Educational Review* 45 (1975): 17–43.

5 C. Fielstra and B. R. Chrispin, *Evaluation Report on Phase Two of the Secondary School Project*

for an Introduction to the Allied Health Professions, 1972 (ERIC Document Reproduction Service number ED 075 665).

6   J. Adwere-Boamah, *Project MACK: Final Evaluation Report, 1974–1975* (ERIC Document Reproduction Service number ED 140 415).

7   R. A. Gibboney and M. Langsdorf, "The Career Intern Program: An Experiment in Career Education That Worked," *Journal of Research and Development in Education* 12, no. 3 (1979): 103–05. See also M. Langsdorf and R. A. Gibboney, *The Career Intern Program: Final Report—Vol. I: An Experiment in Career Education That Worked,* NIE Papers in Education and Work, No. 7 (Washington, D.C.: National Institute of Education, 1977; ERIC Document Reproduction Service number ED 142 795): and P. G. Treadway et al., *Study of the Career Intern Program: Final Report—Task A: Implementation,* 1981 (ERIC Document Reproduction Service number ED 206 841).

8   G. Farkas et al., *Early Impacts from the Youth Entitlement Demonstration: Participation, Work, and Schooling* (New York: Manpower Demonstration Research Corporation, 1980); idem, *Impacts from the Youth Incentive Entitlement Pilot Projects: Participation, Work, and Schooling over the Full Program Period* (New York: Manpower Demonstration Research Corporation, 1982; ERIC Document Reproduction Service number ED 236 301). See also J. M. Gueron, *Lessons from a Job Guarantee: The Youth Incentive Entitlement Pilot Projects* (New York: Manpower Demonstration Research Corporation, 1984); M. Pines, R. Ivry, and J. Lee, "The Universe of Need for Youth Employment: The Reality behind the Statistics," in *A Review of Youth Employment Problems, Programs, and Policies, Vol. 1: The Youth Employment Problem: Causes and Dimensions,* ed. B. Linder and R. Taggart (Washington, D.C.: U.S. Department of Labor, 1980).

9   D. P. Sprengel and E. G. Tomey, *Vocational Exploration in the Private Sector: Final Report and Assessment, 1972–73: Comparison of Impact in the Pilot and Experimental Years* (Washington, D.C.: U.S. Department of Labor, 1974; ERIC Document Reproduction Service number ED 143 691).

10   G. Magnum and J. Walsh, *Employment and Training Programs for Youth: What Works Best for Whom?* (Washington, D.C.: U.S. Department of Labor, 1978); R. Taggart, "Lessons from Experience with Employment and Training Programs for Youth," in *Education and Work,* Eighty-first Yearbook of the National Society for the Study of Education, ed. H. F. Silberman and K. J. Rehage (Chicago: University of Chicago Press, 1982).

11   L. S. Lotto, "The Holding Power of Vocational Curricula: Characteristics of Effective Dropout Prevention Programs," *Journal of Vocational Education Research* 7, no. 4 (1982): 39–49.

12   G. G. Wehlage, *Effective Programs for the Marginal High School Student* (Bloomington, Ind.: Phi Delta Kappa Educational Foundation, 1983); and G. Wehlage et al., *Effective Programs for the Marginal High School Student: A Report to the Wisconsin Governor's Employment and Training Office* (Madison: University of Wisconsin Center for Education Research, 1982).

13   A. Körner, "Comprehensive Schooling: An Evaluation—West Germany," *Comparative Education* 17 (1981): 15–22.

14   Der Bundesminister für Bildung und Wissenschaft, *Grund- und Strukturdaten, 1983/84* (Bad Honnef: Bock, 1983), p. 80; idem, *Berufsbildungsbericht 1984, Grundlagen und Perspektiven für Bildung und Wissenschaft* (Bad Honnef: Bock, 1984), p. 43.

15   Deutscher Industrie- und Handelstag, *Berufsausbildung in der Bundesrepublik Deutschland: Das duale System:* (Esslingen/Neckar: Bechtle, 1982), p. 7.

16   S. Williams et al., *Youth without Work: Three Countries Approach the Problem* (Paris: Organization for Economic Cooperation and Development, 1981).

17   P. E. Barton, "Youth Transition to Work: The Problem and Federal Policy Setting," in *From School to Work: Improving the Transition* (a collection of policy papers prepared for the National Commission for Manpower Policy) (Washington, D.C.: Government Printing Office, 1976); and P. Osterman, *Getting Started: The Youth Labor Market* (Cambridge, Mass.: MIT Press, 1980).

18   J. W. Gardner, *Excellence: Can We be Equal and Excellent Too?* (New York: Harper, 1961).

19   J. Rawls, *A Theory of Justice* (Cambridge, Mass.: Belknap Press of Harvard University Press, 1971).

20   J. E. Rosenbaum, "Social Implications of Educational Grouping," in *Review of Research in Education*, vol. 8, ed. D. C. Berliner (American Educational Research Association, 1980).

21   National Education Association, Research Division, *Ability Grouping* (Research Summary S3) (Washington, D.C.: National Education Association, 1968).

22   W. E. Schafer and C. Olexa, *Tracking and Opportunity* (Scranton, Pa.: Chandler, 1971); and A. B. Hollingshead, *Elmtown's Youth: The Impact of Social Classes on Adolescents* (New York: Wiley, 1949).

23   T. L. Good and S. Marshall, "Do Students Learn More in Heterogeneous or Homogeneous Groups?," in *The Social Context of Instruction: Group Organization and Group Process*, ed. P. L. Peterson, L. C. Wilkinson, and M. Hallinan (New York: Academic Press, 1984).

24   T. Husén, *The School in Question: A Comparative Study of the School and the Future in Western Societies* (Oxford: Oxford University Press, 1979), p. 87.

25   B. S. Bloom, *Human Characteristics and School Learning* (New York: McGraw-Hill, 1976)

26   R. C. Rist, "Student Social Class and Teacher Expectations: The Self-fulfilling Prophecy in Ghetto Education," *Harvard Educational Review* 40 (1970): 411–51.

27   F. Erickson, "Gatekeeping the Melting Pot," *Harvard Educational Review* 45 (1975): 44–70.

28   D. C. McClelland, "Testing for Competence Rather than for 'Intelligence,'" *American Psychologist* 28 (1973): 1–14.

29   J. E. Rosenbaum, *Making Inequality: The Hidden Curriculum of High School Tracking* (New York: Wiley, 1976).

30   J. D. Jones, E. L. Erickson, and R. Crowell, "Increasing the Gap between Whites and Blacks: Tracking as a Contributory Source," *Education and Urban Society* 4 (1972): 339–96; and R. N. Evans and J. D. Galloway, "Verbal Ability and Socioeconomic Status of 9th and 12th Grade College Preparatory, General, and Vocational Students," *The Journal of Human Resources* 8 (1973): 24–36. Compare R. A. Rehberg and E. R. Rosenthal, *Class and Merit in the American High School* (New York: Longman, 1978).

31   Compare E. J. Haller and S. A. Davis, "Does Socioeconomic Status Bias the Assignment of Elementary School Students to Reading Groups?," *American Educational Research Journal* 17 (1980): 409–18; and K. Alexander, M. Cook, and E. McDill, "Curriculum Tracking and Educational Stratification," *American Sociological Review* 43 (1978): 46–66.

32   Rosenbaum, "Social Implications."

33   Rehberg and Rosenthal, *Class and Merit;* and J. E. Rosenbaum, "Track Misperceptions and Frustrated College Plans: An Analysis of the Effects of Tracks and Track Perceptions in the National Longitudinal Survey," *Sociology of Education* 53 (1980): 74–88.

34   Rosenbaum, *Making Inequality.*

35   H. Dickinson and M. Erben, "An Aspect of Industrial Training in the Federal Republic of Germany: Sociological Consideration on the Role of the Meister," *British Journal of Sociology,* in press.

36   J. E. Berryman, "The Equity and Effectiveness of Secondary Vocational Education," in *Education and Work;* W. Conroy, "Some Historical Effects of Vocational Education at the Secondary Level," *Phi Delta Kappan* 61 (1979): 267–71; J. Grasso and J. R. Shea, *Vocational Education and Training: Impact on Youth:* (Berkeley, Calif.: Carnegie Council on Policy Studies in Higher Education, 1979); B. B. Reuben, "Vocational Education for All in High School," in *Work and the Quality of Life,* ed. J. O'Toole (Cambridge, Mass.: MIT Press, 1974); J. O'Toole, "Education Is Education and Work Is Work — Shall Ever the Twain Meet?," *Teachers College Record* 81 (1979): 5–21; and W. Wilms, "Vocational Education and Job Success: The Employer's View," *Phi Delta Kappan* 65 (1984): 347–50.

37   Conroy, "Some Historical Effects."

38   Barton, "Youth Transition to Work."

39   W. Wilms, "Vocational Education"; and E. Lynton, J. R. Seldin, and S. Gruhin, *Employers' Views on Hiring and Training* (New York: Labor Market Information Network, 1978).

40   Berryman, "Equity and Effectiveness of Secondary Education."

41   T. Davidson and J. Johnston, "High School Boys in Vocational Education Programs: Facts and Fallacies," *The Vocational Guidance Quarterly* 25, no. 2 (1976): 106–11.

42   J. Combs and W. W. Cooley, "Dropouts: In High School and After School," *American Educational Research Journal* 5 (1968): 343–63.

43   J. G. Bachman, S. Green, and I. D. Wirtanen, *Youth in Transition: Vol. 3, Dropping Out: Problem or Symptom?* (Ann Arbor, Mich.: Institute for Social Research, 1971).

44   J. F. Claus, "An Ethnographic Investigation of Attitude Development in Vocational Education: The Importance of Ethnographic Meaning" (paper presented at the annual meeting of the American Educational Research Association, New Orleans, 1984).

45   J. J. Adler, *The Paideia Proposal: An Educational Manifesto* (New York: Macmillan, 1982).

46   See especially Panel on Youth of the President's Science Advisory Council, *Youth: Transition to Adulthood* (Chicago: University of Chicago Press, 1974); and Carnegie Council on Policy Studies in Higher Education, *Giving Youth a Better Chance: Options for Education, Work, and Service* (San Francisco: Jossey-Bass, 1979).

47   R. B. Bucknam, "The Impact of EBCE: An Evaluator's Viewpoint," *Illinois Career Education Journal* 33, no. 3 (1976): 32–37; T. R. Owens, "Experience-Based Career Education: Summary and Implications of Research and Evaluation Findings," in *Youth Participation and Experiential Education*, ed. D. Conrad and D. Hedin (New York: Haworth Press, 1982), 77–91.

48   R. B. Bucknam and S. G. Brand, "EBCE Really Works: A Meta-analysis on Experience Based Career Education," *Educational Leadership* 40, no. 6 (1983): 66–71.

49   D. Conrad and D. Hedin, "The Impact of Experiential Education on Adolescent Development," in *Youth Participation and Experiential Education*, pp. 57–76.

50   S. F. Hamilton, "Adolescents in Community Settings: What Is to Be Learned?," *Theory and Research in Social Education* 9 (1981): 23–38.

51   A. A. MacKenzie and R. T. White, "Fieldwork in Geography and Long-term Memory Structures," *American Educational Research Journal* 19 (1982): 623–32.

52   J. Agnew, "Better Education through Application," *Synergist* 10, no. 3 (1982): 44–48.

53   S. F. Hamilton, and R. S. Zeldin, "Learning by Watching: Knowledge and Attitudes of Local Government Interns." (paper presented at the annual meeting of the American Educational Research Association, Montreal, 1983).

54   K. Sonntag and E. Frieling, "New Ways of Vocational Training in the Federal Republic of Germany: An Empirical Research Comparing Training Systems," *International Review of Applied Psychology* 32 (1983): 289–306.

Taking Stock: Renewing Our Research Agenda on the Causes and Consequences of Dropping Out

GARY NATRIELLO
Teachers College, Columbia University

AARON M. PALLAS
U.S. Department of Education, Washington, D.C.

EDWARD L. MCDILL
Johns Hopkins University

Gary Natriello, Aaron M. Pallas, and Edward L. McDill provide an assessment of the findings and suggestions presented in this special issue on school dropouts and outline an agenda for the next steps in research on the problem. They argue that a comprehensive program of research should include data on student characteristics, school processes, the act of dropping out, and the economic and cognitive consequences of the failure of large numbers of students to complete high school.

As the articles in this volume clearly indicate, the problem of students leaving school prior to graduation is one that has long been with us and one that shows no sign of abating in the near future.[1] While some have suggested that dropping out is an inevitable feature of modern American schooling and a phenomenon that may cost our society less than is often believed,[2] we are forced to agree with Wehlage and Rutter, Fine, and others writing here that the individual and collective disadvantages that accrue when a significant portion of students fail to complete their high school education are impossible to ignore, particularly in a society committed to equality of opportunity and to the full participation of all citizens in political, social, and economic affairs.

Because we view the dropout phenomenon as damaging to a democratic society and because it appears to be an enduring social problem, we believe that the time has come to subject it to sustained investigation aimed at alleviating its worst manifestations. While the articles offered here and many others are testimony to the considerable efforts to attack this problem in the

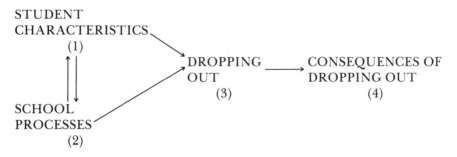

Figure 1. Key Elements for a Renewed Research Agenda on Dropping Out

past, researchers, policymakers, and educational practitioners must join forces in the kind of coalition described by Mann in his article to plan, implement, and assess programs and policies that will encourage students at risk to complete their high school education. It is time to renew our research agenda to address the dropout problem.

The articles in this volume have a great deal to contribute to the building of that agenda. They review many of the most important research and policy issues bearing on the dropout problem. Our reading of these papers and of other recent work in the area[3] leads us to argue for increased attention from investigators and educators to four aspects of the dropout phenomenon.

These four aspects or components of the dropout phenomenon are depicted in Figure 1, which thematically represents our framework for a renewed research agenda on the dropout problem. This figure suggests a pattern of reciprocal relationships between the two antecedent components, the personal and social characteristics of students, and the process aspects of their school environments. In one way or another, each of the articles in this volume have touched on the background characteristics of students most likely to leave school before graduation and on the experiences these students have in school. Indeed, much of the analysis in several of the articles focuses on the relative contributions of these two components to dropping out. What our diagram emphasizes is that these two components themselves are not independent. The background characteristics of students determine the kinds of schools and educational processes to which they have access, and the characteristics of schools play a role in attracting students with certain characteristics.[4] Each of these components is shown to have an impact on the third component, dropping out. Since dropping out is, of course, the central element in any research agenda focusing on its causes and consequences, it is important to consider the identification and measurement of this phenomenon. Several articles in this volume make it clear that there are serious difficulties to be overcome before we can obtain valid and reliable data on the extent of dropping out in U.S. schools. Finally, the act of dropping out is presented as influencing the subsequent personal and socioeconomic well-being of the early-school-leaver. While most would agree that dropping out carries a host of immediate negative consequences for the individuals involved, it is only through longitudinal studies of the impact of the decision to drop out that we can fully appreciate the total costs to individual dropouts and to the nation of this failure to complete high school. Although, as we shall point out, studies related to each of these aspects or components of the dropout phenomenon have been conducted in the past by the authors represented here and by others, the serious and enduring nature of the dropout problem argues for renewed efforts to gain greater understanding of each of these aspects.

STUDENT CHARACTERISTICS

Previous studies of dropping out have revealed a now familiar story of how students with certain background characteristics are more likely to leave school prior to graduation than students with other characteristics.[5] In this volume the articles by Ekstrom, Goertz, Pollack, and Rock, by Fine, by Wehlage and Rutter, and by McDill, Natriello, and Pallas make it only too clear that minority students and students from economically disadvantaged backgrounds are much more likely to leave school early than are other students. In an attempt to reach some solid conclusions about where to target educational resources and research energy, it would be tempting to say that we now know enough about the characteristics of dropouts, and that as Wehlage and Rutter point out, more research on student characteristics will not help us to solve the problem, or that as Fine observes, when the majority of students in certain groups leave school, knowing the characteristics of likely dropouts is not terribly useful. Indeed, we would agree with Wehlage and Rutter that more studies that simply link dropping out to student characteristics are unlikely to move us closer to solving the dropout problem.

However, there are several reasons why it is crucial to continue monitoring the characteristics of dropouts if we are to understand the problem. First, there is evidence that the dropout population is not remaining stable. Certain groups may become more prominent among dropouts. For example, recent figures from the U.S. Bureau of the Census indicate that the dropout rates for black males and females and for white females are the lowest recorded for these groups in the last fifteen years, while the rates for white and Hispanic males are the highest recorded over that same period.[6] Thus, the dropout phenomenon may be changing in ways we have yet to understand fully.

Second, if we are to begin isolating the contribution of other factors to the dropout problem, it is important to control for the effects of student background characteristics. As the articles by Mann, by Ekstrom, Goertz, Pollack, and Rock, and by McDill, Natriello, and Pallas report, it is quite clear that students in certain socioeconomic groups are much more likely to drop out than students in other socioeconomic groups. It is impossible to ignore the impact of background characteristics on dropping out.

Third, as Morrow and Hammack point out, in most school districts data on student characteristics are not currently considered in analyses of the dropout population; yet, according to Mann, such analyses must include student characteristics if we expect schools to assess the degree to which their educational programs are meeting the needs of various groups in the community. As Mann further notes, dropping out of school prior to graduation is the result of many quite different kinds of problems. To understand what schools are doing to exacerbate these problems as well as what schools can and should do to ameliorate them requires carefully assembled information on the backgrounds of the students who eventually drop out.

Fourth, as the analyses by McDill, Natriello, and Pallas and by Hamilton show, new school reforms designed to improve the educational experiences of all students may have positive effects for some students and negative effects for others, thereby aggravating already pronounced inequities in the schools and ultimately in the larger society. Requiring greater time in school, enrollment in narrowly defined academic courses, and achievement of higher standards by students whose background characteristics suggest they cannot meet current demands is likely to lead to greater numbers of students leaving school prior to graduation.[7]

All of these concerns make it more important than ever to collect accurate data on the background characteristics of students who fail to complete high school. Such data, now routinely collected as part of national surveys of secondary school students,[8] must also be part of the data-collection activities sponsored by school districts.

SCHOOL PROCESSES

Wehlage and Rutter and Fine make clear the importance of understanding the impact of school processes on students if we truly want to understand the causes of dropping out. The discussions by McDill, Natriello, and Pallas and by Hamilton of the features of programs that appear to be effective in holding students in school until graduation demonstrate the utility of a greater understanding of the impact of school processes on the development of programs to tackle the problem.

While Wehlage and Rutter properly raise the question of the role of the school in contributing to the dropout problem, the data set they use for their major analyses, the High School and Beyond study, contains little information on school processes. Indeed, data on the experiences of students and teachers inside of schools are notably absent from the High School and Beyond study. The absence of these indicators severely limits the use to which researchers interested in the impact of school processes on dropping out can put such a data set.

To advocate additional research on school processes is to provide very little focus and direction for either researchers or policymakers. School processes encompass a wide range of phenomena, but there are certain features of schools that seem particularly worthy of investigation as we seek to develop a better understanding of the causes of dropping out. First, characteristics of school processes that fit under the general rubric of "responsiveness" should be considered.[9] Fine describes situations in an urban public high school in which the staff failed to respond at all to student decisions to leave school. Wehlage and Rutter argue that the feedback students receive in schools often leaves them little opportunity to experience success. McDill, Natriello, and Pallas and Hamilton list characteristics of successful dropout-prevention programs that include small size, individualized approaches, small student-teacher ratios, and more counseling resources, all of which tend to make the school organization more responsive to the concerns and problems of students. Mann's second C for care suggests similar strategies. Others have pointed to additional specific school processes that might make a difference.[10] As the articles in this volume make clear, students most at risk of dropping out often live in turbulent family and community environments where reactions to their own actions are swift and forceful. When these same students find themselves in environments that are markedly less responsive to their needs and problems, they find it all too easy to withdraw gradually from the school.

As discussed earlier in this volume,[11] there are a number of particular school practices that appear to affect the responsiveness of schools to student needs. First, smaller schools and programs appear to permit greater responsiveness to students. Second, greater individualization of curricular and instructional strategies that involve the tailoring of course content and the method and pace of instruction to individual students results in more responsive learning conditions for all students. Third, when school programs are consistent with the cultural and community conditions under which students live, educators are able to be more responsive to individual students. Fine's description reveals the problems students encounter when the staff and program of a school are unable to relate to the very real conditions in which students find themselves.

Perhaps the most crucial aspect of the school organization in being responsive to the needs and concerns of students lies in the capacity of the school staff to assess on a continuing basis the impact of their program on students, including dropouts. Hammack notes that only one of the six large urban districts in his study actually attempted to link data on dropouts to various school problems, and Mann views this omission as preventing the development of cumulative knowledge of dropout-prevention efforts. Gottfredson[12] and others have argued that we can only begin to make progress in developing effective school programs for any population of students if we engage in the systematic design, implementation, monitoring, and evaluation of school programs. As schools seek to develop the capacity to assess their own programs, there is a great opportunity for researchers and practitioners to collaborate to generate evaluation processes that increase the responsiveness of schools to students.

DROPPING OUT

On the face of it, there would seem to be few phenomena easier to measure than whether or not a student has dropped out of school. After all, a student is either physically present or not. However, as the articles by Hammack and Morrow make painfully clear, we have a long way to go to arrive at standard measures of dropping out. The variation in school district practices described by Hammack and the implications of such variations illustrated by Morrow should make us more than a bit uncomfortable about relying on current dropout statistics.

Typically, there are two approaches to the measurement of dropping out: individual and organizational. Individual approaches to measuring dropout rates involve surveys of individuals or households. The High School and Beyond study used by Wehlage and Rutter and by Ekstrom, Goertz, Pollack, and Rock is an example of this approach. Organizational approaches to assessing dropout rates involve calculations of statistics from aggregates of schools, such as school districts. The articles by Morrow and Hammack document many of the difficulties that arise in the comparison of dropout rates across school districts.

Inevitably, tabulations of dropouts by schools and individuals will differ.[13] Student enrollments in school are becoming increasingly complex as patterns of school attendance depart from traditional patterns.[14] "Stopping out" has become more common, and there now are several ways to acquire a high school degree, including obtaining a passing score on the General Educational Development (GED) examination. Because schools and school districts lack the resources to track the educational experiences of students who have left school, they cannot account for the complete educational histories of individual students.

Some of the problems in measuring dropout phenomena are technical; it is difficult to collect data on individuals who leave any setting. Other problems are practical; it is hard to arrange for individual districts to use the same practices when there are no standards. Finally, many of the problems that frustrate attempts to obtain valid and reliable measures of dropping out are political; it is often in someone's interest to minimize or exaggerate the dropout statistics, but seldom in anyone's interest to produce precise figures.

The technical problems in measuring the dropout rate can be attacked with greater effort and attention as well as through regional and national agreements about methods for following student transfers. The practical problems can be alleviated through the adoption of standards, perhaps along the lines suggested by Morrow.[15] But the political problems may be the most difficult to address.[16] They would seem to require a new set of incentives for the careful and accurate collection of data on dropouts. These may arise in the context of the kind of coalition-building activities advocated by Mann. Such incentives may be generated by a new generation of district-based and other research efforts that will link data on student characteristics and school processes to data on the dropout phenomenon. Since previous efforts to collect dropout data in school districts have generally failed to connect such data to the school program, there have been few uses of dropout data at the school and district level except for public relations purposes. In such a context there was much to be gained and little to be lost from distorting the true picture. But if schools and districts mobilize efforts to address the dropout issue in a serious way through variations in programming, then perhaps the collection of accurate data will assume somewhat greater importance. While we are neither naive nor optimistic enough to suggest that such will be the case in all districts, in those districts that make a major effort to deal with the dropout problem the collection of valid and reliable data on dropouts may assume some priority.

CONSEQUENCES OF DROPPING OUT

There is a clear need for research on the consequences of dropping out of high school. We know rather little about either the economic or social consequences of dropping out. It has long been assumed that the costs to society of the dropout problem are quite large. As the high school graduation rate has increased, however, the population of dropouts in the 1980s may be very different from the population of dropouts in the 1950s and 1960s. Hence, our knowledge about negative effects of dropping out for earlier cohorts of youth may not apply to today's dropouts.

It is desirable to have estimates of the costs of dropping out for policy purposes, and it is important to weigh the dollar costs of dropout prevention against the expected benefits of keeping dropouts in school. Levin argued that the costs of the dropout problem to the nation far exceed the estimated costs of programs to keep youngsters in school.[17] Levin's figures are now quite dated, and although our attempt in this volume to estimate the costs of the dropout problem still suggests that it would be cost-effective to invest in dropout-prevention programs,[18] we need more current figures on the monetary costs of dropping out.

We expect a primary source of information of the consequences of dropping out to be the ongoing High School and Beyond study being conducted by the National Center for Education Statistics. As noted by Wehlage and Rutter and by Ekstrom, Goertz, Pollack, and Rock, High School and Beyond is the only current study of a nationally representative sample of youth surveying substantial numbers of high school dropouts. The recently released second follow-up of the sophomore cohort provides information on the educational, occupational, and social experiences of dropouts and graduates for the two years after the expected high school graduation date for the sophomore cohort. These data are well suited for the analysis of the early labor market consequences of early school leaving.

The articles in this volume have already documented some of the early consequences of dropping out revealed by the High School and Beyond study. Ekstrom, Goertz, Pollack, and Rock and Wehlage and Rutter showed that the self-esteem of dropouts in the High School and Beyond study rose after leaving school. Ekstrom, Goertz, Pollack, and Rock also corroborated the findings of Alexander, Natriello, and Pallas regarding the cognitive costs of dropping out.[19] Although it is nearly impossible to calculate the dollar costs of the cognitive shortfall of dropouts, the aggregate long-term costs may be quite large.

Finally, the High School and Beyond follow-up will help shed light on the question originally posed by Bachman, Green, and Wirtanen. Is dropping out of high school a problem or a symptom?[20] Given that most high school dropouts are socially, economically, and academically disadvantaged, can we isolate that portion of the economic and academic shortfall of dropouts relative to graduates that can be attributed to dropping out itself? In order to do this, we need detailed information on the experiences and characteristics of dropouts before they left high school, as well as data on their labor market experiences, cognitive performance, and attitudes and behaviors after leaving school. The High School and Beyond data are by far the best available for this purpose.

While each of the aspects of the dropout phenomenon noted above — student characteristics, school processes, dropping out itself, and the consequences of dropping out — have been examined in a number of studies, each requires intensive investigation. Moreover, if we are to understand fully the dropout problem, these components of that problem must be studied together. Studies of the dropout problem tend to be quite involved and expensive since they require following individual students over time and since these students leave the organized settings of the schools where they can be most conveniently contacted. To achieve the greatest returns from future dropout studies, it is important that all four components of the phenomenon be included in any study.

We need to know what kinds of students leave school early after encountering what kinds of school programs and processes and with what long-term consequences for individuals and society. As Wehlage and Rutter remind us, knowing only the background characteristics of dropouts will not lead to an understanding of how current school processes contribute to decisions to leave school before graduation. Knowing only the processes that seem to lead to dropping out forces us to ignore the complex nature of the dropout phenomenon and consider it a single problem instead of recognizing it as an outcome of multiple problems as suggested by Mann. Accepting current dropout statistics without question subjects us to the shifting sands of data-collection procedures documented by Hammack and Morrow. Failing to follow dropouts over time to ascertain the long-term consequences of failing to graduate from high school prevents us from understanding the true magnitude of the problem and impedes attempts to marshal public support for efforts to attack the problem. For all of these reasons we advocate a comprehensive and sustained effort to examine the dropout problem. Greater understanding of the problem will not guarantee the adoption and implementation of effective dropout-prevention programs, but the failure to understand the problem will guarantee a great deal of wasted effort on the part of educators and the continued squandering of human resources.

Notes

1 For additional insights into the background and scope of the dropout problem, see L. Hersov and I. Berg eds., *Out of School: Modern Perspectives in Truancy and School Refusal* (New York: John Wiley, 1980); J. L. Kaplan and E. D. Luck, "The Dropout Phenomenon as a Social Problem," *The Educational Forum* 47 (1977): 41–46; S. B. Neill, *Keeping Students in School: Problems and Solutions—AASA Critical Issues Report* (Arlington, Va.: American Association of School Administrators, 1979); R. W. Rumberger, "Dropping Out of High School: The Influence of Race, Sex, and Family Background," *American Educational Research Journal* 20 (1983): 199–220; and D. Schreiber, ed., *Profile of the School Dropout* (New York: Random House, 1967).

2 See, for example, J. G. Bachman, "Response to Levin," in *The Costs to the Nation of Inadequate Education*, ed. H. Levin, Report to the Select Committee on Equal Educational Opportunity, United States Senate (Washington, D.C.: Government Printing Office, 1972).

3 Our assessment of the research and program development literature in this area and the implications of the recent school reform movement for potential dropouts are presented in Gary Natriello, Edward L. McDill, and Aaron M. Pallas, "Uncommon Sense: School Administrators, School Reform and Potential Dropouts," *Educational Leadership* 43, no. 1 (September 1985): 10–14; Edward L. McDill, Gary Natriello, and Aaron M. Pallas, "Raising Standards and Retaining Students: The Impact of the Reform Recommendations on Potential Dropouts," *Review of Educational Research*, Winter 1985.

4 For studies of the interdependence of "recruitment" and "socialization" processes in schools, see Edward L. McDill and L. C. Rigsby, *Structure and Process in Secondary Schools: The Academic Impact of Educational Climates* (Baltimore, Md.: The Johns Hopkins University Press, 1973), chaps. 4 and 5; and J. L. Epstein, "Friendship Selection: Developmental and Environmental Influences," *Process and Outcome in Peer Relationships*, ed. E. Mueller and C. Cooper (New York: Academic Press, 1985), pp. 129–60.

5 S. B. Neill, *Keeping Students in School: Problems and Solutions*, AASA Critical Issues Report (Arlington, Va.: American Association of School Administrators, 1979); A. M. Pallas, *The Determinants of High School Dropout* (Ph.D. diss., Johns Hopkins University, 1984); H. C. Quay and L. B. Allen, "Truants and Dropouts," in *Encyclopedia of Educational Research*, ed. H. E.

Mitzel, vol. 5, 5th ed. (New York: The Free Press, 1982), pp. 1958–62; and Rumberger, "Dropping Out of High School."

6   U.S. Department of Commerce, Bureau of the Census, *School Enrollment—Social and Economic Characteristics of Students: October 1981* (Advance Report), *Current Population Reports,* Series P-20, No. 373, 1982.

7   Harold Howe, "Giving Equity a Chance in the Excellence Game," Martin Bushkin Memorial Lecture (Washington, D.C.: Education Writers' Association, 1984); and McDill, Natriello, and Pallas, "A Population at Risk," in this volume.

8   See S. S. Peng, W. B. Fetters, and A. J. Kolstad, *High School and Beyond: A National Longitudinal Study for the 1980's: A Capsule Description of High School Students* (Washington, D.C.: National Center for Education Statistics, 1981).

9   For a general discussion of the responsiveness of secondary schools, see J. McPartland and Edward L. McDill, eds., *Violence in Schools* (Lexington, Mass.: Heath, 1977).

10   See, for example, recent studies focusing on performance evaluation processes by D. R. Entwisle and L. A. Hayduk, "Academic Expectations and the School Attainment of Young Children," *Sociology of Education* 54 (1981): 34–50; S. J. Rosenholtz and C. Simpson, "The Formation of Ability: Developmental Trend or Social Construction?" *Review of Educational Research* 54 (1984): 31–64; and G. Natriello, "Problems in the Evaluation of Students and Student Disengagement from Secondary Schools," *Journal of Research and Development in Education* 17 (1984): 14–24. For a study examining the role of rules and procedures in schools, see G. Gottfredson and D. Gottfredson, *Victimization in Six Hundred Schools: An Analysis of the Roots of Disorder* (New York: Plenum, 1985). For studies of the impact of peer networking processes on students, see J. Coleman, *The Adolescent Society* (New York: Free Press, 1961); M. T. Hallinan and N. B. Tuma, "Classroom Effects on Change in Children's Friendships." *Sociology of Education* 51 (1978): 170–82; and J. L. Epstein and N. Karweit, eds., *Friends in School: Patterns of Selection and Influence in Secondary Schools* (New York: Academic Press, 1983). For studies of group processes in schools, see S. Sharon, "Cooperative Learning in Small Groups: Recent Methods and Effects on Achievement, Attitudes, and Ethnic Relations," *Review of Educational Research* 50 (1980): 241–71; S. Sharon, P. Hare, C. D. Webb, and R. Hertz-Lazarowitz, eds., *Cooperation in Education* (Provo, Utah: Brigham Young University Press, 1980); and R. E. Slavin, "Cooperative Learning," *Review of Educational Research* 50 (1980): 315–42. For studies of instructional strategies, see T. Good, H. Edmeier, and T. Beckerman, "Teaching Mathematics in High and Low SES Classrooms: An Empirical Comparison" *Journal of Teacher Education* 29 (1978): 58–90; and T. Good, "Research on Classroom Teaching," in *Handbook of Teaching and Policy,* ed. L. S. Shulman and G. Sykes (New York: Longman, 1983), pp. 42–82. For studies of the impact of time on academic tasks, see N. Karweit, *Time on Task: A Research Review,* Report No. 332 (Baltimore: Center for the Social Organization of Schools, Johns Hopkins University, 1983); and N. Karweit, "Time-on-task Reconsidered: A Synthesis of Research on Time and Learning," *Educational Leadership* 41 (1984): 33–35. For studies of the impact of standards for performance, see G. Natriello and S. M. Dornbusch, *Teacher Evaluative Standards and Student Effort* (New York: Longman, 1984); and G. Natriello and Edward L. McDill, "Performance Standards, Student Effort on Homework and Academic Achievement," *Sociology of Education,* in press.

11   McDill, Natriello, and Pallas, "A Population at Risk: The Impact of Raising Standards on Potential Dropouts"; S. Hamilton, "Raising Standards and Reducing Dropout Rates," in this volume.

12   G. D. Gottfredson, "A Theory-Ridden Approach to Program Evaluation: A Method for Stimulating Researcher-Implementer Collaboration," *American Psychologist* 39 (1984): 1101–12.

13   C. Cooke, A. Ginsberg and M. Smith. "The Sorry State of Education Statistics," *Basic Education* 29 (1985): 3–8; A. M. Pallas and R. R. Verdugo, "Measuring the High School Dropout Problem" (Paper presented at the Annual Meeting of AERA, San Francisco, 1986).

14   B. Birman and G. Natriello, "Absenteeism in High Schools: Multiple Explanations for an Epidemic," in *School Crime and Violence,* ed. K. Baker and R. Rubel (Lexington, Mass.: D. C. Heath, 1980).

15   Indeed, the current review of the data-gathering efforts of the National Center for Education Statistics has prompted calls for greater attention to the development of a standard definition of a dropout as reported in T. Mirga, "Researchers Propose New Federal Statistics Agenda," *Education Week* 5 (September 18, 1985): 10, 14.

16   Systematic biases affect the collection of all kinds of school attendance data. For example, Meyer, Chase-Dunn, and Inverarity have pointed out that attendance records are unreliable for two reasons. First, not only do teachers and students tend to protect students from the negative consequences of being listed as absent, but school records may also systematically exaggerate attendance in order to protect the school's resources, which are based on measures of average daily attendance. As a result of these two factors, they note that "many students who make only an occasional or brief entry into the school may be continuously listed as present" (J. Meyer, C. Chase-Dunn, and J. Inverarity, *The Expansion of the Autonomy of Youth: Responses of the Secondary School to the Problems of Order in the 1960's* [Stanford, Calif.: The Laboratory for Social Research, Stanford University, 1971]). Indeed, a team of auditors from the office of the California State Auditor General found that physical counts of students in classrooms showed actual attendance substantially below that reported by school districts for the allocation of state funds. See also S. B. Neill, *Keeping Students in School: Problems and Solutions,* AASA Critical Issues Report (Arlington, Va.: American Association of School Administrators, 1979).

17   H. Levin, "The Costs to the Nation of Inadequate Education," Report to the Select Committee on Equal Educational Opportunity, U.S. Senate (Washington, D.C.: Government Printing Office, 1972).

18   McDill, Natriello, and Pallas, "A Population at Risk."

19   The cognitive deficit of dropouts compared to graduates is estimated to average about one-tenth of a standard deviation or three percentiles on a standardized achievement test. See K. L. Alexander, Gary Natriello, and Aaron M. Pallas, "For Whom the School Bell Tolls: The Impact of Dropping Out on Cognitive Performance," *American Sociological Review* 50 (1985): 409–20.

20   J. G. Bachman, S. Green and I. D. Wirtanen. *Dropping Out—Problem or Symptom?* Youth in Transition Series, vol. 3 (Ann Arbor, Mich.: Institute for Social Research, 1971).

CONTRIBUTORS

RUTH B. EKSTROM is a senior research scientist in the division of education policy research and services, Educational Testing Service. Dr. Ekstrom is co-author of the study, *Determinants of Achievement Gain in High School*, and author of a recent study of the impact of public high school guidance practices on student outcomes.

MICHELLE FINE, assistant professor of psychology and education at the University of Pennsylvania, is actively involved in educational research and advocacy, with interest in gender, race, and social class as they operate within the lives of urban adolescents.

MARGARET E. GOERTZ is a senior research scientist in the division of education policy research and services, Educational Testing Service. Dr. Goertz is a policy analyst specializing in the fields of education finance and governance and school effectiveness.

STEPHEN F. HAMILTON is associate professor of human development and family studies in the College of Human Ecology, at Cornell University. He does research and develops programs related to adolescent development in school, work, and the community. He was a Fulbright senior research fellow in West Germany during 1983–1984.

FLOYD M. HAMMACK is director, Program in Educational Sociology in the School of Education, Health, Nursing and Arts Professions at New York University. His current research interests revolve around issues of equity in educational reform.

DALE MANN is professor in the department of educational administration at Teachers College, Columbia University. A long-time analyst of education improvement, he is working on a book combining that topic with the recent evidence about the characteristics of the instructionally effective school.

EDWARD L. MCDILL is professor of sociology and co-director, Center for Social Organization, Johns Hopkins University. He has a long-standing interest in the sociology of education, especially the effects of the social organization of schools on the academic productivity of students.

GEORGE MORROW is the director of the management information systems in the South Orange-Maplewood, New Jersey School District; prior to this he was research assistant in the development of a simulation based doctoral program at Teachers College, Columbia University called Inquiry in the Educational Administrative Practice.

GARY NATRIELLO is associate professor of sociology and education in the department of philosophy and the social sciences at Teachers College, Columbia University. His recent research has focused on the impact of evaluation processes on teachers and students.

AARON M. PALLAS is a statistician at the National Center for Education Statistics. His recent interests include reconciling differences in dropout rates, the determinants of high school dropouts, and the measurement of school climate in American high schools.

JUDITH M. POLLACK is a senior research data analyst at Educational Testing Service.

DONALD A. ROCK, a senior research psychologist, Educational Testing Service, has recently been the project director of the study of "Excellence in High School Education," funded by the U.S. Department of Education. His research interests include the development and application of statistical models for program evaluation in training and education.

ROBERT A. RUTTER, Ph.D., is a project associate at the Wisconsin Center for Education Research. His recent work includes causal modeling of positive school climate, analysis of secondary school improvement programs, and studies of the effects of community service on student's social development.

GARY G. WEHLAGE is professor of curriculum and instruction and principal investigator at the Wisconsin Center for Education Research. His recent work includes teacher education program development, research on effective programs for potential dropouts and workshops for educators concerned about dropouts.

INDEX

RAP